G000149191

Acknowledgements

I would like to say thanks to a number of people in the writing of this book: Thanks to Mike for enabling me to study by covering my shifts so I could attend courses. Thanks to Jo for your support and Fran for opening the door. Lastly, thank you to my Emma for your belief, encouragement and understanding, and for being you.

Contents

Introduction

Do you ever wonder how it is you have got here and reading the words on this page? Why it is you've decided to choose a book on personal development instead of one on history, the environment, or politics. Perhaps you have chosen this book because of a desire somewhere in yourself that you want to know yourself better, to gain an awareness of who you are? Or, maybe that your life now, or for some time hasn't felt right, and you feel that your life is without purpose or meaning. Maybe you are reacting to situations with anger or resentment, or are feeling anxious or depressed, or, why you continue to have failed relationships that start off so well, yet seem to end the same way.

I could have focused this book on a "how to" method to overcome these issues and more, but I believe that just as an event creates anger in one person the same event may lead to anxiety, stress or depression in another. I believe that it begins with the self and how you view your self, and more precisely how you exist in relation to a person or in a situation.

So with that in mind this book is a culmination of experiences, contemplations and reflections, and the knowledge gained from gaining an awareness of my self, as well as my work and studies in a field of mental health. This book is about who we are and how we develop, adjust and adapt to live in the world we are born into, as well as adjustments later in life. As I see it, when we become a person we have taken in an extraordinary amount of introjections and adjustments that enable us to live in whatever world that we are born into, as to how to be a person. For example the girl who is treated like a princess growing up may have that expectation of her self and in relationships with other people, she may find a suitable partner who will treat her as such, but there is another side to this, for the girl may also restrict her own development, her problem solving skills, her communication skills, how she speaks, her beliefs, the use of her words, her choice of clothing and occupation so that she can fulfil the purpose of being a princess, and may react in a certain way if her expectations of how she should be treated are not met. As she creatively adjusts to this she may become bitter and angry as people do not treat her to her own desires. This image of her self is not real, but a collection of beliefs and values that has formed her self-concept.

We are continuously adjusting to new encounters and experiences whatever stage in life we are at, so a person who believes they have to be of value to society to win the approval of others may enter a crisis when they reach retirement age and view their self as redundant or worthless, or the effects of a person who has endured the erosion of her identity from being in an emotionally abusive relationship.

How we adjust to life from many introjections and creative adjustments can become fixed, how we see ourselves can become stuck and may create significant problems when in relation to others. If the girl in the earlier example can no longer be *a princess* then she may be affected by depression, anxiety or anger if she is not treated this way. She may also seek some support from other people or the government as she has the view that people should look after her, or she may become ill which may mean that her family or partner will focus more attention onto her. Another person though in the same circumstances may introject the same message not as *you are a princess* but *be what other people want you to be* as she creatively adjusts to the view that she has to do what her parents say, despite her own desire to have autonomy. Each person adjusts throughout their life in their own way and in that each person has their own truth and their own way of being in the world.

In this book I hope that it helps you to find your own truth and way of being, with the potential to grow against the boundary of your own self-concept, which is the collection of beliefs about how to be a person, as well as to understand how you configure your world to give these beliefs meaning.

It is my belief that by becoming the role, we adjust ourselves; how we think, how we express ourselves, our beliefs, how we listen, the sensations we feel and how we understand our experiences. This is also relational I believe as well, i am sure we all know people who change how they speak depending on who they are speaking to, and when a person adapts how they speak to different people, how do you know when they're being authentic?

In this book we shall explore the origin of this, and how you have adjusted to your own way of life, and in later chapters a focus on the experiential (learning from your experiences) communication skills, how you exist now and what you do to maintain your *self,* we shall experiment with not being your *self* through exercises developed to increase your awareness, not only of who you are, but also what maintains this. It is my belief that when a person has an awareness of who they are then a choice becomes apparent, whether they would like to continue to be this way or challenge that. When a person develops their own autonomy they also become more responsible for their own life, that is to say, the responsibility of being a person, and the path towards authenticity.

The way I see it is that you are the expert in you, and together we can work collaboratively to help you discover who you are. This book then is as much about self-discovery as it is about overcoming the issues that may be affecting you. I have no intention of trying to change you or to direct you into a certain way. My intention is only to provide an awareness of how you exist, and then to leave you with the choice, and the responsibility of *how* you would like to be.

To protect privacy and confidentiality, identifying information has been altered for all examples, except for my own examples. For the same reason, each example is actually a composite of several observations or reflections about the nature of being, to illustrate the various theories and themes in this book.

Also, I believe that you are the expert in you, and what I propose is an idea from a Gestalt perspective about a person's way of being and how they exist, and also the person's capacity for growth beyond the *me* of the self-concept. There is nothing concrete and no absolutes in this field. I therefore encourage you to discover your own truth, and I hope this book can assist you in your own search towards authenticity.

Chapter 1

Creative Adjustment and Introjection

When we argue for our limitations, we get to keep them.

Evelyn Waugh

Adjusting, the very word may suggest a lack of choice, that we are being guided in a certain direction, we are having to adjust to the circumstances that we find ourselves in. The question I'd like to ask is what we are adjusting from, and what we adjust ourselves to. That comment would suggest that there is some agency in that decision, and it's my belief that we adjust to our world, not because we want to, but because we have to, and then we create our own world from that. I believe that although a person may be born with a certain level of intelligence, physical or biological limitations we are restricted not by our own potential but from the world that we are born into, and how those influences, be it social, cultural, religious, political or any other means of conformity hold us in place and create rigidity. For me i consider the implications and consequences of how the person adjusts to this, whether they are born as i was, in inner-city Belfast during the 1970's or a child born in Dhaka in Bangladesh.

Now, before I continue I'd like to say that i am not a natural writer, or would say that i have any particular proficiency in this field, i read, reflect and contemplate in my spare time and am amazed of how writers can articulate a description about something that i could say in a sentence. Perhaps it's my upbringing to keep in simple and i have to be honest with you, i have no plans to expand this book out beyond what's necessary, as in light of the first paragraph there i *choose* not to adjust to my idea of what a writer is (or indeed to compare myself to an introjected idea of what a writer is) and instead to just be myself, to be authentic and to keep it real. Saying that of course, it's taken me the past six years to learn more about myself, or rather my self and that involved 4 years studying to become a counsellor. To cut a long story short, i was listening to the radio one day and a person was saying that she wrote the book that she wanted to read, she had said that she wanted to travel somewhere and she couldn't find a book of being a lone female travelling in that part of the world (I think it was a country in South America) so she decided to travel there anyway, and write the book that she wanted to read.

Now, this was a important moment for me, i remember that i was driving home from work at the time and thought to myself, yes, that's a fantastic idea, i had the same thoughts about wanting to find and read a book that encapsulated my ideas of personal development and the growth of a person with some direction as to how we become who we are, how our self-concept or identity is formed, and how that idea of our self forms our relationships and the world around us, how the messages we receive in our development can be construed in many different ways, and then to become introjected and integrated into the person's own self-concept or identity, and can influence among many other areas how they speak, the structure and purpose of their words, how they hear, how they experience and deal with difficulties, what creates fear or anxiety, how they experience events and how they think or give their self meaning. I've written this book because I had many notebooks of ideas compiled over the years and wanted to put them all together, to create a linear model and I have used this to understand myself and the nature of the self, and lastly because I wanted to assist other people who desired to gain a better understanding of who they are, their influences, how they are shaped by their influences and also how and why, that is to say the meaning in which they interact with others, what others they choose to interact or form relationships with, why they are affected by events, how a person may *create* events to give their self meaning, how they interact with others, and also, how a person communicates with others. For example, growing up in inner-city Belfast I had to adjust myself to be physically tough, because of the environment at the time, and later became a Firefighter, and associated with people who were also *tough*. I write that in italics as it's a subjective term, and my own view of this was physically and emotionally tough. Did I become a Firefighter to give that self meaning, did I form relationships with others from that position, or that self-concept, did I have the idea of what *tough* meant and tried to live up to this with the words, stance, movements and posture of a man who encapsulated that, how such a man would speak or relate to others, and also what happened to the opposite polarity in my self-concept what happened to the aspects of me that were fragile or vulnerable, or the feelings of tenderness, kindness or compassion, where did they go? I creatively adjusted in relation to my environment and introjected what it meant to be a man in that city at that time. In that world

5

though there was a certain amount of normality in this way of being, and therefore my environment supported my self. I am reminded of a quote "does a fish know it's in water?" and why would it, it is happy swimming along and living its life, it's only when it gets stranded on a beach or plucked out of that water does it realise how much it had adjusted to that environment. I like the fish analogy as I think as the water sustains the fish, which has adjusted itself to survive in that environment, and when it leaves that water, the source of its survival it can no longer sustain itself, gills don't work in the air after all. Just as myself growing up in inner city Belfast and being a certain way to survive there would be out of place or redundant in an affluent area of London or in an ashram or peaceful community somewhere.

Have you ever noticed that politicians mostly talk about politics, beauticians mostly talk about beauty, gamers talk about gaming and housewives talk about parenting or their house, each person has a belief about who they are as a person and I believe that how we view ourselves, our self-concept is based upon a multitude of introjections and adjustments made throughout life, either by necessity, choice or survival. Has the person who has introjected and creatively adjusted to life made a conscious choice as to their personality and how they relate to others? Do they ever get the chance to create their self, to become a person?

We as people can have an insight into our self, we unlike the fish can become aware of the water that is our environment we can observe ourselves and gain an awareness of ourselves in our relation to that world, and to ourselves, how as I did and focus on developing one aspect (being tough) which meant the opposite polarity of being soft or sensitive was underdeveloped, and in fact that part of me was rationalised, with powerful introjects such as "only girls are soft" or "men don't cry" I had learned more about myself experientially (learning from experience) both in action, and from action, that is to say reflecting on events and my impact on them or their influence on me, as well as actively putting myself into situations, or developing an awareness of my self when i was in a situation, and these situations were from a broad field, such as interacting with senior managers, or colleagues at work and how i was in relation to them, negotiating at a meeting or talking to a sales person, but not only understanding why i was for instance anxious about talking to a senior manager but also how it was that i would put him into a position that enabled me, or rather affected in such a way that I felt the feelings of

6

anxiety when in relation to him, that was absent when I communicating with a colleague of the same role as myself.

I'll tell a quick story that highlights this: I was working in a company and a senior manager was a very autocratic and dominant person. He was criticising a colleague who he felt should have been doing a different task, or rather, that he was engaged in essential work duties other than the task that the senior manager wanted him to do, and was talking about him to other managers and colleagues in a critical way. I felt this was wrong, that i wanted to say something in defence of my colleague, but was holding back, and even in the process of holding back i felt very anxious, feeling that i wanted to, that I should say something to this person, as I am engaged in active experiential learning I thought this would be a good opportunity to just give it a go, to feel that vulnerability and anxiety, to become aware of my own processes in relation to another person.

I tried to approach him in an assertive manner trying to understand how he saw the situation the way he did, I tried to include my own perspective, and to try to engage in conversation, but the way in which he was responded to me was to challenge and critique my opinion, and I felt under pressure to conform to his point of view. It wasn't my purpose to try to change his opinion, but merely to open up the possibility to another's perspective and to convey my feelings that my colleague was being judged unfairly. The conversation ended pretty quickly, he was rigid in his view, and was talking to me not in an equal way, but in a somewhat dismissive manner. I considered whether to highlight this, but thought of my intentions for doing so, and for what purpose, and if I did respond in the way he was inviting (for it to develop into an argument) was I happy with that invitation, and I wasn't, so I ended the conversation saying that it looked like that we had different views of my colleague, and that I respected that this was his opinion.

So, what did I learn from this, the manager had learnt from somewhere that to interact with people, especially people that he viewed himself as more important than, he behaved in a dictatorial and autocratic manner, and that this way involved speaking a certain way, how he may have become a manager to be able to relate to people in such a way his reaction to people to whom he believed weren't doing what he thought they should do, his reaction to me trying to support my colleague and how he communicated his ideas about my colleague to other members of staff. There is also a particular question I would like to ask that what would

7

happen if this manager could no longer maintain his idea of his self-concept or if was challenged, would anxiety, depression, anger or stress ensue? This example isn't a world away from my own adjustments to become tough to survive on the streets of Belfast, and this manager's adjustments or introjects to become the way he has, and just as my *toughness* affected how I spoke, how I interacted and my beliefs about the world, then so it is the same for this manager, he is being in a way that is getting his needs met. What was important in this interaction I felt was that from my observations the manager communicated in different ways, he talked in an competitive one-up way to managers at his level, talked in a dismissive and condescending manner to subordinates and seemed to ingratiate himself to senior managers in the organisation. This person's self-concept, just as with many people is very complex, and there is a shift when in relation to different people or situations, and this shift is based on his own idea of himself. I am writing now with the image of this manager and how his world is based on his beliefs about himself, and other people. Is this image of his self-concept a rigid composite image? I would say that it is as he shifts between roles as to his belief of himself in relations to others, based on his belief of his self. So here is a man with the potential to be anything engage with others from an idea of who he is, and he responds to others from that. Is this real contact with another person, does he view the other as a unique individual and respects their right to exist. No I do not believe he does, and by doing so engages the other like an object, an object with the purpose of giving his self meaning, and when we see a person and believe that we can judge them, order them or manipulate them to fit into our way of seeing ourselves we turn ourselves into an object as well.

I would like to introduce to you a symbol and talk about the first section and introduce two concepts:

This is a symbol that i first thought about when contemplating how a person adjusts to life, as when a person is born they can become anything within their own personal limitations and whatever environment a person is born into will inevitably affect how that person develops and becomes a person.

A person always has the capacity to creatively adjust all through their life and in the multitude of possibilities that life may thrust upon us. This symbol could be used when a person is affected by a traumatic event, or a relationship breakdown. For example, a woman whose partner has been unfaithful may creatively adjust, or take it as an introjection and believe that men can't be trusted, and any man she meets in future may be viewed with suspicion, the woman may hold herself back or restrict herself emotionally in relationships with the expectation that this may happen again, she may become cynical, and if she believes that men cannot be trusted, then she may begin to associate with nefarious men that indeed cannot and should not be trusted, or she could adjust to the belief that it was her own fault that he was unfaithful, and become depressed in her belief it was her fault the relationship ended or endured difficulties, it may also affect her self-confidence or self-esteem, if she believes that her husband no longer thinks of her as attractive or desirable (or that he prefers other women) and if the relationship fails and she becomes single, she may carry that belief (a creative adjustment or introjection) of being unworthy onto future relationships, she may also believe that as she cannot rely on her husband (or men if she becomes single) she had to become very independent and as such this will affect her in future relationships, as she may be unable to trust herself to rely on her new partner, for fear of being hurt again, perhaps moving from dependent to self-supportive and independent as the trust in others diminishes. The example could be used for a person who has been taken into care and learned that he is his own support, the child of alcoholic parents who has had to take responsibility for their younger siblings and forms the belief that it is his duty to take care of people, the person who has been bullied at work because of his sexuality, then changes jobs and keeps that part of his self hidden or undisclosed. In these examples there is a mark of rigidity, that is to say there is no flexibility in how the person views themselves or their environment and their self-concept may become fixed, and they may have beliefs about who they are and the world around them, the woman whose partner has been unfaithful use of language and belief about men may change as she becomes more cynical, the child in care may feel that he has to do everything himself, the way in which he communicates and his behaviour may keep people at arm's length or have people actively distance themselves because of his behaviour and the person who has the alcoholic parents may become a nurse, become a volunteer or gain employment in another caring profession.

It is from this that i want to include these two concepts, these are Introjection and Creative Adjustment, and is it these two areas that i believe are influential in the development of our self-concept or identity, both in our idea of our self, and who we are in relation to other people, and while there are boundaries there is an amount of fluidity with our self-concept (just as with the manager who relates to others based on his belief of himself) the introject or the way in which a person creatively adjusts may become fixed and part of their idea of who they are, and they may start to own it, or become it.

Creative Adjustment is a term that involves changing as the person's situation changes and that we ideally are constantly adjusting in relation to our ever changing environment, that we create new ways of being in response to new situations (Mann 2010 p8) and in the picture I will try to illustrate this.

The tree that has grown on top of a hill has had to creatively adjust to survive in that environment. You can see that when it was developing and young (the top part of the tree) it has bent in relation to the wind, it didn't have a choice really I think, it had to bend in the prevailing dominant wind to survive, you can see that when the tree gained sufficient strength it was able to grow normally with the trunk straight. The tree has also had to creatively adjust in relation not only to the wind, but also to the nutrients in the ground. Growing on a hill means that any water will drain away at a faster rate, meaning that this will affect how the tree grows and develops. This is apparent if you look at the tree to the left looking healthy and having grown slightly lower. So, even though the tree was able to take root in that position it had to grow in the conditions in which it found itself. Similarly a child who is born in a certain environment will also have to creatively adjust to survive and as we shall explore in this chapter and throughout this book there are as many possibilities as there are people as to how a person adjusts to life, as well as the implications on the person's self-concept and how they relate to the world around them. As we shall see in later examples in chapters the process of creative adjustment may become an issue when the person becomes stuck in the way they adjust, or just like the tree become fixed in that way of being, or in relation to a person they may become frozen in the way they respond to, and how they influence the world around them. In fact one of the purposes of this book is so a person can become more aware of how they have adjusted to their world, and what introjects they have assimilated.

In the Growing Edge of Gestalt Therapy (1997 p222) Laura Perls states that these *fixed Gestalts* in time can become a block, and in block she refers more to the *habitual and automatic behaviour patterns, and social attitudes that have become second nature,* as well as *the fixed attitudes, habits and principles that pervade our whole culture and confine, and define the so called "normal"*

I have included this as any adjustment or change as the person's world changes is healthy, however the creative adjustments (and introjections) that influence how we see ourselves (our self-concept) which in itself suggests a fixed way of how we see ourselves.

Now, before I go further to explain to talk about creative adjustment I'd like you to consider the picture below;

As a species this cactus had to adapt it to survive in the harsh climate that it is native to, it has developed a deep and complex root system so it can search for nutrients and water deep in the earth, then stores that water for future use, it can even swell to accommodate more water and the cactus also shrinks in times of drought. It has also had to adjust to the intensity of the sun by developing spines instead of leaves (the water in the leaves would evaporate in the sun) and the spines also collect moisture in the air and then drip down towards the roots. The spines also protect the plant from predators and it has that tough protective coating. The cactus can also become dormant in really dry conditions and becomes active again when it rains.

Such is the adjustment or adaptation of the cactus that it can survive in those harsh conditions that it is a real survivor. However, as you can see this particular cactus is in a pot and as such has no need for any of these adaptations, there are no predators here and as I water it regularly this means that the deep root system is now redundant. The spines and tough protective coating also now have no real purpose. The environment of the cactus has changed, yet the means of survival, the creative adjustments or the adaptations have not, they have become fixed. This is how I see the role of creative adjustment in people that the person has had to adapt or adjust in whatever world the person was born into (or for adjustments later in life) and may have become fixed. Just like the cacti having to adjust, adapt or evolve to survive, and then it becomes fixed, so it is for a person, especially in relation to their identity or self-concept. Unlike the person this cactus can't decide that it doesn't need spines anymore and shed them, and doesn't need that tough skin. It would be hard to change though as if it did so then it would become something different, something new. It would also have to realise just what the function was of its varying defences to survive, how it adapted or adjusted to survive and then decide that these were no longer necessary. Now if we put the manager in place of the cactus, how like the cactus he has creatively adjusted to survive in his world, how maybe in place of the barren terrain in which the cactus had to source water he had to adjust to become dominant, to become authoritative to his younger siblings (the same style of parenting as his parents) and in doing so he adapted to speak a way that reinforced this, but also to adjust again when he was interacting with his parents or any other persons he viewed as being in authority. This belief of himself could easily have given him the message *I am more important that people below me, but less important that people above me, so for me to be a person of worth I have to be important.* I wonder if he would want to know how he interacts with others, because if he gained an awareness of the purpose and meaning of how he related to others, how he viewed himself and his belief of himself, then it may lead to the question "if I am not this, then what am I?" and I believe that when we gain an awareness of how we live, how we communicate and interact with others, as well as our idea of who we are then we can have a choice as to the person we would like to be. So if we view that this person is taking a role that has integrated into his self-concept then this would be limiting as he would be restricting himself from a number of other possibilities of how to exist, and how to simply be a person.

The cactus has adjusted to life in its harsh environment to be able to survive, but why are there other species? This is another view of creative adjustment, for just as the cactus adapted in its own way so it is that another species adapted in a different way under the same conditions. This is the complexity of people, that we all, under the same conditions will adjust in different ways.

Imagine the adaptation or the creative adjustment of a child who lives with 4 brothers and sisters in a busy and hectic family environment with little boundaries. How could she be listened too when she would in competition with her siblings for the attention of her parents, and while there are significant possibilities I shall focus on one outcome I have observed. The child began to speak louder and louder to be heard, and of course as this was the way of the family means of communication then her other siblings also talked louder, to also be heard. To substantiate and reinforce this (and also as a measure of an introjection) the mother also talked in a loud voice also. So, walking into this family home was just a wall of noise as each person was in competition to be heard, and volume was the medium of this. Now, what would be the implications of this person when she went to another environment, say perhaps she visits her friend for dinner, and this particular family who are quieter and more reserved in comparison. If like the cactus and the manager her behaviour is fixed then her volume would be more noticeable, or even appear loud and boisterous when in relation to the quieter family. If the girl can adjust flexibly she could adapt, however if the underlying message for the adjustment is *for me to be noticed I have to be speak louder than everyone else* then when under pressure (or what she experienced to be pressure) then she may revert to that loud speech volume.

Another aspect of creative adjustment would be a person who lives in a busy and congested city, and perhaps the person lives in a deprived area where the crime level is high. How would this person adjust to this environment? Does the person filter out the traffic noise so as not to be overwhelmed by the incessant noise of the cars, buses, and commercial vehicles as well as the exhaust fumes, walking down the busy street, negotiating a path to avoid other people, keeping their head down as they try to carve a path through the crowd. As the person lives in a deprived area she has had to adjust to this as well and prefers to be home before it goes dark, something which is difficult when autumn and winter arrives so she chooses a path of least risk from her place of work to her home. If there are a group of people stood on a corner she feels she has to cross the road to avoid them, her way of seeing and sensing may also adapt so she can judge whether the person has any hostile intent, or just loitering. What are the implications of adjusting to this environment, does the person not *hear* as well, so when she is walking in the countryside as she is so used to filtering the sound around her she misses the sound of the birds, crickets, bees and the flowing river. She is so used to keeping her head down when walking through the city while planning a path through the crowds she now misses the trees and hills and clouds, by filtering out the smells of the city she misses the aromas of the countryside, and also visually, when as she has adjusted to the drab greyness of the city she doesn't see the colours of the countryside as well. She has in all these cases adjusted her senses to filter out stimulus that is unwanted or would otherwise be overwhelming. The antithesis of this would be the farmer or other rural countryside dweller who has adjusted to living in a traffic free, noise free, pollution free and relatively crime free area and then to be dropped in the middle of a busy city, their senses would be overloaded I think.

While writing now on the means of adjustment and the impact of living in the city and how the person adjusts to survive, in the case of living in the city and the *dulling down* or *switching off* sensory awareness I now ask you to consider the impact of the adjustment of a woman who is in a relationship with a dominant controlling man and invite you to conduct the following experiment before we go onto a further exploration of the impact of this adjustment. There are also areas of introjections that I shall also highlight.

Awareness Experiment: Being Controlled

I ask you to find a partner for this, ideally a partner that you are willing to relinquish control too.

Stand up and ask the person to stand behind you with their arms on the side of each shoulder at the top of each arm. Now walk around the room you are in with the person following. Now have the person gently at first start to slow down your movement and as you are walking slowly have them guide you in a direction that you were not walking, so if you are walking in a straight line have them guide you to the left or right. (What are you experiencing as you are being guided, do you go with the subtle shift in the person controlling you, or do you want to push against the controller?) Start to push against the person to go in the direction you want, but the other person reacts to this and presses harder in the direction that they want you to go, the more you choose your own direction the more they stop this. (What are you experiencing now that the person is more active in controlling you? Do you want to push back or do you just give in and go with the person?)

Now, have the person totally stop you and each time you attempt to move have them restrict you. Now, please don't push too hard, this is just an experiment after all!

(what do you experience in what you are sensing in your body, you are trying to push, but in all directions you cannot move, do you resent the controller? Do you lose energy to push against the person? Do you start to play games pretending to go with the controller but change direction quickly so as to try to trick the person or do you start to believe that he is in control?)

Now have the controller begin to guide you again, but instead of pushing against him start to believe that he is in charge and do what he wants, imagine that you want to push against him but he is charge and that he is right. (What are you experiencing now as you believe he is in charge?) Now push against him but note that he still only lets you walk in the way he wants you to walk, and you can make small adjustments, but only adjustments that he agrees to, or doesn't challenge you. (What are you experiencing now, that you can only walk in the directions that he agrees to?)

You can now stop the experiment. What did you learn about yourself? If you are normally a strong and confident person how was it for you to be guided at first, you thought you were in charge but as the experiment continued the controller became more and more dominant how was this for you? Finally, how was it for you to be allowed to walking only in the direction that was agreeable to the controller?

If you are not so confident or normally a passive or easy going person how was it for you to have control over someone and have them follow you, and what was it like as they gradually exerted more control, until they directed each way you were walking. Was it reassuring to have them take control and guide you, or did you believe that as they were in charge then it was their way you had to walk.

Finally, ask yourself that if you did want to assert yourself, how would you creatively adjust to take control of some aspects of your self and your environment, especially with a person in this experiment who is physically dominant over you? Now change physically dominant for other means of control. Imagine if the person used their own self-justifiable role (such I am a husband and the person in charge) to dominate you, or after undermining or challenging your intelligence and ability in your self, saying you are incompetent then they dominate you with *their* intellect and abilities. What about instead of being physical they used your children to control you, or sees himself as being in charge of the house, or if he bullies you by shouting, swearing, glaring if you give the *wrong* answer or say the *wrong* thing that challenges him. What about if the controller uses insults and put downs to emotionally abuse you then you give in to his control, or starts to cry to get his own way. Or controls you through your friends. On the surface he is the charmer and helpful to all your friends (so you have little support if you tell them about him) but in private he is manipulative to put himself in charge. This could be an exhaustive list of how people are controlled, especially in personal relationships, but I hope I have highlighted how people can be controlled outside your awareness.

The example below is how a person may creatively adjust to a dominant and controlling man.

When they first met the man was very supportive and helpful, she had a child previous to when they met and he reinforced to her that he would take on the responsibility for the child (this had the message that she should be grateful to him) and as the relationship developed he took over all the responsibilities for paying the bills, rationalising that it would be easier if they were all in his name, she did question this but his complex answer was difficult to follow and she eventually gave in. As this was the case he needed access to her account to transfer money to his account and pretty soon she had to adjust to this by asking him for money for shopping, of which he also took care of and she was relegated to simply pushing the trolley. When they went on holiday he always gave reasons why they should go to the places he wanted to and discounted her suggestions and when she did try to state her opinion of something that was important to her, he also challenged this, not by listening and valuing her opinion but by his usual "but what about..." and his old chestnut, saying what he was doing was for her and the children, and that he twisted her opinion to state that it was selfish. If they ever visited her family he would start an argument so they leave early, and if her family visited her in their family home he would make them feel very uncomfortable, sometimes swearing in front of them and calling her names. He would also discipline the children and if she ever questioned his authoritarian methods he would say that if she didn't agree then it meant she was bad parent. He would sulk and throw a tantrum if he didn't get his own way The message that he was saying was that he was in charge of the house, the finances and who they visited, there was also the manipulation that if she didn't agree with him he would sulk or throw a tantrum. This was his way of controlling her and as with the Being Controlled experiment she eventually gave in. The only area that she could assert herself (within the boundary of his control) was to do the menial jobs in the house, so she cooked and cleaned and adjusted to not challenge any area that he put himself in charge of. She also had dreams of going to college and starting her own business but this was a challenge to him, so through coercion he managed to keep her in a job in a shop stacking shelves. As she had adjusted to little more than a servants role (a role that did not challenge his) this also had the impact of affecting her belief in herself, her self-confidence and her abilities. She noticed that she never got excited any more, or was enthusiastic towards holidays or other family outings (as it was always his idea of what they did or where they went) and as he wasn't interested in her (except for sex) she never spoke or made conversation with him on the topics that were of interest to her, or of her opinions and thoughts. When he came in he would sit and tell her all about his day, and this affected her hearing as though she was sitting there she didn't actively listen to him, as she was just a sounding board for his ranting and complaining, she would also ask questions on the topics he wanted to talk about. She has adjusted to her life with him to the belief that she should keep him happy (or else he would throw a tantrum) never challenge him (as it would cause an argument) and to just endure the menial life she had with him. The other implications of this were that as the introjected message was *you are not important* this also had the impact on her children who talked to her the same way their father did, and also viewed her of being less important, and only capable of menial tasks, and that her thoughts has no value. For many years she had adjusted to this relationship, which had the consequence of influencing her beliefs of her self (of being little more than an opinion-less servant) and much like the cactus when she did have the courage to leave that dominant and controlling man she carried those beliefs with her, and it took some years for her to assert her own importance and belief in her own self and her own right to state an opinion and her thoughts without the fear of a person attacking this. As she had survived this relationship the introjections and creative adjustments had a lasting effect and she became highly sensitised and aggressively reactive to any man she thought was controlling her the same way he had. After leaving him she realised that all her fear of challenging him was like trying to appease a petulant child, a selfish child who just wanted to get his own way and expected all others to adjust to his needs (his own introjected belief about himself perhaps?) and that all his threats were just that, empty threats with no substance.

Did this change happen overnight, and what was the impact of these creative adjustments for the woman? The dominant partner was very subtle in his *need* to have his partner adjust to his way of being, for her to fit into the way he thought she *should* be. Initially it was out of her awareness as outwardly he was being helpful and offering guidance, then after some time the guidance became directions as to what to do in situations and then after this was accepted (as he would through a tantrum, start an argument, or to give a complex reason as to why his view was better) This eventually became a controlling relationship where the woman knew not to challenge his authority. The impact of these adjustments were many, she tried her best not to upset others, even to feel the anxiety at the possibility of upsetting others, whether this was her employer (and could never say no to their request to work extra hours) she didn't give her opinion when speaking to others and instead stayed quiet and merely listened. At the thought of starting college she became anxious, as the thought of putting herself first, instead of being in a menial role (both in her employment as well as in her family) that she has adjusted to. When she did speak, it became apparent that she didn't make statements such as "i think" or "i believe" that is to say owning what you a saying, and instead phased her thoughts as questions such as "what do you think of?" such as such to gain the person's idea of the topic they had an idea on before disclosing her own thoughts and adjusted them so as not to upset the other person. The person this lady was when she first met this man had gone, and it was not through growth to become something more, but the opposite, that she had become restricted by a dominant controlling man, and had to adjust to this life. The repercussions of this was that some beliefs and behaviours had become fixed into the how the woman viewed herself, that it was not an immediate or overnight change but a very gradual process that was outside the person's awareness. The other aspects of this adjustment was that she never treated her self, and rarely bought new clothes, when she did she shopped in discount or charity shops. Also, when a person showed an interest in her, or a concern for her well-being she immediately deflected this, normally with the quick answer "i am fine thanks, how are you?" and began to focus questions on the other person, or on topics or interests that she knew the other person was interested in and therefore lead the conversation. The woman, after having adjusted to her life with the dominant controlling man knew which questions to ask the other person to focus on their own needs or topics instead of her own. The person's self-concept had adjusted because of her life with the controlling man.

One of the aspects of creative adjustment (and introjections) is that when it becomes a rigid view of how they view their self then their actions becomes a *should,* that is to say, they *should* behave a certain way, speak a certain way, they should have their house clean and tidy at all times, to never challenge their parent, employer or other authority figure. These rules of how to be a person guide their behaviours, thoughts and actions, even how the person will walk, talk, structure sentences, hear, feel and remember. I shall cover this more in a later chapter on polarisation, assertiveness and the contact functions, however to give an example, a person who believes themselves to be in charge, or more important than others may start or guide conversations to the topic they would prefer, or if the person has an agenda (for example a salesperson who pretends to listen to the customer however it is just part of a game for them to interject at the right time so they can fulfil their own motivations) to let the other person lead before taking over. Some people who have adapted to believe they are in charge may become a manager or other authority figure and in contrast a person who has adjusted to be the opposite may adjust to an occupation with little responsibility or authority.

In his book People Skills (1979 p70), Robert Bolton discusses what I would call creative adjustment and introjection:

Ours is a culture that teaches people to repress their feeling. From an early age, children are taught to distort or repress their feelings. "Be nice to your sister" "stop crying" "how many times have I told you not to get angry!" "let other children play with your toys" "i don't care how you feel – do it" "you don't know what is good for you" "stop acting like a scared cat" "Stop that silly laughter"

Though this is from an older book I believe the words of the author are still relevant today. We all receive messages that we integrate and assimilate all through our life and it becomes part of our identity or self-concept. The example above of the person being told not to get angry may have to creatively adjust to this and believe that to be a person they cannot get angry, then if they inhabit the polarity of *being nice* then they may actively avoid getting angry and become passive or non-assertive. The person may sit on the fence and not commit to an answer or make a statement that can be challenged, and this in turn will affect the person's contact functions, that is to say how they speak, the tone, pitch and speech rate of their voice (so as not to challenge others) how they interact with people and may appear bland and weak as they refuses to state their beliefs. The occasions when they do feel anger they may feel guilty for being this way, and may also get anxious when this does happen, as it challenges the view of their self or identity. The person may rationalize and believe that it's ok to get angry if it is for a noble or righteous cause and release their aggression for an environmental or human rights cause. Of course all those times when the person wanted to get angry but felt those pangs of anxiety he may in fact bottle up those feelings and then explode, or contain those emotions for years and collapse with the weight of carrying them. All those years of covering their anger with a fake smile and choosing the right words to placate the other may take their toll.

In all the examples above the person who is being addressed, that is to say the person who is being talked to is being put by the other person into a submissive role while the speaker is in a more dominant role and telling the other how to be a person. The submissive person therefore has to adjust to these rules for them to survive in this environment. Then, when these rules are integrated into the person's self-concept they start to become it, or own it.

In his book Gestalt Therapy Mini Lectures (1976 p74) the author James Simkin gives an example of Creative Adjustment in a person that pleases others for his own gain. He states;

Many people think, "i am afraid the other person won't be there when I need him" so the game they play is pretending to be interested in the other person so he will be there when they do want him. They don't really want the other person all the time. As a matter of fact sometimes they wish the other person would just disappear or go take a swim or leave them alone. "i'm afraid, however that if I get my hooks out he will disappear"

As a young man I saw this example a few years ago from a woman in my home country, she pretended to be interested in a neighbour who was adept at property repairs and fixing cars, and would flirt with him and charm him to keep him interested. It never went any further than this flirting as she wasn't that interested in him in an intimate way, but just for what he could do for her. As the lady didn't have the skills or technical aptitude to conduct repairs on her property and on her car she adapted to entice another person to do this for her. She would play coy and ask questions that enticed him into a responsible and knowledgeable position. The media has a common portrayal of this in films with the beautiful woman at the side of the road with a flat tyre looking flustered or in tears and a kindly motorist stops and offers to change it. She stands there, observes with praise and thanks, and never gets a hand dirty. In the case of my old neighbour she would flatter him with compliments and innuendo. This was her way of adapting to cover a deficit in herself I believe and to manipulate support from those around her. My neighbour could have learnt the skills to maintain her house and car (which would have cost her time and money to enrol on courses or to read books on these subjects, as well as a belief in her own abilities and potential) or to source a reliable plumber, electrician, builder or motor mechanic (which would have also cost money or create anxiety dealing with these skilled professionals) but instead she adapted or adjusted to flirt and charm a person she knew had the skills and aptitude to help her, she also maintained their relationship by appearing helpless to entice the man to help her. While I shall cover this more in a later chapter for her to fulfil her need to be taken care of, or to cover what she saw as her own shortfalls she adapted herself to be able to get support from others. For this lady her way of speaking to her neighbour meant talking in flirty conversation, making herself look attractive and dressing in a somewhat sexual way as well. I observed that she would talk in a normal manner to other people but *shift* to a flirty helpless person when she wanted something from the male neighbour. So, here is a woman who is getting her needs met from those around her to cover a deficit in herself and also to keep the man on hold for when she needs him. There are probably many beliefs about herself originating from introjections such as not believing in herself, her ability to talk in an assertive manner to others and so became passive, and playing a role with games (being helpless) she may even have had a dominant ex-partner or an authoritarian parent and she was never allowed to develop skills that meant independence and assertiveness, so she had to creatively adjust from this position and develop skills that meant she could survive in her world. This also meant an intuitive understanding of being able to ask the right person who would be able to help her. In this case a man who she was could sense would respond to her way of (manipulative) communication and who he himself was lonely. So in this relationship we have a man whose need to help (perhaps to fulfil his own needs) and a woman who need to be helped (through a low sense of worth) The woman had previously had an aggressive partner and for her to survive in his world she had to become very sensitive to his moods and to be able to *read* him. So here she is now after honing her skills to survive in that world with her previous partner to know which way to communicate with the capable man who could help her. She could sense that he was lonely and that he would help her given the right stimulation. One of the introjected messages that drives this creative adjustment is *you can't do things alone* or *you need other people as you are incapable of overcoming problems yourself* and so here she is now, not being independent but relying on others for support through manipulation (the difference between self-support and environmental support) and has developed her contact functions to fulfil this need or self-concept of herself. There may also be a factor in her pleasing the other person to get needs met, in the case here of pleasing the other person through flattery, flirting and admiration, as she talks about his positive qualities, we will explore other areas of *pleasing* others, particularly in relation to the how the person's identity or self-concept and how they please others, either to fulfil a need in their self, to play a game, whether this is situational, that is to say pleasing some people but not others, and importantly the circumstances in which this takes place.

Another aspect of this and creative adjustment is from people who only want to get their needs met temporarily and are then happy discard the person (seeing the person as an object to use rather than a unique individual). I remember once encountering a person who exhibited this, he would appear very interested in a person if they were either a manager or a person he wanted information from. There was once a person he worked with and never really acknowledged that person or showed any interest until he found out that person could help with a project he was working, he then asked questions about the person's family and interests, spoke about the topics the person had an interest in and would again flatter and charm the person with compliments, sometimes putting himself in a less knowledgeable position so he could ask the person if they knew the answer to a question, and also asking opinions of the other person. This was just another means of manipulation as he flattered to get his needs met, and he did so through his use of contact functions, the way he spoke, the syntax of his words (such as finishing statements in a question) and would often act with a sense of being aloof and humorous, but also weak and needy. This was interesting to see actually as he would be able to turn this on depending on who he was talking to, and immediately switch it off. When the project was completed he went back to how he was prior and no longer showed an interest in the person. I noticed as well that when he was in dialogue with a manager at work he would immediately ingratiate himself to the manager, acting in his usual aloof and jokey way and asking questions that very often he knew the answer to, he would also ask advice about the problems in his personal life to the manager. It seemed that when he spoke to the manager he went into a child type personality and would again appear quite helpless when asking for advice. I often wondered how this creative adjustment came into being, and later learned that his father was a very strict parent with whom he had to praise, adulate and on occasions have to grovel to gain attention from him or recognition. He could never talk to him as an equal and he very way of being reflected this and he would often put himself into a subservient position with those he wanted information from, or from those he viewed as being more important that himself. This was interesting to me as he adjusted himself to this position and again he very rarely made statements and asked for a response, he asked a question and listened to the reply before stating his opinions, which were of course in line with those person's views. This was part of this person's manipulation to fulfil that role he saw of himself (especially with those people who he saw a being more important or with something he wanted) and by putting himself into a more submissive or non-assertive role and how his actions substantiated and reinforced this, his style of being and the way he spoke as well as the questions he asked tried to invite the person into a more dominant role, a more decision making and influential role. In the first example he flattered the other to get help with the project (putting himself into a lower role to ask for advice) and in the second example with this person he acquiesced responsibility to act like a child when in relation with a manager. Both these creative adjustments had their origin in his development as a child, a child whose parent was strict, authoritarian and dominant.

Simkin (1976 p50) writes *sometimes I stop myself from expressing myself because of my fear of expressing myself because of how the other person will react.*

I view this is another aspect of both introjection and creative adjustment. Somewhere is a person's development they learnt to hold back from expressing themselves. For example a man who feels that he will be laughed at or ridiculed for showing a sensitive understanding of an issue, but stops himself from doing so. Environmental or political issues that he may be passionate about may never be disclosed if they are not shared by the person or group he is interacting with. He may have the idea that he is a masculine man and not be able to express his deep love for his wife. If a crisis occurs and she is in a distressed state he may resort to giving practical advice or solutions rather than be loving and supportive towards her, or feel that he has to strong so she is able to be emotional.

In fact, Polster E. and Polster M. (1973 p121) explore this further and have used the term Expressive Boundaries. They write briefly of the expressive limits of a person who is a model and is hanging on to her youth (or teenageness as stated by the Polsters) and as such she has adjusted to this belief, moreover her contact functions and how she expresses herself are based on this. When she tries to develop herself as a singer as well as a model she discovers that it has a light tonal quality and not a mature fuller voice a woman her age would have. At 21 she is still expressing herself as teenager (trying to look younger as a model) and as a result it had implications for her singing career.

Writing this reminds me of a particular aspect of creative adjustment, and how person adjusted themselves as a means of expression. It was a lady who for a number of years had known she was attracted to women and had encapsulated masculine qualities (or her experience of what masculine was) and expressed herself from this way of being, as she identified with this masculinity she wore men's clothes. Typically women's jeans have a different cut and style than men's jeans and as such she only wore men's jeans, she would wear polo neck t-shirts or thick jumpers, and also went to a barber to cut her hair in a masculine style. I think she must have been observant of how men moved and sat as she seemed to copy this and would walk in a manly way and also sit the same way a man would. Although women sometimes now drink from pint glasses (in the north of England anyway) when she did go to a pub she would stand at the bar and roll a cigarette while drinking a pint of lager. I noticed as well that any girlfriends she would have were blonde, petite and very feminine. The lady had the idea of who she was and expressed herself this way (as a means of creative adjustment) however as she owned the more masculine aspects of a person (tough, strong, resourceful) the more feminine polarities such as sensitivity, understanding and warmth were deficient in how she interacted, both with herself and others.

How we express ourselves, as well as our values I believe is inextricable from our self-concept and the many introjections and creative adjustment that influence how we see ourselves and how we want to be seen.

I once knew a person who had creatively adjusted to an interesting position which affected both his relation to others as well as had implications for his life. He grew up with an introjected message that he was less important than others, and in particular his relation to women. He had a very stern and again authoritarian mother and he learnt from an early age the introjected message *you are less important than women,* this was reinforced by the way in which he was treated less favourably than his sisters. That is to say his sisters were treated as more important than he was. He adjusted to this by pleasing women in later life, however he would please women by having sex with them. He would sense of what the woman's intentions were, by her suggestive remarks, inferences or suggestions and fulfil them. It was not that he was intentionally sleeping with women, but falling in line with what they wanted, and in effect he was passive and gave himself to how they wanted him. His worth came from how women viewed him and what he could do for them. As he was an attractive and athletic person this is why it became sexually orientated. Of course this became integrated into his own way of being and as he viewed himself as doing what women wanted he become charming, superficial and pleased women through flirting during their interactions. When I met him, even though he was married he was having relations with other married women who he believed were unhappy in their marriage and also women who were single and with whom he could help. (he viewed himself having sex with women as helping them to satisfy their needs) He was a promiscuous man which had a detrimental impact on his relationship with his wife. Due to the nature of creative adjustment this introjected message had become integrated into his self-concept and after his marriage had failed he went from relationship to relationship in his endeavours to please women, as he viewed his own happiness as less important that women he would not focus his efforts on his own needs or care, but instead to again put himself second to the wishes of women who he viewed as in need or that he could please. His contact functions adjusted to this idea of himself, and the way he spoke when in relation to women was soft and flattering, highlighting attributes they exhibited. His contact functions also meant the creative adjustment of his body, which has become toned from many hours in the gym, mainly because this is how he believed women wanted him to be. The creative adjustment that had originated from the initial introjection had profound and lasting effect on this person in his search for affection, approval, worth and recognition. (much like a woman who becomes promiscuous because of a low self-worth and need for affection from men, and becomes sexual as she believes that is all they want from her)

In his book The Miracle of Dialogue (1963 p52) The author Reuel Howe discusses a person who has the view of his self as a person of authority, that is to say that as he views himself as an authority figure then he has the belief of himself to be able to exercise that authority. Such is the case of people who become teachers or educators and their adjustment to which this position is attained and that they can now direct others. If the person fulfils any type of role in a field where they have to educate others there is the possibility that to be in that field that a person must give answers to questions or to follow a syllabus as a means of education, instead of helping the person to educate themselves. If they are following a syllabus then the person has the requirement of adjusting to the requirements of this. This may have the benefit if the purpose of teaching aligns to how the person views their own self, that is to say if they have the idea of their identity as being more important that others (students) or that they gain a sense of worth from this role, maybe even they have felt they have to follow in their parents footsteps, if they were teachers or by following the advice or guidance as to what to be (an introjection) though of course this could be used for any profession or career path. There may also be the possibility that if the person believes that they have to be noticed and listened to, then standing in front of class may fulfil this. If the teacher has the purpose of answering questions instead of helping others source their own answers then this could become an introjection or creative adjustment that they cannot develop their own resources to support themselves, and instead to ask for another's advice or opinion. As a simple example of this I have observed a person who has been searching for a product in a supermarket immediately ask for help from a member of staff, instead of using their own resources to find the product they are were looking for. If we put this example onto the teacher then this would mean when the student encounters a problem then their first response is to ask the most immediate person who can give a solution rather than try to solve the problem by themselves. A teacher who *needs* to be a person in authority may encourage the former, at the cost of developing the person's own creative process to solve problems or issues. On a slightly different area I have always tried to solve my own problems, be it fixing my car or doing maintenance projects in my house such as plastering, plumbing or joinery, however I have noticed that many people take their car to the garage to get repaired and call in a skilled trades-person for minor house maintenance at their property. Although there are of course other factors I feel that the belief of a person to be able to overcome their own problems is diminishing and the easy answer if to ask another person to fix something, or answer something instead. Is this an indicator of the creative adjustment our society today, or a mass introjection that if something breaks then one must call a professional to fix this.

As a measure of creative adjustment and how one can adjust without really being aware of this I have noticed that at my local supermarket the checkout staff have the method of work to scan the items as quickly as possible onto a small platform at the till. Although this is a very simple example it provides a clear indicator to me of creative adjustment. Imagine the person who applies for a job at this budget supermarket and is told that this is the preferred method of work, to process and scan goods very quickly at the checkout. The person who works here has to adjust to this to be able to work there, they have to change their self to the company expectations and as such move faster when at the checkout. The company's rationalisation is that by being faster on the checkout then fewer staff are required, and as such prices are kept lower.

So, much like the person whose job it is to greet customers entering a store with a pleasant "good morning" or "hello" even though it is easy from the way a person speaks that they really are forcing themselves to say these words, for the person to be able to exist in this environment they have to adjust to the *rules* of that company and their contact functions have to adapt (moving quicker at the checkout, or saying a pleasant good morning) as a result of this. This is now passed onto the customer, the first time the customer arrives at the checkout and puts their goods at the checkout and is greeted by a checkout operator who very quickly scans their shopping. The person therefore either has to be assertive and ask them to slow down, or become passive or non-assertive and simply adjust to the unspoken message of the checkout operator, to pack their shopping very quickly. (If they have knowledge of the company message of "less staff - better value" then they may buy into this method of work and introjection) More often than not the person remains passive and falls in line without much fuss, they are merely also following the *rules* of the store without question. Now, the next time the shopper enters the store his is aware of this and adjusts himself when at the tills and proceeds to pack his shopping to the method and speed of the checkout operator.

Creative Adjustment is also relational, I once encountered a person who had the idea that she *should* be in charge, however because of the circumstances in her life she was unable to follow a career path that would have given this adjustment meaning, and as the need organises the field so it was that she did indeed put herself in charge, but it was as a very strict parent and she also associated with people with whom she saw as lower in status and as such she put herself in charge of people who had alcohol and drug problems, as well as people who had mental health issues. Her contact functions developed as part of this adjustment and when she spoke to these people then in doing so was with a very authoritative and knowledgeable voice as she told people what they should be doing. This adjustment occurred as a small child as she lived with relatives as her mother was unable to look after her, so this trauma as well as the reinforcement of being told that she was living temporarily with her then caregiver. So the adjustment for her was to exert control on her environment by being in charge, she found if difficult or anxiety provoking to engage or interact with a person in the spirit of equality and dialogue and so she chose to put herself in control, and thus to be in charge of people who she viewed herself as being as more important than. Part of this also involved developing an active dislike and avoidance of people who were in a position of authority (such as police officers, doctors, council staff or educational officials) and this also affected her contact functions when in relation to this types of people as she became aggressive.

However, many women (as well as men who have had strict parents) have been brought up to question their ability to take control and to be a voice of authority and as such avoid positions where their voice can be heard, or feel anxious telling another person what to do. If this adjustment becomes fixed then the person's self-concept develops with this possibility, this also has the impact on the person's contact functions and I have observed that some women and men talk with a very softly spoken voice and actively avoid saying or doing anything that would mean they have to be in charge of anything. I have noticed that eye contact is diminished in these people as well their style of dress. The term "wall flower" comes to mind here as the person adjusts to this belief about themselves and they adapt to this and stay off the radar. This adjustment is also alive in many controlling relationships as the person endeavours to stay out of the limelight, for the fear of the controller viewing them as competition.

Painful learning can become both introjection and creative adjustment and may the person may adjust to block this. This has become apparent to me when I see people who have endured painful relationships and avoid becoming involved in any new relationships as they have associated intimate relationships with a hurtful or damaging experience. I recall a person I once knew, her husband had been very aggressive, dominant and emotionally manipulative, she had been married to him for over 20 years before he passed away, but instead of her meeting another person she remained single. As she was an attractive woman she had her share of male admirers but she rebuffed them and kept herself single as she kept men at a distance. This was the repercussions of the painful experiences she had endured with her previous husband and her avoidance of any new relationship.

I remember once coming across a person who had previously had a relationship with a woman who he described as moody and selfish. He had been a very warm and caring person prior to meeting this woman however as she was self-centred and very difficult to please nothing that he did was good enough for her (perhaps her own creative adjustment that meant keeping herself for being happy, or enticing a partner to acquiesce to her control by trying to please her) even though he was a very attentive and considerate man. This became very draining for him and he would sense what mood she was in when he came home from work as she would give him a look that he interpreted as a sign to keep quiet or an argument would ensue. He eventually started to arrive home later and later, telling his partner that he was working overtime, taking up running that meant he could spend time alone. Eventually he finished the relationship but this painful learning of relationships had left its scars and he creatively adjusted to this by not entering into any relationship again for over 7 years, though as he missed having intimate relations with women this left him in a dilemma of a want to be intimate with a woman but was scared of entering into a relationship with a woman (after the experiences of his previous relationship) and so this meant that he entered into meaningless relationships with many women, when they wanted to develop the relationship he felt the tremors of anxiety and he would end the relationship with excuses or him not being ready to commit to another person, of having a difficult childhood and not being able to get over the experiences of his ex. These responses became almost scripted to him and he would manage his transient relationships with great skill, so he could be intimate with a partner without having to enter into a meaningful relationship, as this went against his morals he eventually started to question this behaviour and how he was treating women as objects to satisfy he own desires and was surprised when he gained an awareness of how much he had adjusted from the considerate, caring and warm person he initially was before meeting the lady who was selfish and as he described moody. He eventually had to learn to trust again and the last I saw him he had spent some time alone to become the person he wanted to be and had entered into a loving relationship with another person. I wonder sometimes that he had not questioned his own behaviour and how he had adjusted to the impact of being in a relationship with this woman. He initially spoke to people with respect and consideration, but after the relationship ended and he adjusted to seeing women as objects he style of talking changed and he became flattering and charming, knowing which way to speak to women to get his needs met, he also became to know just which women were likely to succumb to his charms and he would cast his net far. This adjustment also altered his contact functions, in his style of dress, way of questioning and purposes of self disclosure. He would tell women about the painful experiences of his life, though only for the purpose of hoping to make them feel sorry for him and therefore more likely to engage in an intimate relationship. Another person would have been controlling and picking passive women to enter into intimate relationships with, but he became the victim to entice women, with the benefit that he could use the same role (playing the victim through the use of disclosing his hard luck stories) to end the same relationships. The was also part of his way of creative adjustment for as he was entering into temporary relationships using his own difficult stories to manipulate the person to feel sympathy for himself this also meant that he had to change the way he spoke (speaking in a needy and helpless way) and this was apparent when he was speaking to people with whom he was not trying to manipulate, that is to say instead of playing the role of helpless he talked in a very confident, warm, articulate and intelligent manner. It was this shift that he became aware of was an indicator for him the impact of how much he had adjusted from his previous relationship with the self-centred and moody woman.

The means of creative adjustment can have many origins, at any point in a person's life, such as fear of, or an avoidance of making errors or mistakes (the person may adjust to this by becoming specialised or expert in a chosen field and, or to stay in a role where it is difficult to make a mistake) a fear of making the wrong decision (originating from a controlling and punitive parent and the repercussions of adjusting to a role where responsible decisions are not made, or becoming passive and enticing the other person to assume responsibility) Adjusting to a need to have an orderly and disciplined life (from a fear to being out of control or losing a routine for their way of life, or a role that gives their self meaning) After the person may have been emotionally hurt (as with the previous examples) they may become restrictive emotionally or reticent about displaying emotions. If the person has had to adjust to a strict or disciplinarian parent the person may feel they should follow the rules whatever the situation may be, which may also evoke feelings of guilt or anxiety if these rules cannot be followed. The person who has also been heavily criticised at some point in their life may creatively adjust to this and become a perfectionist with a need to have everything in their life done right, but also possibly to become highly sensitive to when a person is criticising them, as well as not taking risks. This example would also highlight the person's contact functions and how they hear or listen, that is to say, if the person becomes sensitive to any criticism then may (outside their awareness) filter anything said by another person that gives any suspicion of a critical comment. The person who is sensitive to this may also develop their response to criticism by having a number of quips or comments (being defensive) as a retort, and they may build up a bank of criticisms against significant others that they can "fight back with" should they be criticised by another. The same would be for a person who has been called stupid or dumb growing up (or any other point in their life) and may again feel they have to develop themselves in a field to prove they are not stupid, or begin to own these comments and not pursue their hopes, ambitions and dreams or any particular career path as they have believed they are incapable of, and instead resign themselves to a mediocre life. The way in which they interact with people (their contact functions) may also be affected. They may not converse with other people on meaningful or topical issues as they feel they do not have the ability to engage.

These creative adjustments and introjections may influence how the person interacts with their world and beliefs, the child who is criticised may learn that to be a person they have to criticise or judge another and therefore condemn them based on their own personal set of rules. If the child or person has had an environment of aggressiveness or hostility then they may become hostile to others (or passive to a person who they view as being more aggressive) if a person has encountered ridicule or being the brunt of person's jokes they may then withdraw from others or learn to ridicule others. If the person had adjusted to a world in which they are accepted and loved then they may adjust to accept others regardless of their circumstances. Also if a child is rewarded for behaviours (such as being responsible) then this they may adjust to this reinforced behaviour, however with the influence of peers, family or media the reinforcement of behaviours or beliefs that are questionable the number of introjections and creative adjustments is immeasurable. I have noticed on the new reality programmes that seem to have overrun mainstream television that to be a woman one has to wear skimpy clothes and flaunt their body and are judged on this. Men on these programmes are judged on their attractiveness and their ability to get these women into bed as well as what clothes they are wearing and the superficiality of the interactions. This is the power of the introjection, for if a person who is growing up views this as how to be a person then they may focus on the superficial rather than anything of substance and meaning, that is to say, a person may integrate into their beliefs that that have to look pretty to gain attention or acknowledged rather than just to be acknowledged for being a person. The person may seek confirmation or acceptance based on the popular values such as attractiveness and promiscuity and if a person integrates these then they may judge others on the same, and thus it becomes vicious cycle or the person feeling that have to live up to others expectations, as well as judging others on those same rules. Such is the means of adjustment, and is a form of conditioning and reinforcement, propagated by the media, whatever peer group or other association the person identifies with, or the changing circumstances of a person's life. In all of this the person is a passive receptacle from their world, from the introjections of their world and have to, or feel the need to adjust to their world.

This is how I see creative adjustment, the person enters an environment and either has to, is manipulated into, or feels obliged to follows the rules, sometimes as the case of the supermarket a somewhat valid reason, or in the cases previously for their own good, to gain affection or worth, or to survive. While this may be healthy and we all have adjusted to our way of life it is when this becomes fixed and the person has a rigid way of being in, reacting to and seeing the world that we can encounter problems in life. This is the nature of learning from experience, and all the examples up to now the person have been influenced by their world, and when a person can take charge of their life the nature of experience become different, and they can actively and consciously learn how they exist, they can learn from action and in action, how the values that they hold about themselves, how they have adjusted to life and the introjections that have been a driver for these creative adjustments, as well as how these have become fixed into how they view their self, and when we challenge this fixed behaviour that is integral to our self-concept we reach the impasse, the anxiety when we reach the boundary of what is not us. The introjection and the creative adjustment as a means of learning are the building blocks of this self-concept or identity.

Now, I may have jumped forward a little previously with my talk of introjections, and please forgive me, as while I view creative adjustment and introjection as on having a similar meaning, they are also separate and while a person can take a message from our environment as a introject and creatively adjust to this, then so it is that a person can creatively adjust and use is as a form of introjection.

I shall explore introjection in a moment I would like to illustrate this first. I try to keep in good shape physically and my body has adjusted to this. Most of my interests are based in the outdoors and I regularly run, enjoy walking with a weighted backpack as well as cycle and lift weights. My body has become conditioned to be able to exert itself in these ways, and my cardiovascular system has adjusted to be able to meet the demands of what I require. Imagine if I was in an accident and lost that ability to be so physical. This is the introjected message from my world, that I cannot be as physical and have to adjust from this. I won't press the point now, but it is an example of my self taking in the messages from growing up in Belfast and having to be fit and strong (an introjection) and adjusting to that by becoming strong and capable. My occupation in the emergency services gave this a meaning and purpose, and sustained this belief. If I got injured and could no longer maintain this self-concept I would either have to accept this and take this as another message from my environment (that I could not be as strong and capable) in the form of an introjection and adjust to this as well, perhaps by having a less physical job and interests. It is when I come into conflict with my beliefs that I may encounter problems, for if I *must* be strong and capable as it is fixed and integral to my self-concept (and my job and interests sustain this belief and gave it meaning) and I cannot due to injury then I may enter an existential crisis and anxiety or depression may ensue, or if I am exposed to a trauma and I feel that I *should* be able to overcome this that a crisis may also be encountered, as I struggle to give meaning to, or make sense of my world, as the introjections that I have swallowed into how to be a person, as well as the adjustments that this meaning and purpose are in question. They do in effect restrict our ability to choose other options of being or alternatives, or choices, the self-concept can become a straitjacket for our life.

I have often considered how it would be for a number of children in the same household and how they don't adjust the same way, (much like different plants going under exactly the same conditions) I have a number of examples to illustrate this and how even in a family or social group the person may creatively adjust or accept introjections to and from their environment. I remember once a few years ago I knew a family in which the parent were heavy drinkers, every day the father would walk past my house on his way to the off licence to buy bottles of cider for he and his wife to drink. They had six children who were exposed to this lifestyle of drinking, shouting, arguing and violence. Nowadays this would be a safeguarding issue but 30 years ago nothing was done about this. So, how some of the children creatively adjust to the environment they were born into? The eldest daughter became a replacement mother for the younger children, it seemed that she took on a role that was negligent in the household as the mother was drinking most of the day. That would be an important introjected message, that she was only of value taking care of other people and the last I saw of her a few years ago she was a carer in an old peoples home and had 3 children herself. She looked harried and worn out and this reminded me of her as a child, she would finish school and immediately tidy the house and start to prepare dinner for her younger siblings. She had also become involved in an abusive relationship with a controlling and aggressive man though luckily she had been able to free herself from him and was now living alone. The eldest of the family was a boy and he would join in the parents drinking sessions. He took the mother's side in the arguments and would fight with the father, as it as a way for the mother to get her own way in the family. I suspected this as when the mother and father were drunk and arguing she would involve him in the arguments and try to get him to take her side. The last I saw of the eldest son he was working as a labourer in a mill. He had become involved in a relationship with a much older lady who was also involved in drinking and arguing and he seemed to be replicating his time spent with his mother and father. He had developed a bad stammer and when I saw him in the area he was always drinking.

The second oldest son had it quite tough as he was not the biological son of the father. The father would also get the second son drunk and then bully him and physically beat him when he was drunk. The second son also began working as a labourer in a mill and was also a heavy drinker. He adjusted to that life by using humour in an attempt to get his step father to like him (I had asked him why he would try and have a joke with him, even though the step father would physically abuse him) he also started to lift weights and became quite muscular. Unfortunately this person became alcohol dependent and is still living his life this way. He still tries to placate his mother and father who continually deride him and talk to him in a patronising manner, reminding him that he is a failure. The 3 younger children also grew in similar ways and all 3 drank alcohol heavily and seemed to argue to communicate.

There are number of introjections and creative adjustments here, though I think firstly the children grew up and learned to be less important than their parents, they had to adjust to what was expected of each of them. The daughter as a stand-in parent to younger children in the household, cooking, cleaning, ironing clothes and other household chores. She had to become very responsible yet have no authority. Her mother was happy to have her daughter look after her children and to keep the house clean, but it was more as a servant. What would it mean for a child to gain recognition only as a servant focusing on the housework and childcare? How would this impact on her identity or self-concept? The eldest son again had to follow the mother's direction, for him to gain acceptance and worth is was as a drinking partner and back up, to enforce the mother's opinions against the father. What a strong introjection this would be, to not be valued as a person with their own hopes and aspirations but just someone who has to fit into the needs of another person, in this case it was that of their mother and father. Interestingly, the daughter never got as involved in alcohol the same way as her siblings, it seemed that she fulfilled the role of being the caring and supportive parent that was missing in the family home. The younger brother who had been bullied by the step father tried to fit in by becoming the joker and trying to gain attention and worth from trying to make others laugh. He always tried to live up to his mother's expectations, though she talked to him in a very demeaning and derogatory way, criticising him for his dependency on alcohol and lifestyle. The two older sons also entered into relationships with dominant women who they tried to please. This meant that they would put themselves into a lower position than the woman, that is to say, they never put their own needs first in a relationship, but rather became submissive to the needs and desires of their partner at the time. I noticed in all the 3 older siblings there was never any desire or ambition to have a career or to progress in a job role. They were satisfied to work in menial roles (the daughter as a carer and the two sons as labourers) or had no self-belief or drive to try and do better for themselves. I wonder sometimes if they saw the relationship of the parents in which the mother was in charge and the father more submissive as a model, or if for them to be of any worth they had to fit into the idea of what their mother wanted them to be. If they had tried to progress in a career then this may have meant that they would be in competition (as their mother saw it) for authority in the house. This may have also been an aspect of the introjection and creative adjustment of the family, for they may have received the message from the mother that working in a menial and physical role was a good job and this may have been the manipulated message from the mother so she could be the matriarch of the family, a family in she was firmly in charge. While I write this brief example of the impact of 3 siblings having to live in an environment and how they have been influenced. This example could have been written in Chapter 2 and the nature of a person's self-concept and how the mother manipulated her field to get her needs met (to be in charge) and to not have anyone challenge her authority, for this she met a man she could be in charge of, and of children who would fit into her world, but highlighted the nature of creative adjustment and introjection. There are of course many different creative adjustments for each of these children in relation to their mother and father. How would they have to adjust their way of talking to their parents so as to placate and not antagonise them both? As they were living in an aggressive oppressive household did they adjust to ask questions instead of making statements, the purpose being that if a question is asked, either for permission or to ask for an opinion it has the effect (in this type of environment) of dis-empowering the person asking the question, and enforcing or empowering the other person, in this case the purpose being to say that mum was in charge. If one of the children stated an opinion then this could be attacked, criticised or derided, and for these children to survive in this world they had to adjust to this. The also had to adjust to develop a sensitivity to *know* when to speak, when to stay quiet and know what to say. In my experience this is a how people have to adjust living in with a dominant person whose tool is emotional abuse to enforce their position. This was as well as how they adjusted to express themselves. I shall explore this further, especially the use of questions and use of expression in a further chapter on the contact functions, but right now I would like to talk about creative adjustment a little more before discussing introjection more fully.

In his book Psychotherapy and Process (1978 p7) the author James Bugental states;

in the process of our development from infancy to adulthood, we each work out ways of surviving in the world, of avoiding harm as much as possible, and of getting some satisfactions. These ways become the structure of our lives, they are importantly part of how we see our own identities and how we believe the world to be.

Much like all the examples so far this is how I see creative adjustment to be, a way to survive in the world, and at any point in a person's life. A person who may have a low self-worth (perhaps through a series of introjections) or searching for excitement or danger may create a world which means putting themselves in a harmful environment, or engaging in some type of self harm. Maybe in the world they have had to adjust to has meant that they have had to become desensitised, and the lack of feeling has meant that engaging in harmful behaviour is the only way for these people to be able to feel anything.

The way in which a person may creatively adjust is endless but here a few examples:

- a person who is afraid of his feelings of being attracted towards other men may identify with a strong polarity towards masculinity and "being a man's man" This may have originated from an introjection that feelings towards men is unnatural, or something that creates shame.
- A person with a need to be special may adjust themselves to be noticed, to search for stardom, to be in a position of authority, or to create a family in which they are the person in charge. A person may become the victim to focus attention to themselves, or become adapt and knowledgeable.
- A person who has a lack of belief in their own abilities may avoid learning, and search for others who may be able to answer their

38

questions or to resolve issues.

- A person who does not want to draw attention to themselves may adjust to appear dull, boring or interesting. They may involve themselves in a type of conversation that would mean the other person is the focus of attention. They may also develop their listening skills, to be able to keep the direct attention on the other person.
- A person who is afraid to show his feelings may adjust to become analytical or place themselves into a role where that possibility is reduced, they may work in a field of science or behaviour, they may put also put themselves into an authoritarian role. They may not express their feelings in an emotional way, but in a safe verbal manner. They may think their feelings instead of feel their feelings.
- The person who feels they should be taken care of may become a victim or helpless, to manipulate their environment so they are taken care of. They may seek a partner who will take care of them.
- The person who has adjusted to rely on technology such as using a smart phone to source their queries, or to fill their time by going on Facebook may become anxious if their cannot access this, the first question they would ask a person if they visit their house is "have you got wifi?"
- The person may adjust to not be lonely may have many children or become very helpful so that others need them. They may also become passive, believing that if they state their thoughts that the other person won't like them and leave.
- The person may adjust to get their needs met by becoming angry, and shouting or screaming, or by becoming tearful or crying.
- The person may have difficulty adjusting to a health problem or injury and they need care or assistance in doing things, especially if their self-concept is believing their self to be capable and self-reliant.
- The person who is afraid of anything negative or critical may instead filter what they hear so as to focus on the positive.
- The person who is looking to blame a group or a certain ethnicity may filter any information so it gives them a justification to feel the feelings of hate or anger to those people (rationalisation)
- The person who is afraid to enter into relationships with other people may adjust to view them as objects and to place their own personal meanings onto them (such as people as no good, they always use me)

as a means to not enter into relationships. They may also stick to small talk and talking about football, beauty, cars, or other gossip to avoid any meaningful conversation and dialogue.

- The person who is afraid of any type of criticism may say nothing, do nothing and be nothing, so as to avoid a person looking at them, or judging them in a negative light.
- If the person has been raised in an environment where anger, tears, swearing or other forms of aggressive behaviour was present, they may adjust to actively avoid any of those behaviours.

The person may adjust through life, such as the child adjusting to live in the parent's world, just as the parent who has to adjust to the needs of the child. The person adjusting to the requirements of a job or working pattern, the single person adjusting to life in a relationship (no more leaving the dishes in the sink for a week!) the police offer who adjusts to being exposed to criminals and reoccurring traumatic experiences. The person adjusting to view their own personal history in a certain way, so as to make it more palatable.

In many of these bullet pointed examples who the person has adjusted into could be viewed as the abeyance of anxiety, the person fulfils a role or function to stop feeling the feelings of fear or anxiety. If the person has had to adjust because of age, an injury or circumstances they there may be the fear or what they may become, anger or resentment at what they are giving up (such as an athlete who can no longer compete and no longer knows what he is, or a mother who can no longer be a mother) there may be the fear of "if I am not this when what am I?" or in the first bullet-point of the man who is afraid of his feelings towards men and creates a world in which he can become a manly man, and have a role that exemplifies this such as joining the army or a physical hard working job. This is easier than touching his feelings towards men and what they mean to him personally. It may go against his (introjected) values of how to be a person, or he may feel that his friends judge him based on his sexuality. At a deeper level he may have these feelings because he may have never felt the love of his father, who may have had his own difficulty in showing his feelings towards his son, and the son now is projecting this desire of love and acceptance onto other men. The love and acceptance he wanted from his father is now displaced onto other men as a type of unfinished business.

The creative adjustments that mean that people can survive may occur in a multitude of ways, though this is often outside our awareness or informed choice and when these adjustments that were necessary become fixed so it is that we limit our own potential and restrict our ability to grow or become a person.

Now I have alluded to the term introjection previously and I would like to explore this further now, as I have said previously, introjections can originate from a self-concept based on creative adjustments, or conversely introjections can lend themselves to the necessary conditions for a person to adjust to survive.

Introjection is a term that means to take in and assimilate messages from our environment that is to "own it" and become it. The psychotherapist Fritz Perls likened introjection to eating and digesting food (Perls 1973 p32) in which we introject indiscriminately, for example while i was out earlier today on my bike and became thirsty i bought a can of soft drink, but upon reading the ingredients which included aspartame, potassium sorbate, caffeine and sodium citrate. I realised that i was taking ingredients into my body that i have no real knowledge of, or how it will affect me and my body, that is to say how my body assimilates this drink, yes it quenched my thirst but i was unaware of how else the ingredients would affect me. So as I see it in relation to a person, they have introjected so much that is outside their awareness that is never questioned, because it's part of who they are. Just as my self in my belief, based on my own introjections of what it meant to be a male in Belfast that i had to be tough, and then looked for an occupation in which this "toughness" had a purpose (just as the soft drink had quenched my thirst).

Introjection isn't necessarily a bad thing, for i *had* to survive in that world, and that introjection meant that i could, but what is the impact of this, for although this can be beneficial there are some areas that may stagnate or not develop, the manager mentioned earlier had introjected or adjusted how to be in the world, and this has impacted on how he communicates, in fact i'll go further than that and suggest that how he communicates may be relational in *how* he sees the person, does he talk in a dominant one-up way to people who he considers *lower* than himself, and neutrally to people who he feels are at the same level, and lastly does he acquiesce, flatter or charm those with whom he considers superior. I am aware that this person wasn't born this way, he grew through childhood or later in life and became this person. Just as the soft drink i had consumed had hidden ingredients that affected me without my awareness, so it is with the manager, who is simply *being* (just as with the fish in the water) and it is this being without choice but influenced by introjections and creative adjustments that creates the self-concept.

Erving and Miriam Polster in their book Gestalt Therapy Integrated (1974 p73) stated that "*learning exclusively through Introjection takes an impossibly favourably environment, one which is which is invariably suited to the individual's needs*" and that any introjection is nourishing and promotes growth and acceptance for the child, and if this was the case then the symbol above would be a rectangle instead of a trapezoid. The child would be born and be free from, or have an informed knowledge of their influences and develop their own way of being, explore their own choices and arrive at a person that they would have chosen to be, they would be able to discriminate between the many messages as to how to be a person and be able to filter as to what they would like to integrate and assimilate into who they were, the child would have a defined choice and a freedom as to how they would like to exist, and for this the ground would have to be fertile and nutritious so that the person could grow in an organismic way. The child however cannot discriminate between what is beneficial and what is detrimental for their development and must simply accept (without awareness) the messages that are received, from both other people and their environment.

To introject something is to *take it in whole, to absorb it, to copy it and to swallow it without reflecting upon it* (Korb, Gorell, De Reit 2002 p56) and these introjections can and do cover i believe all areas of a person's existence, how a person communicates, how they listen, the way they speak, how they move, the clothes they wear, how they view themselves in relation to others, their patterns of relating and beliefs about who they are and others, even their physiological responses to the environment, other people or situations. For example the person I wrote about earlier who had the negligent parents and became the responsible care giver to his younger siblings inhabited a role that was missing, but why would he take on such a role? He may be projecting his own desire to be taken care of (but of course hasn't as his parents have only one concern and that is their own needs) onto his younger siblings, he may be rewarded by his parents who offer praise for taking on this role (an introjection) although conversely they may also criticise him or resent him for embracing the role of which they were reticent or have reneged. He may have the idea or introjection of how families *should* be, and is trying to fulfil that idea, he may also have an existential awareness of his own being and chooses to take on this role because of his independently formed beliefs, (even though these beliefs may be in relation or response to his world) and the introjection may still be there in that he has taken on responsibility, but with very little authority (and may be a driver for him to enter into a job that has a lot of responsibility but very little authority) and the beauty of humanity is that each person lives in their own individual world made up of these introjections and adjustments and therefore, you, me and everybody else have their own way of existing and relating, and it is only us who knows these configurations, and it is only us who can truly understand ourselves and know our own truth.

I'll give a quick example of this from my own experience. I have observed that in major conurbations in the UK such as London, Manchester and Glasgow in the inner-city areas that were considered "working class" the speech rate tends to be faster (this isn't based on empirical data, but from my own experiences) than other areas, and being born in Belfast this was no exception, and a powerful introjection, for i "swallowed whole" something as innocuous as speech rate. This was outside my awareness and i had no conscious choice on this area of development, but was beneficial in that environment. I just copied or introjected how to speak from the people around me, (my environment) this wouldn't have been have an issue if i had stayed in that area, however we decided because of the troubles in Northern Ireland to move to a small town in North West England during my teenage years. The people here i found upon moving here talked at a much slower rate (from perhaps 120 words per minute in Belfast to 70-80 words per minute in England which of course relationally meant that i was talking so much more faster than the locals here. It seemed sometimes like we were talking different languages! Of course now i talk in a more measured and considered manner but, it took about many years to slow my speech rate to a level that i could communicate effectively. Such is the strength of an introjection i feel. Without jumping ahead too far I feel that this also offers an example of being able to gain an insight into one's own being from our own perspective. We see the world from our own eyes and it's not normally until our environment changes that how the many facets of how we live comes more into focus and therefore our own awareness. (just as the fish out of water)

Another example of an introjection which may at first seemed favourable in a particular environment would be a young man who when growing up and into his adult years had the luxury of having his parents satisfy his needs, they spoiled him with buying him games consoles, branded fashion clothing, buying him his first car and paying for his car insurance, cooking his meals and preparing his sandwiches for his lunch at work and when he got into trouble with the police after committing an offence and appeared in court his parents paid the fine for him. On the face of it this young man had quite a favourable life with his material needs met, yet it later transpired that he had no idea of responsibility, and in fact admonished his responsibility to his parents, the message, or introjection he had received from his parents was *don't be responsible, we'll be responsible for you* and that also *you are very important* the parents had for want of a better phrase wrapped him in cotton wool and any point in which he tried to do things for himself was reprimanded by his authoritative father and his mother who strongly identified with their role of parents. The parents were in fact trying their best not to let their son grow up (which would has made their own roles redundant) and when the man entered into relationships he had that same expectation of his partners, and playing a passive role invited the other person to take care of him as he was more important or special, fulfilling this very powerful introjection from his parents.(this is what I call a manipulation of the environment, that is to say, the person has a fixed idea of their self, and tries to change the world around them so that self has a meaning) If this became more pathological he may transfer this onto the state and develop a mental illness so that the state takes care of him, or enter into romantic relationship with a woman who has a low self-worth or self-esteem who would be grateful to be in a relationship with this man. Another aspect of this introjection is the message of *don't be yourself, but become what your parents want you to be* and though this young man may have wanted to look after himself, to grow as a person and to be responsible in making his own decisions free from the influence of his parents (who had their own motives) he instead had to adjust himself to survive in their world. The parents, far from allowing a person to develop in to a person with autonomy, assertiveness and self-direction were in fact rewarding, and encouraging his passivity, under the rationalisation that he wasn't giving in to anything as he was getting his material needs met, and allowing his parents to spoil him and treat him with importance also gave him the message that he was more important than other people. On a slightly different aspect the parents were treating their child as an object to satisfy their own needs (a manipulation of their environment) to fulfil their own idea of who they are (a mother who was fixed in her role as mother and in which created anxiety if she couldn't be a *mother* and authoritarian father who needed someone to be authoritative too) and to manage their own anxiety, from the mother's perspective that if she couldn't be a mother then what would she be, and from the father if he couldn't be in charge then what would he be. I shall say more in a further chapter about this anxiety and how a person manipulates both their self and their environment to sustain or give meaning to the self-concept.

Introjections are not necessarily something that is bad, as they are a way in which we learn our manners, morals and values. Different religions and cultures around the world have their own belief systems about to be a person and provides rules for how a person should live their life (even though these may also be restrictive) they provide a message about how to live in whatever environment a person find themselves born into. A person may search for an introjection also, for example, as my father was a heavy drinker growing up I would read books to source information, to be able to provide me with answers. This could also have been an creative adjustment about becoming independent and self-supportive as having a lack of support when growing up meant that when I encountered a problem I learnt how to overcome it myself, so as my father was not around I often wondered about how to be a person, so I read many books on manners and etiquette, learning the *rules* of good manners and etiquette in different situations that are accepted as to how to behave in a certain situation or towards another person. (An introjection)

For example, is it good manners for a child to correct their parents, and if so in which manner must a child must conduct themselves when doing so? As I recall a child should courteously say to his parent that they believe the parent is mistaken and then tactfully make a suggestion without injuring the feelings or authority of the parent. This introjection is still relevant now as if you are reading this and are a parent, do you believe that your children should talk to you in certain way to show you respect, and in which would you like them to speak to you?

As a child in which way did you have to behave in relation to your family, what was regarded as good manners for you? If you grew up in a household where good manners was not recognised how was this for you, and you grew up in a house where you could say and do what you anything (I know some people where is was acceptable for them to swear at their parents, to interrupt them to make demands) and what happened when you behaved the same way when associating with other people? I remember once a young girl whose father was a very dominant man expected absolute respect in his family home. His daughter had to adjust to this expectation and follow the introjected message of *I am more important than you and you should follow my rules* and so the young girl was never able to challenge her father, or state her opinion, she had to follow the rules of the house. This affected her confidence and her belief in her self and also how she viewed herself in relation to other men.

Manners and etiquette also cover such areas as customs and desirable behaviours for men, women and children, customs at funerals, how to speak on the phone and good correspondence via letters and invitations. There are also *recognised* ways to organise and conduct oneself at dinners and parties, as well as weddings and christenings. This area of manners and etiquette are relational to western values and in different cultures they have their own ways of being also.

These are not composite and fixed but an introjection that is fed to a person about how to behave in situations and as such the person creatively adjusts to these expectations. Now, as most people *buy into* these rules about how to behave and what etiquette and good manners are, if someone goes against this and say for example wore jeans and t-shirt to a formal wedding this would raise a few eyebrows, and much the same if the young girl went against what was accepted as good behaviour (in the form of a parents dominant control of his family) this would also create tension, though the repercussions for not following the rules would be more severe for the young girl. For many people having good manners may be beneficial to the person as is a societal introjection, though if this is enforced as in the case of the girl of the dominant parent then this may cause resentment as the person feels they have to fit in to what is expected of them. Also, if a person is raised with no rules, or maladjusted rules of what constitutes good manner this may have a negative impact of their relationships with other people who do not share these.

Another example of an introjection would be a person I knew some years ago, she had been plagued by depression for a long time and it had affected her relationships to the point where boyfriends had left her because of her negativity, at the time I knew her she was in a relationship a with a person who did not share her plans for her life, that is to say that she had a strong desire to have children and her current [then] partner had strong beliefs that he did not, he was supportive though, and understanding towards her. The lady being aware of this still carried on a relationship with him, even though it made her feel low. I was interested as to the need that was being met in her by being in a relationship with this man, and also the meaning of her depression, as well as how this was being maintained. I asked her about her family and she had little contact with her mother or father, she said that her father had suffered with severe depression for all the time she knew him, and that her mother was always very attentive to him, and took care of him when he had episodes of depression. I could see a pattern forming in her own way of being and patterns of relating with that of her father and asked her to describe herself, however I did so in the form of a quick experiment which I have called "The Shirt"

Awareness Experiment: The Shirt

The purpose of this experiment that I have created is to highlight introjections and creative adjustments that may be outside our awareness, but never the less are still a driver for the values and beliefs we have about ourselves, as well as our Zones of Awareness (more about this in chapter 1b) and when we extend it further we can she how we configure our lives around those beliefs of how we should be. The Shirt experiment is quite a simple experiment and I invite you to try it yourself. If you are wearing a shirt, jacket, jumper or similar article of clothing I would like to take it off and place it next to you, and upon doing this I would like you to imagine that if someone else had to _put on your shirt,_ what type of qualities, values, beliefs, attitudes or aptitudes would they need to have to be you? To be your gender, (since gender identity is largely an introjection) part of you religion or sexuality and what they would they need to be to _be you._ Now I would like you to write this down into a list and then look at this list and consider to yourself if this list is made up of qualities that you have consciously made a choice as to how to be a person, if some of these qualities are beliefs that you have held about yourself as to the way that you should be, or if you have taken them without question. Ask yourself if you are aware of where these came from and if you are aware perhaps you could then reflect on how you have assimilated them into your own self. To expand of the meaning of this experiment I shall say what the lady had been affected by depression found out about herself.

She described herself as independent, tactile, morose, not interesting, sad, argumentative, picky, quick to anger and added that she went from job to job but had always wanted to work in fashion but was working in retail, which I was surprised at, as her clothing she wore was always dark and bland) So I then asked her which of these qualities she had made a choice in becoming, and her answer was that she had always been this way, with an "i don't know" as she sat in silence as she contemplated where these qualities and attributes had come from (a sign of an introjection) and after she sat in silence for some time, I asked if she could name a person who also exhibited some or all the list that she gave then who would this be, and to some surprise she had said her father. This for me is an indicator of the powerful nature of an introjection, for in the person above there was no discrimination of what qualities to adopt and assimilate, and which to discard, but a wholemeal taking on board, from the person above there were many introjections from her father, how to look, how to dress, how to speak, how to view the world, how to interact with people, how to look after her self, and her own self-care, that is to say, that as she was negligent in her own self-care this had the purpose of fuelling her feelings of low self-worth. When I first encountered her and talked to her about herself, she could have chosen any area to focus on, but as you have seen the messages she was giving out as well as how she was *seeing* her self were readily apparent in her self-description.

As another opposing view of this outcome of the same awareness experiment, I will give the example of the young man whose parents had reneged on their responsibility towards their children. The young man, for far from becoming *just like* his parents he exercised and developed qualities that were missing from these parents, and while they were out drinking and socialising with friends he looked after his younger siblings. I offered the same awareness experiment to him asking him to remove his sports sweatshirt (even his wearing an sports sweatshirt was an indicator in itself of how he saw himself) and to describe the beliefs, qualities and attributes a person would need to have to if they were to put it on, he considered this for a moment, and these are what he disclosed. The person would have to be: responsible, strong, resourceful, respectful, moral, brave, tough, be able to defend or protect the ones they love (he was proficient at boxing) caring, to be a good role model and to consider other people and their feelings.

Now, this was quite a what I would say a very positive list, and when I was sitting with this person I could sense no badness or arrogance, and I felt like I was sitting next to a saint (who was good at boxing) so I asked where these qualities had come from and he drew a blank, and he didn't have a clue at all, so I asked if he could think of a person or people who were the opposite of the qualities he described in himself, and at this he started laughing, and said his parents. Another person who had said the same qualities may have gave the reason for introjecting and assimilating these qualities because they are what the parent expects from the child, even if the parent doesn't exhibit them himself. The child adopts qualities that are favoured or preferred by the parent, and restricts the development of qualities that are disapproved of, for varying reasons.

Introjections and creative adjustment can happen through life, consider a confident and self-assured young lady who marries a man who is controlling, but of course he doesn't start the relationship by being directive, authoritative and restricting the autonomy of the young lady, but he does so shrewdly and manipulatively, he suggests initially in a helpful way that he will arrange the home and car insurance, then set up a joint account so as to have access to her finances, he may direct the topic of conversations and choose what programmes or films to watch, he may choose the restaurants to go to, or restrict the options so that it appears she has a choice, he goes on to arrange holidays away and when they don't go somewhere he specifically wants to he makes it known to her, or complains so that next time she just gives in to his preference. He suggests what car to buy and where to live. The introjected message that the husband is giving the wife is that he is in charge, and by the way he communicates with her the introjection is also that her opinion or beliefs do not really matter, that it is only his way or his opinion that counts. While not being exhaustive on the possible reasons for how he comes to hold these beliefs about himself the expectation is that his wife has to adjust to his beliefs, and because he has been sly and calculating to become the person in charge it has been a gradual process. I say calculating but that would mean a conscious decision in the man's awareness to be that way, when he actions could be outside his awareness and he may have gone from failed relationship to relationship previous to his marriage because of his controlling nature, because he may rationalise his behaviour and instead on controlling he may see this as protecting or helping the other, that is unless he has no regard for the rights and opinions of women or others. The adjustment for the wife having to live with a man who views himself as being in control may be given the following introjected messages; *your opinion and views don't matter, you are incapable of being responsible, you need me to make decisions or to validate your views, don't be you, be the way I expect you to be, don't be important, don't think for yourself (I will make the decisions for us)* and then this in turn may mean a creative adjustment, the woman's self-confidence, self-esteem and belief in herself will be affected which would make her even more dependent on her husband, and perhaps part of the husbands means of control is to isolate her from others who may offer her support. In effect what has happened is that the husband has the idea of himself (his self-concept) based upon numerous introjections and creative adjustments and is manipulating the other or himself to give this meaning (a manipulation of the environment) Of course, this is just one side of a coin, for what if the woman in this example has the idea of herself that outwardly she appears confident but this is just a show as that is just the *face* she projects to others (perhaps seeking worth or confirmation from others) but underneath that *role* she presents to others she believes herself to be of little worth or self-esteem or belief in herself and her own autonomy. She may entice the man she meets to take control, by being vague or confused about plans or her choices, manipulating the man to take charge, she may give say "i don't know" or "it's up to you" to avoid giving a preference and therefore leading, or rather coaxing or inviting the husband to take charge, to be in control. (Another example of a manipulation of the environment, as well as a manipulation of the self) There is also the possibility that as in the example above the person who feels the need or desire to be in control may actually develop a relationship with a person who wants to be controlled or happy to be told what to do, they are looking for someone to be in charge. Problems may of course arise in that relationship if the person who is in charge finds themselves out of work through redundancy or ill and needs the support of the other, this may create anxiety (existential anxiety) or depression, and that the person who has been quite happy to be told what to do may encounter anxiety when they now have to take a more dominant position as previously their partner was in control of everything. Another area of complexity (as with the woman who has been controlled) is that she may harbour a resentment towards men (an introjection or creative adjustment from her dominant or negligent father perhaps) and manipulates herself to be weak and thus entice her partner to be in charge, so she can through rationalisation feel justified in showing resentment towards him.

Although I will examine this further throughout this book it is my belief from this example that we all have an idea of who we are from numerous creative adjustments and introjections that forms our self-concept and we look to give this meaning, because we have the capacity to assimilate introjections and creative adjustments through our life, which is often outside our awareness it is possible to try to manipulate others to fulfil our idea of ourselves, but also we are open to manipulation from others to fulfil their idea of who they are as well. (This is an area called Field Theory that I will touch on in a later chapter)

This is a very intricate process that encapsulates all that a person is and how they relate to the world around them, how they shape their world and how they relate to other people. Also as we have seen in the example above how the introjections and creative adjustments that help to form the self-concept may mean that support is needed from the person's world to give that meaning (such as with the controlling husband manipulating the other so he has someone to control) and I will call this environmental support, and that the need, whatever that need is organises the field. It begins though with creative adjustment and introjections and the messages we have received about how to be a person, how we walk, talk, move, dress, think and so on, and in that is something that is called our contact functions. I will cover contact functions in a later chapter however they are in essence all that we are and how we relate to the world and our own thoughts about ourself and our self-concept. Have you ever noticed how a woman sits a certain way, she doesn't sit with her legs splayed open, more than likely she sits with her legs crossed or one leg carefully folded behind the other. How many ladies do not dare go out without make-up or not looking presentable? This amongst others are powerful introjects about how to be a person in their world. These can of course become more toxic when there is a message that to be accepted or to win the approval of others one should have a thin build, dress in named brand clothing and fulfil other areas that are deemed *important* just to be of worth or for confirmation or validation. The person who has taken the introject that to be a person of worth you *must* fit into other's expectations is inevitably adjusting themselves to this toxic message. I remember watching a programme on television before about a group of women who were being criticised for being overweight by a well-groomed muscular man who worked in the fashion industry. So who is the victor here? Is it the man who believes that to be a person of worth he must wear such clothes and go to the gym 5 times a week to have a socially valued impressive physique, or the women who also *buy into* this message and judge themselves against this message, to view themselves in a critical negative light for not living up to these expectations? No, for I think there are no victors here, just people who feel that to be accepted they must adjust themselves to the introjects of a culture or society (and society is just other people) or any other smaller more niche' group that the person chooses to identify with.

On a separate thread to this there was once a person I knew that used to wear very expensive clothing (just like the fashion conscious person above) and on one occasion while speaking to him he disclosed that he *wanted* to wear such clothing, so I asked him if he would wear my jumper to walk through town? Now my jumper was an old walking top that had seen better days, but it was comfy and I liked it. He was aghast at this and said that he couldn't, and when I enquired why he said that if he wore that then people wouldn't think much of him and wouldn't notice him. I then asked him if he *wanted* to wear expensive clothing or did he *need* to wear them? Such was the power of an introjection for this person, that he was only of value because of how he dressed, I remember an old quote of "when you make someone your judge, you also make them your master" and this person, as well as the persons above did just this, they had made introjections from *society* their master, and in doing so were living a less free and self-accepting life.

I have observed that there are people who try to become the antithesis or the opposite of what they think is mainstream, of what is fashionable, and some people form groups with the purpose of actively not *fitting in* and I ask myself if the person is making a responsible choice to be this way? I once encountered a person who embraced an alternative lifestyle, talked in an esoteric language, dressed in clothing that made her look like a witch, described herself as a shaman, was a vegan and was a strong advocate of spiritual cleansing as well as a devoted care of the environment as well as a staunch feminist. When I say feminism, her construct of feminism was not for the equal rights of women but was simply anti-men, or misandry (a dislike of, contempt for, or ingrained prejudice against men) and her friends were people who also shared this view. As I was interested in her history and the introjections that influenced her I discovered that when growing up she had been ill for a long period as a child and spent a lot of time in her bedroom when she often fantasised about being special and later became interested in the occult. She said also that her father was distant as he was always working. I had noticed that when she spoke to women she did so in a warm and nurturing way, however when she spoke to men her voice was a lot sharper, defensive and critical. So considering all of this I asked if she could wear normal clothes for one day, to become mindful of her use of language and when she talked in an esoteric language and what purpose it served. I also asked he to start a conversation and to focus on topics that was ordinary such as the weather, children, favourite television programmes or what her plans were for going on holiday later in the year. Part of the reason for this was to experience *not being her* and to experience what it was like to do so, to go about her everyday activities. I could have focused on other areas but a person's dress and way of speaking seem innocuous but is actually an indicator of how they relate to their world, and how they want the world to see them, as well as how others interact with them. This can be self-sustaining as it reinforces how they see themselves and their self-concept, and of course the self-concept is made up of a number of introjections and creative adjustments. The next time I saw the person I asked if she was able to wear ordinary clothes and to speak without using specialist language to people she encountered. I had the idea that as a man she was keen to prove me wrong or that my suggestion was stupid and not worth the effort (as what I had observed as her way of speaking to invite conflict with men) however she said she had, and as she was walking around in town she was normally aware of people looking at her but, when she was dressed in normal clothing and had her hair tied back instead of wild and unbrushed she felt that she had become ordinary, that people didn't notice her like before, and that also people didn't keep their distance so much. I asked her about how she spoke to others and she realised that the way she spoke kept people also a distance, for they didn't know how to speak to her, but when she tried to speak about everyday topics instead of the occult and shamanism that people seemed ok to engage with her. She told me that she carried on this as work and engaged with people who normally she didn't speak to and talked about holidays and other ordinary topics of conversation and was surprised that people were interested in her without wearing her uniform (she now started calling the way she dressed previously as her uniform)

I asked her what she was experiencing when she interacted with people on what she saw as boring trivial topics, and she said anxious, as at first she didn't know what to say but never the less wanted to find out more about herself, especially in relation to other people. It became apparent then that her choice of being, her self-concept made up of these introjections to dress and speak in a certain ethereal manner also had the purpose of the abeyance of anxiety from her normal interactions with people, and when she talked with men she came to the realisation that she was resentful of her father who never seemed to be there for her. I saw her a few months later and she had toned down the way she looked, and seemed comfortable talking to what she thought were normal people. Here was a person I thought who had become aware of how she related to the world and made a choice to understand herself, then as she was not a cactus or a tree she decided to change herself, and to grow as a person. The introjections and creative adjustments that had formed so long ago had become fixed and rigid, and it was only through her own awareness of how she related to others that this was questioned.

Perls, Hefferline and Goodman (1951 p189) stated that an introject *consists of material – a way of acting, feeling, evaluating – which you have taken into your system of behaviour, but which you have not assimilated in such a fashion as to make it a genuine part of your organism*

I would agree with the majority of this, that we do indeed learn from introject ideas about who we are as a person, and that sometimes the way we act just doesn't feel right, such as the lady in a previous example in the book who had been in a relationship with the dominant controlling man and when eventually she didn't accept that this was part of her she resisted his controlling behaviour and left him. However, it is when this introjected idea of who we are become integrated into our identity, our self-concept that it becomes part of us and it not questioned.

When I first came to this country I came across a man who was also Irish and had worked as a labourer and worked at building roads and on building sites, he was also a heavy drinker,. His son had followed in his footsteps and became almost a kind of carbon copy of his father, that even though he was reasonably intelligent he still worked in a manual physical job in a factory, and more recently his own son when leaving school had followed in what I thought was a generational introjection, as he also worked in a manual job. I asked the son what he thought about going to university and to attain a degree in a subject or a field that he enjoyed, but his reply was that his dad had told him he should get a job and learn a trade. So he got an apprenticeship in engineering and worked fixing machines at the same factory as his father. All three generations of men worked in a manual job with no real desire to improve or to break free of these introjections. There was a glass ceiling, but it was ceiling made by themselves and their view how they thought there were lead to a restriction of what they thought they could be and curtailed the possibilities of what they could become. Interestingly, they were all heavy drinkers and sat in their garden drinking cans of lager, I used to think about the power of introjection and creative adjustment, and if any member of their family would ever break from this and push the boundaries of what they could become, but have considered that another aspect of creative adjustment is when a person actively doesn't fit into what is accepted of considered normal. The drinking father may say "what's wrong with you, you're not drinking?" and the creative adjustment may be a means to make him follow the family rules or introjections.

I have noticed something similar here in the town in which I live, that there are many people that have many children early in their life and have never worked. I have noticed that their children follow this introjections as well and become the same as they have been exposed to, it seems like the introjected message is *be like me* and while there may be reasons for this, such as if the child is just like the parent then it gives the parents choices and life meaning, or that if the child excels and surpasses the parent then may create feelings of animosity in the parent (if the parent has the belief that they should be in charge) so any feeling that the child can do better is quashed by the parent. This is never questioned though as it seems that the person creatively adjusts to the introjected message and becomes the person that is expected of them. However, there are occasions when the introjection and the messages from a person's environment does not sit well with the person and they actively challenge these beliefs and rules about how to be a person, they believe it is their life and their choice as to how to be a person. I look at children sometimes and wonder where in life they will go, will they follow the spoken or unspoken rules of the family, society or peer group they are involved in and learn from this as to how to be a person.

Such introjections and the creative adjustments that a person integrates into how they view their self has but one outcome in the formation of their self-concept that is to say, it is limiting as to the person they will become, and restricts the potential of the person.

This is where I had the idea of this symbol, that a person at any point in their life can integrate and assimilate introjections and creative adjustments and just as the symbol becomes narrower so it is that as people when we creatively adjust to our circumstances or environment, or integrate and assimilate introjections (and become fixed to how we see ourselves) that we limit the way we interact with the world around us, as well as how we react to the world. How our beliefs, thoughts, values and way of being becomes limited and restricted. This way of being reduces flexibility and the growth of a person, especially in the areas that are not valued, approved of or avoided.

*

The range of what we think and do is limited by what we fail to notice. And because we fail to notice that what we fail to notice there is little we can do to change until we notice how failing to notice shapes our thoughts and deeds.

R. D. Lang

Chapter 1a

The Contact Functions, Zones of Awareness, Assertion and Polarisation

People are not disturbed by things, but by the view they take of them

Epictetus

So, in this chapter I would like to talk about the Contact Functions, Assertion and Polarisation, and how they are integral to a person's self-concept, and give this meaning, substance and purpose.

I spoke about the Contact Functions a few times in chapter 1 when giving examples of Creative Adjustment and Introjection and would like to expand on the meaning of this term; put simply it is how we make contact with ourselves, other people and the environment we are in based on our own beliefs about our self. These are relational as we may adjust to the person we are interacting with or whether it is for example a work, social, personal or intimate environments or relationships. Gestalt Therapy Integrated (1973 p128) listed the contact functions as looking, listening, talking, moving, smelling and tasting, and here in this chapter I shall explore these further and expand onto other areas of contact.

There are many books and sources of information on assertiveness so I will assume that you the reader will not need me to describe this in detail, and instead will relate assertion to a style of contact, and in this context is integral to how a person makes contact with their world, this is to say whether they are assertive, non-assertive, passive aggressive, aggressive or passive and how this impacts on how they listen, speak, move etc.

Finally there is the area of polarisation. In an emotionally healthy and fully functioning person they may be able to choose between opposing polarities such as masculine and feminine, strong or weak, happy or sad depending on the situation or requirements of the situation. However for others if they identify or have creatively adjusted through a series of introjections with a particular quality then the opposing quality may not be developed or used, and may have atrophied. As a simple example it may be easier for some men to identify with masculine qualities, to have integrated the qualities inherent with that characteristic from a number of introjections and creative adjustments in their development assimilated them into their self-concept. However the deficit in the opposing emotional or feminine side may be unexplored, projected or avoided, and the person may be unaware of this as it is rationalised as "that's a woman's job" or "i'll get the wife, as she is better about talking about emotional stuff" or instead of offering emotional support to a person they may steer the conversation towards a role they can fulfil such as problem solving or advice giving. This rigidity of polarities is also apparent in women who makes comments such as "that's a man's tool" or "that's a man stance" (used by a woman I over heard recently as she was looking at a man sitting on the train with his legs spread wide in a masculine sitting position) and it is in this context I would like to explore polarities, as identification with a certain polarity with affect how a person interacts with their world and forms the person's self-concept as well as a fixed way of seeing themselves and their relation to others. I will also talk about the Zones of Awareness (inner, middle, outer) and how these relate to how we make contact with others and the world around us. Now, I would like to take us back to the symbol from Chapter 1

and in particular the first section. As I described in chapter 1 the nature of Introjections and Creative Adjustments influence the formation of our self-concept and limit the ways in which we make contact with others and how we view our self, as the first section narrows as we accept and integrate introjections and creative adjustments so it is that we limit the ways in which we interact with others and our world, namely in the ways in which I have asserted above. I shall explore first the Zones of Awareness (Skills in Gestalt 2010) and I believe Contact Functions, Assertion and Polarities will flow from this.

Imagine if you will a person divided into the outer, the middle and the inner zone, such as the symbol below and I will elaborate on each of these zones below.

The Outer Zone:
This outer section is the outer part of a person, such as speaking, moving, seeing, listening, hearing, smelling, touching, behaviours, posture, spatial awareness, expression (how we express ourselves) appearance, physical proximity and so on. It is this outer zone that we contact with the outside world, how we are seen by others, as well as how we communicate. A person looking at us cannot be aware of our beliefs, unless the way in which speak, or our way of dress or appearance or posture etc is an indication of our beliefs, and even then this can only be an inference or assumption.

The Middle Zone:
In this zone we have our beliefs (about our self and others) values, reasoning, introjections, knowledge, memories (and intrusive memories) expectations, fantasies, how we think and cognition, how we feel, our emotions, our experiences (how we view events) intuition, reactions, anticipations, imagination, self-talk and so on.

The Inner Zone:
In this zone are our sensations, tensions, moods, heartbeat, thirst, adrenaline surges, breathing, visceral reactions, elation, sweating, anxiety, palpitations, shivering, excitement, fear and other bodily effective states, concentration, hypervigilance, freezing, disassociation, nausea, fatigue.

Of course there is also an environmental or social context to this. Before I go on I shall give a quick example of this and holistic nature of these 3 zones.

I knew a person a number of years ago who was affected by social anxiety, his father had been a very dominant and controlling man who used aggression and emotional abusive tactics to enforce his dominance of the family. There was no encouragement from his father, and sarcasm and criticism was the way in which he communicated. Any time the young man tried to better himself the father would put him down and say that he was too stupid to go to college, but that he should get a job in a mill instead. The son developed a lack of self-esteem and no confidence in his own abilities. The introjected messages from his father may have been *don't be a person, don't argue, dad is always right, you aren't capable of anything as you are stupid, don't believe in yourself, I am more important than you* and any time the son showed any masculine qualities the father saw this as competition and took it as a challenge to his dominance.

The son developed a difficulty in speaking to others and when stating his opinions (as he was always criticised when speaking by his father) and instead would agree with the other person or ask questions to gauge the person's reaction before saying something.

As he had these beliefs of his self he would start to have palpitations as he prepared to speak and would occasionally stammer, though he knew which words would trigger his stammer so he avoided these. His heartbeat would increase when he was speaking, and he would talk quickly to rush out his words, he listened for any reply that could be construed as a criticism and I noticed that when he spoke to men there would be an agitation in how he spoke, this was in relation to women when he spoke much softer and more confidently.

With regard to polarities he was often criticised for any masculine characteristics and instead creatively adjusted to a safer feminine way of relating and communicating, a way that was not challenged by his dominant father. Imagine that his father had encapsulated masculine qualities and these were now off limits to his son. (though another father may have encouraged his son to instead integrate these, as it sustained his idea of what men should be, though I am aware that qualities or characteristics are just that, it is the person's own interpretation of these, and the gender identification of these that puts an masculine or feminine prefix or meaning/value) What is important to me is that in this case the father has identified with characteristics he determined as masculine and though his words and actions tried to manipulate his son from integrating these characteristics into himself.

So imagine the masculine qualities or characteristics that may have been off limits for this man when he was growing up; tough, muscular, rigid, robust, protective, violent, straightforward, sexual, forceful, athletic, courageous, daring, rugged, brave, aggressive, decisive, confident, adventurous, strong, powerful, and firm. Now imagine how the person if the son did display any of these? There would be an uneasy feeling and his heartbeat rose as it felt unusual, maybe even guilty. He could certainly speak sharply or with sarcasm but in doing so it created tension for himself so he avoided this way of speaking. He often took a passive role in conversations and when relating to people. He had creatively adjusted to avoid qualities that created anxiety for him, from the introjections from his father. He may have identified with what he construed as feminine qualities such as; understanding, empathetic, soft, emotional, nurturing, sensitive, intuitive, compassionate and gentle and incorporate that part of the polarity spectrum.

All these 3 zones are integral, from here the person's beliefs about himself that influence how he speaks, listens, how he dresses, how his thinks and reacts to people, and what situations create anxiety, tension, flushed skin or sweating. Even the person's intuition, his internal thinking process may alert him with an uneasy feeling in his stomach as he encroaches on the edge of his self-concept (the impasse) in this case if he decided to challenge someone in an aggressive manner, or if he decides to go to college or further study, the introjected beliefs he has about himself (or being incapable and stupid) may come alive at the thought of college, and the avoidance of this can only substantiate the introject. For if he believes himself incapable, an is unable to challenge those introjected beliefs then it may be interpreted as a failure (his own internal voice of criticism inherited from his father) Additionally, if he has assimilated these beliefs and becomes passive, non-assertive or submissive when in relation to others (and fulfilled by the contact functions) he may invite the other person to become critical, and this would again reinforce his view of himself. (Field Theory)

Now, I realise there I am heading onto chapter 2 and the self-concept with that example, so I'll take us back and further explore the contact functions, which incorporate the zones of awareness. The contact functions then, are the means in which we communicate, and how we relate to others, how we express ourselves and as I am writing this I am imagining overlapping circles with contact functions inextricably linked to zones of awareness, assertion and polarities, and that they are all derived from our creative adjustments through life and the many introjections from a multitude of different sources. This way of communicating give an insight as well as give a meaning to the person's self-concept and how they structure their world.

The Contact Functions.

The contact functions covers different areas, of which some overlap, while I am aware this could be an exhaustive list I shall highlight areas that I have observed, both in myself and with others, often with the explanation of "this is just the way I am" which suggests a fixed and immutable way of being. It is my belief that creative adjustments and introjections influence how we interact with others, as well as the shift between interacting different ways with different people (as in the example of the manager from chapter 1 who talked one way to managers at his level in the organisation, and talked in a discounting manner to those with whom he viewed as beneath him) for instance a person who communicates through ordering or directing others may be view himself as being more superior to others, and to do so he may influence the conversation, or distort the interaction to give that ordering self meaning. He may also try to become a manager so ordering others is a part of his role, and therefore he has a reason to tell others what to do. He may also have the introjection of *don't trust people* or *I am important or special* and the creative adjustment of this by putting himself into a position in which he can order or direct others creates a distance between him and those with whom he is ordering or directing, as immediately there is no equality or mutuality. He is firmly in charge. There is also the creative adjustment of *how* he may put himself into a position of authority, either by a functional role such as being a supervisor, manager or expert in a role, or when in communication with for example his friends, neighbours, partner or children. I knew a person once who would associate with people who she viewed as less important so she could order or command them (often said in a manipulative way through helping or supporting others) this also influenced her partner as she chose a very passive man who she could tell what to do, and much like the controlling partner example in chapter 1 this may be done gradually as the person who feels the need to order those around him may chip away at their partner, until they eventually give in and take on a passive role in that relationship. The person may become knowledgeable in different areas so as to be able to competently tell the person what to do or behave aggressively so that the other person acquiesces or gives in. I have observed such people who exhibit this type of behaviour become discounting when a person challenges them, and it becomes a tit-for-tat if two people who both want to be in charge state viable arguments against the other, to dismiss each other's ideas or suggestions. I knew another person who became a manager in an organisation who no matter what was said I to him, he always manipulated the conversation so as to be trying to tell me what to do. It seemed like he found it difficult to just talk to another person about shared interests or leisure activities, or if the other person was genuinely interested in him. It seemed easier for him to inhabit the manager role rather than two people just talking and taking an interest in each other. I imagine as I write this that simply talking may have created some anxiety for him, and the safe role was the managerial role.

Such a person who feels the need to order or direct others isn't viewing the other person in an assertive manner, that the other has the right to form their own opinion and choice of direction, but towards the aggressive end of the assertiveness spectrum as the other person inevitably becomes an object that serves to reinforce the person's self-concept, and in that the abeyance of anxiety. There is no real dialogical connection here as the person who controls or dominates is managing the relationship. I have found that people who behave this way listen with a judging attitude and highlight any area that they may then interrupt to tell the person what they should be doing instead, there is no communication, merely pretend listening and waiting for a chance to interrupt to fulfil their need. So with all this in mind, I would like you the reader to consider the following ways in which a person communicates as a result of the many creative adjustments and introjections. A child isn't born telling other people what to do and so becomes the person that incorporates this means of communication through the many messages from their environment, as to how to be a person.

Talking/Speaking:

The way in which we talk to others, (as well as our own self talk) is an import aspect of how we may communicate and make contact, there is also much about how the person talks to others, and the paralanguage associated with each style of communicating, for example the tone of voice, how different words will be focused on to deliver a certain message, whether the person whines or is unusually negative etc. when talking to another. I will explore this further in this chapter, but will focus for now on how we communicate, such ways of talking include:

- **Ordering, directing, bullying, dominating or commanding**

As indicated in the previous paragraphs about controlling behaviour, an order is a direction through coercion or force, this can be done from the person's role if they are in a supervisory capacity, or if they are *in charge* in some other capacity, such as the patriarch or matriarch of a household or the leader within an organisation. When the person is giving an order it is a form of dominating the relationship, and may sustain the person's self-concept, and, as with some other ways of communication this may bolster the person's self-esteem, as if they can tell another person what to do it means that they are important. In any case, there is still a manipulation of the other person, for if the person feels the need to order another person, then this is seeing the person as an object to use to give their self meaning. There is also the implication of what the effects are for the person or persons that are ordered, commanded, dominated or bullied. Does the person become compliant or submissive, does it affect their self-esteem and belief in their self (both a form of introjection and creative adjustment) as they cannot live their own life and rely on another person who tells them what to do, do they stop thinking for themselves as another person will tell them what to do, or does the person become resentful, reluctant or resistant to the person giving the order or dominating the relationship? Ordering a person may also give the message that they cannot overcome an issue or problem, and this may also undermine the ordered person's self-esteem or self-belief. I have seen this type of communication in emotionally abusive relationships, as one person takes charge through the domination of another person (but rationalised with the message *i am only trying to take care of my family*) when the real purpose is to be in charge of the relationship. The person who is passive aggressive may control or dominate others through playing sick, he may have an illness that he uses to enable him to be taken care of by others, the other person may feel obliged or duty bound to help, and if this is relational as in a husband and wife relationship, the husband may use his *illness* as a means to dominate the relationship.

- **Needing to win, hating to lose**

Much like the person who has to give orders or dominate the other person there is a fear of losing, through the many introjections and creative adjustments that leads to this, such as the effects of overly praising a child as they are developing. If this is the case then there as I see it an introjection of *you are only of worth if you succeed or win* be that in a career, in conversations, in appearance or physically. This can be a pretty flimsy self-concept as their view of their self is dependent of their relation to another person. I have observed this in conversations as the person guides the subject to a topic or area in which they have an expertise or proficiency (such as antiques, cycling, cooking, football etc.) and they can therefore dominate and therefore *win* the conversation, I have observed that there is a shift when this takes shape as the other person is viewed as competition and the person's voice changes to talk louder or more pronounced, or uses *banter* to dominate the other person. If the person has a drive to win, they may have a number of contingencies, and have a mental log of failures or ways to challenge the other person so if they feel they are losing the conversation (viewed as competition) they can talk about that failure to bring the other person "down a peg or two."

This competitive way of being is also apparent in some people who have hobbies and will practice and practice, not because of a love of the hobby, but so that they will not be seen as a failure in comparison to the other. If the person viewed losing in whatever field as a failure, then this would create anxiety at the thought of losing. There is no real contact with the other person, as each person is just a object to win against. I remember once a man had separated from his wife and their child had started taking violin lessons from the wife's new partner. This man had the *need* to win at everything he did and so he bought the child a violin so she could play it when at his house, and also arranged private tuition from a violin teacher. This wasn't because he wanted to make his daughter happy, but because he viewed himself as a failure if he lost his daughter's affection, and his fear was that his daughter would show affection to his wife's new partner instead of himself. Even though he had never met this man he still had to win in that relationship, as the fear of losing meant a feeling that he was not worthy and therefore anxiety.

Needing to win, and to not lose may have many origins, especially in our reward or recognition based society, how many people now have a drive to be famous, not through accomplishment or achievement, but for the desire to be noticed. I am aware of the number of reality based television programmes where the participants all take part just to be noticed, and if they are noticed by others then they are of worth, to be special, however having to win, as in this case is that one has to step on the shoulders of others for this recognition, and in that the person treats the other as an object to win against. The drive to look prettier, to be more intelligent, more knowledgeable, have a better body, have a better job, earn more money can only exist in relation, as the girl isn't just pretty, for she is having to win against the other person and to be prettier, to be noticed, or the person who wants to earn money so he can buy an expensive car and clothes, and again this can only exist in relation to another person, and in that is the need to win, and the reticence or hating to lose.

- **Clichés**

I have observed entire conversations that revolve around the cliché, in fact it is one of the 5 Layers of Communication in Gestalt (Simkins 1976 p48) that is to say the first layer, the cliché layer.
Have you ever noticed that some people speak without any connection, with no meaning? I remember when living at my previous house I used to have conversations with my neighbours, such as "how are you?" "Where are you going on holiday?" "How was your holiday?" "What are your plans for Christmas?" "How are the children?" and this was the general conversation style for over 5 years. I have seen this style of communication in relation to other people such as some women who ask or say "i love your new hairstyle" "where did you get those shoes?" "Are you going to Zumba?" or from men as they talk about cars, football, women, sex or the weather. It's all at the surface with nothing much underneath. While this form of communication can evolve to have a deeper meaning and connection to another person, it's like a person throwing a stone that skips on the surface of the water there is no depth to this, the stone just bounces from one place to another, and only have light superficial contact with the water. Although I had an interest in my neighbours, this was the furthest they would go in conversation, and through my observation this was the extent of how they communicated with other people as well. There may be many introjections that would drive this type of relating to other people such as *people can't be trusted*

and the person creatively adjusts this to converse in this superficial manner (much like the person who give orders and has the need to win) there is only empty meaningless communication. I do wonder when people engage in this type of cliché communication but seek spirituality and a deeper connection from a higher source that this connection is here right now if they moved beyond this way of communication. I remember a person who viewed herself as a kind of Buddhist philosopher able to offer quotes of enlightenment from Buddhist text to other people, she was covered in tattoos that had a Buddhist theme, and outwardly it seemed that she had all the answers, but these were all just clichés that kept her at a (safe) superficial level with other people. She would talk about a deeper spiritual connection to others, but could not, or rather would not try to have deep and meaningful connection with a person, I noticed that as a person showed an interest in her she would start to use more esoteric language, to further create a divide. I saw her recently in a supermarket, and as I said hello and how are you, she still replied in this clichéd manner and offered an enlightened quote in reply.

This use of cliché in verbal communication is similar to how people use profound quotes by famous people on social media to express their thoughts or opinions. Contact using another person's words. It's interesting when I see these people make contact with each other through quotes or sayings. Safety by hiding behind words and well-coined phrases, or well used topics of conversation is safe place to live, there is no connection and no risk, and as in the case of the Buddhist person may also serve their self-concept and give it meaning, as well as a purpose to by-pass genuine dialogue with another person in favour of a *connection* with a higher force, perhaps a force that is accepting, understanding and nourishing, something that the person would risk if they tried to engage in deeper communication with a person, and so it is easier to converse through cliché communication.

- **Warning or Threatening**

Have you ever heard some parents when talking to their child, and the parent wants the child to behave in a certain manner, so they speak in a threatening manner, saying such things as "if you don't behave, you won't get any sweets" or "if you don't tidy your room there'll be trouble" and these ways can only serve to tell the child what is expected of them, with a negative consequence of what may happen if they do not comply.

I was due to attend a course, and there was a requisite to complete a test before I could attend. However there was no material supplied or any reference sources that I was to be tested on, and so I raised this issue, that how can I sit a test not knowing the content of the material which I was to be assessed on. The reply I got was that I would be assessed on first aid, and so I asked what resources were available in the organisation (all the other assessments and tests in the organisation have the content in lecture presentations or practical demonstrations and we are assessed after attending these) with which I would be assessed on, or any reference sources from outside the organisation. I received an email from a senior manager saying that I was correct and that there was no reference material available for the test, but that I still had to sit the test prior to attending the course. So I replied saying that if this was the case I would like to cancel my attendance on the course, as I did not agree that a person could be tested with no reference material presented or indicated. Their response I received from the manager was threatening, stating that if I did not attend the course then I may lose my CPD (Continuous Professional Development) for the year and it may impact on any future promotion aspirations. The manager could have replied in any way, but decided to reply in a threatening and bullying manner, informing me of the consequences if I did not attend the course, which would have had a negative impact on myself. There are of course other ways to threaten people, as many people who have been in an abusive relationship know, the ways in which a person speaks that there will be consequences that would adversely affect the person (or their family members) if they do not comply with the demands of the person. I think that the person who communicated through giving orders that threats or warnings would be the likely consequence of if the person does not follow the order. Also, as I shall highlight later in this chapter on contact functions, the person may threaten the other with a glare, a joke, their appearance, nonverbal noises such a grunt or a snarl, a look, their physical presence, a gesture, in writing or by threatening to harm their own self, (such as "if you don't do this I will....) or just as with the girlfriend of an old friend used to do, that if he didn't do what she wanted, she would find someone else who would. There may also be a type of veiled threat, this was used in Belfast when I was growing up, where certain sections of the community would ask for protection money from shop-owners and businesses, not by saying that they would damage the business or set it on fire, but by saying that if the owner paid protection money, then they would protect the shop from thefts and other criminal activities. I remember once the owner of a business who firmly said that he wouldn't pay protection money any more so shortly afterwards his shop was burned down. This also served the purpose of reinforcing any future veiled threats.

- . **Forming Alliances**

I have included alliances here in the talking section of contact functions, though I am aware that this form of communication overlaps into different areas. I have noticed this way of talking and being has the intention or consequence of diluting differences between others, if it serves a particular aim, for example the anti-fracking movement in the North of England, if the alliance has the purpose of being against something or someone. I remember once I was attending a personal development course, and that a person also on the course was highly intelligent and knowledgeable as well as being as altruistic and compassionate as a person could be, and this ignited insecurities in or challenged some of the other members of the group. This was exemplified in that a member of the course saw himself as being extremely intelligent, non-judging and empathetic, and that a lady on the same course said she knew everything about herself, that her role in life was to care for others and viewed herself as being a warm, compassionate and loving person. The beliefs of both these people had been integrated into their self-concept, and of course this self-concept was on shaky ground when they met a person who challenged their beliefs. The person didn't have these values of himself as being altruistic and highly intelligent, he was simply being a person, it was the two other people on the course who had highlighted these qualities of the other person that had a meaning to their own self, and their identity. These two people realised that in relation to this person, the man wasn't that intelligent and the lady not that caring, and so it was that they formed an alliance against the person, the man had no real connection to the lady, or the lady to the man, they only formed an alliance in relation to the intelligent and altruistic person, and so in a sense they were using each other to attack the man, as his presence on this course challenged their own beliefs about themselves. While going slightly off topic here I have often wondered about people who view themselves as having a certain quality that only exists in relation to another, such as the man who viewed himself as being extremely intelligent and empathetic. Instead of viewing himself as simply being a person he became competitive with another person who had these qualities but to a greater degree, instead of actually being empathetic and accepting towards this person. The lady through attacking this man on the same course only displayed that she was not a warm and caring person, as she could only be this way towards people who did not challenge her self beliefs. It's the same as the man who viewed himself as being highly intelligent, instead of seeing himself as merely a person who had a high IQ he became competitive when someone he encountered who was more intelligent. Instead of just being a person appreciating or acknowledging that another person could be more intelligent than he, this man became competitive in relation to the other, and so both these people for their own reasons began a collaborative alliance against this other person.

In fact as I write this I am reminded of an idea I had a few years ago about the competitive nature of some people; imagine the self-professed highly intelligent man scored himself on each of his characteristics or qualities and they each have a score out of 10 such as:

Intelligence 9
Practical Aptitudes 3
Physical Fitness/Strength 2
Being Warm and Caring 3
Listening Skills 2

As he is only setting these scores in relation to another person he focuses on the characteristic that is highest so as to be better in relation, the person who drives the expensive Mercedes and uses money and financial success as a means of comparison to another invariably uses this when in relation, he views the person as he views himself (his own identity or self-concept) and when the person is challenged by this then it can only query their own self-concept, as in the person who viewed himself as being highly intelligent and graded himself as a 9, when in fact he is only for instance a 2 or 3 as he actually meets someone who is a 9 on his scale. As such I believe that as this challenges his self-concept that a type of existential anxiety happens as the person in this case isn't that intelligent. He may of course manipulate his environment and try to advise, order or guide another to give this meaning, but in this case he found another person on the course who shared this anxiety and together they formed an alliance.

This form of alliance is shaky as it is based on a person's insecurity or anxiety as the other challenged their self-concept or identity, and how they existed in relation to another. This type of relationship can only be monological as they are not really interested in each other, only in the ways or reasons that they are in an alliance. It's not too unfamiliar to a Union, the people who are part of this union are in alliance against the employers for fair pay and worker's rights etc. The individual in the union may not really be interested in the other members, but just that they share a common goal or aim. I have seen similar in gangs and other groups as well as in demonstrations as an alliance is formed for a particular aim or goal.

- **Moralising, Righteous Beliefs**

In this way of how the person views their self, especially in relation to others is the way of moralising, where the person takes a higher moral stance and feels justified to judge the other person's life, behaviour, values and actions based on how they belief they *should* be. This may originated in the many introjections and creative adjustments that forms the self-concept, such as *I am always right, I can judge other people, other people have to listen to me, I am more important, I am special.* Some people may have the belief that others should behave a certain way, and if not then morally they have a duty to vocalise this to the person, sit back and be the silent judge or talk to others in a gossiping, degrading or critical way about them, *how* they speak to others is pertinent as they talk in a way that the person should be behaving in a certain way. A person at my previous place of work believed that the organisation *should* be behaving in a certain way, and since they were not then he felt justified to inform the management of this. Some people I have found who have a moralising way of relating feel that they are obliged to tell the other about their behaviour or actions, and then offer a solution, but again, others may state what the person *should* be doing in a self-righteous way without offering any solution or remedy, the purpose being to judge from above. I have seen this in abusive relationships where the dominant partner takes a moral high-ground and says such things or has the introjected message of *as my wife it is your duty to take care of my needs* of course this is nonsense, the person is taking this stance based on their own self beliefs. The person who displays this way of relating to others may also communicate by guiding, ordering, bullying, threatening or criticising and in that they are taking a higher

71

moral stance to the other. I have also seen this in people who are "do-gooders" in that they have found a person or group that needs help (such as people who addicted to drugs or alcohol) and this gives them a role to *help* the other person, but it is not though a genuine concern for the welfare of others, but a belief that their behaviour is wrong and as such they need to be helped. The use of clichés is alive here as well as the person says self-righteous statements such as "respect your elders" and "you must say please and thank you" there is no requirement for a person to behave this way, I am aware that it is nice if a person displays good manners and is polite and respectful, but when the person delivers it as a *should* or *must* then it is a sign of the person moralising to the other. Also in this way of communicating the person is relating to the other in a superior manner, with the expectation that the other should do as they say, if this is part of the person's self-concept then even if someone to whom they can't moralise too then something may be distorted so they are not that good, or they wait for a chink in the person or for them to make a mistake or failure at something so they can feel justified in attacking or morally correcting or criticising their behaviour.

- **Advising, giving solutions, suggestions**

The person who has integrated many introjections and creative adjustments that form their own self-concept, may feel they *have* to advise or give solutions and suggestions to the other, even to filter what they hear to be able advise. They may cherry pick what they hear to be able to offer advice. A person on my old street had this way of being, she would filter what she heard from her neighbours and respond by giving advice or offering a solution. Such a person may become proficient in a certain field be able to fulfil this role, for example the person who has this belief about themselves may volunteer for a charity that offers advice. The person on my old street would only associate with people she knew could help, and as the area was quite deprived she would associate with people who has substance misuse issues and victims of domestic abuse, in this she was believed that she was morally right to be able to offer advice and make suggestions.

The person who communicates this way may have it as part of their self-concept to be more superior to others, and thus offering advice and solutions may be in the same spectrum as ordering, moralising or needing to win. The person is telling the other person what to do, and in that is taking an aggressive stance in that relationship. This isn't to say that giving advice or offering solutions in inherently aggressive, if is offered in an inclusive and assertive manner, but when the person is treating the other person as an object in which they *must* help through offering advice, giving solutions or making suggestions then it becomes more of an aggressive side style of contact, as they are doing something to the person, instead of respecting that the person has the right to take their own path in life, regardless if that is right or wrong by anyone else. I have always thought that sending solutions or offering advice restricts the person's own ability to overcome their own problems and therefore become more independent and confident in making their own decisions. The ability for a person to make their own choice, to discover that they can lead their own life, to find the answers to their own dilemmas or questions can only enliven their self, but, the person who *has* to offer advice, or make suggestions only serves to atrophy or retard this valuable part of the other person.

I have met people who are the antithesis of this, who because of their own introjection and creative adjustments do not belief in their own ability to solve their own problems and find people to whom they have to ask for advice or to tell them what to do. This can become quite a toxic relationship, as the person who has to be a helper meets someone who needs to be helped. There is also the possibility that this is a safe place to be, though this may restrict any type of meaningful contact as the person stays in the *advising* role, much like the other aspects I have talked about so far there is again a certain safety in this style of communication, as the person takes a one up position to be able to offer advice or make suggestions, and unless there is self-disclosure to enable the person to give suggestions (such as "a similar thing happened to me, and this is how I fixed it) the person knows more about the person he is advising than the advised person knows about the advisor. What is it like for the helper/advisor to become the helpee/advised? Do they accept this or do they do so with some reluctance, what is it like for a person who is some accustomed to giving advice to have to ask for assistance. I think this is why some people become very independent, so they do not have to ask for anyone for advice or a solution, yet jump at the opportunity to be able to offer this to someone else. There are also people who are very adept at giving other people advice or making suggestions, yet their own life is

73

chaotic. I knew a person once who as affected by anxiety and panic attacks yet felt ok to give advice to others about how to overcome their own anxiety. Such is someone who may gain a sense of worth, affection or approval, or another need is met by taking on such an advice giving or problem solving role. I have known a few people who feel that it is ok to offer a solution to other people's issues, yet fail to address the similar problems in their own life, there was such a man who had a very negative a nihilistic attitude to life that was never explored or attempted to be understood, yet he saw no problem with advising people who were affected by a similar outlook (it's easier to fix another person's problems than to become aware of their self and way of being) I think as well that the internet if full of people offering life coaching or directive based therapy in which it is easier to advice and make suggestions to others, yet are reticent about following their own advice. Perhaps then this would be a means of projection, rationalisation or deflection as the person avoids understanding their own issues, but yet advises others with similar issues.

- **Judging, Criticising, Evaluating**

A funny thing happened the other day, a friend's daughter came to my house after she had finished school, and upon entering I noticed that she was looking around the house in a somewhat evaluative manner. I was interested in this and asked if this was the first time she had been to my house and she replied that yes it was, and that she liked the colour scheme in the living room, the bathroom was light and airy but that the sofa (the sofa I had bought when I was single and my only criteria was that it was cheap and comfortable) didn't go with the rest of the décor in the living room and it would look better if I changed it. I was surprised at hearing this as she was only 9 and asked if she had always been this way? She relied saying that her mum was exactly the same, and would be critical towards other people and their houses. I thought then about creative adjustment and introjection and how this young girl had integrated her mother's values about how she saw and related to the world, for although this section in on judging, criticising, blaming and evaluating it also overlaps into the person's beliefs, values, how they see and experience their world and cherry-pick or filter all the information from their environment to be able to judge the other. In the case on the above example of the little girl who didn't just come into her friend's house for dinner to play some games with my own child, but to enter the house in an evaluative and judging position. This would be similar to a person who *has* to own an expensive mountain bike because it sustains their own identity or self-concept, then, when they meet another cyclist the first thing they consider is the brand or make of the bike that they are riding. (A form of being competitive) I remember when I first became a Firefighter, we had attended a serious road traffic collision and we were extricating the driver with the use of a spine board. As I am a practical person I enjoy getting hands on and was assisting moving the person onto the board. I noticed that some of the older Firefighters were standing behind me and talking about me in a judging and evaluative manner. I thought about the purpose of doing this, what would be the purpose of evaluating someone from a critical perspective (as opposed to constructive) highlighting only their faults, and how all the information presented was filtered or distorted so that they could judge another person from a superior position (as they had been in the job a longer amount of time and therefore more *experienced* this was the basis of their judging attitude and beliefs) I remember laughing to myself as my previous job was a recovery mechanic and I had attended many road traffic collisions, knew in detail the construction of many different brands of car, and also that I had volunteered for a charity that delivered first aid at community events, and was highly proficient in advanced first aid. These Firefighters had filtered the events so that as they had more *experience* in the role it gave them an unspoken permission to judge me and other people who had been in the job for a less time than these people. They were offering their approval or disapproval of the other from the perspective of *experience* and nothing else. I've never agreed with judging another person or criticising them, each person has a right to live their life whatever way they please. Judging, criticising or evaluating a person can be a barrier to meeting the other person, rather than with an inclusive and dialogic attitude. Judging others may mean that one believes themselves to be more superior and to *judge from above* as in the case of the Firefighters. I realise that it important to evaluate situations or to judge if a person is honest or dishonest for example but feel that a block to understanding or communication may occur when a person takes a superior attitude about how the person *should* be, or the judging attitude reinforces their own position, identity of self-concept. Pre-judging is also a part of this style of communication and may lead to discrimination and therefore blaming the other for societal issues or problems, when the person judges the other on their role, job, colour of their skin, gender, gender identity, appearance, status, religion or beliefs. I have seen this sometime in when observing conversations, the person asks the other "what do you do" or "how many children do you have?" and this isn't asked because of a genuine interest in the other person, but in an evaluative way, for if the person replies saying "i have a part-time job and 2 children" then the person can feel free to criticise them by saying they are a drain on society. Feeling they are being judged they may offer an excuse or explanation by saying "but I am planning on going to go to college soon" or "my husband has just left me so I need to work and look after two children" though she is not answering in a conversational manner as the person is openly enquiring in the spirit of dialogue, but in an explaining manner as she feel she has to explain herself and justify her position or her life. The person asking the judging question or criticising the other may not come from a superior position, but from feelings of inferiority, those Firefighters may have been surprised at my practical aptitude and first aid knowledge and relied on their *experience* to bolster their self-esteem, the lady asking the question may already know the answer and has asked that question in a critical stance as she does not want anyone to be superior to her, she therefore asks questions in a judging way to try to deflate others or look for a chink or fault from which to attack. The person much like the previous examples may discount positive attribute in favour of highlighting any negative aspects to criticise. This style of communication may originate from the many introjections and creative adjustments from the person's life and also affects how the person sees other people, how they hear and how they talk, as well as their beliefs about who they are as a person (as in a self-judging or self-critical way as the person believes they *should* be a certain way) which may result in feelings of guilt, shame, anxiety, retroflective anger (anger turned towards themselves) or depression if they cannot live up to their own expectations. (In a self-judging way)

I have to say that the capacity to judge others, as well as the self judgement of how we *should* be is one of the biggest barriers to communication and stops people from meeting each other and knowing, understanding or discovering each other, to lean into their experience and to acknowledge that the other person is a unique person who has the right to live their own life and to experience the world their own way, as well as the self judgement and criticism as we struggle to live up to our introjected ideals of how we should be, and the struggle for self-acceptance. I think that judging and criticism others restricts us from forming relationships. A senior manager at work is normally a very accepting and understanding person, however a junior manager started work on our team and as he previously working in the training department he had an intricate knowledge of all the policies and procedures in the organisation. This created a sense of inadequacy in my senior manager who started to critique him, saying that although he knew everything and had all the answers he didn't have the *experience* that he had (a sign of being competitive) and that he had poor people skills. The senior manager had perhaps feelings of inferiority and was judging him to find an area that he could attack and criticise, and this is something I have noticed about the judging nature of some people who compare themselves to others, they look for faults from which to criticise. He was therefore only focusing on the weaknesses, instead of the strengths of this person.

I knew a lady who would only associate with people like herself, that is to say people who shared an interest in philosophy but this rigid belief of the people that she would associate with restricted the possibility of contact with others, we all have our ideas about life and who we are, but she didn't talk about her thoughts to *ordinary* people, as she believed they wouldn't understand, and instead discussed these topics with her learned friends. If this is not pre-judging then I am not sure what is as I remember having the most involving conversation about the wonder of people with a music teacher! The lady here by her decision to only talk about her passion for philosophy with a few select people whom she judged worthy meant that meaningful contact on her favoured subject with others was unlikely, as it was based on her beliefs about herself and others. I have been reading in this area for many years, but a friend has only a passing interest and it's so interesting to hear her perspective on the way people adjust to life and how it affects them in the way they relate to others. These conversations would not happen if I had the same beliefs as the lady and only communicated with other people who shared this interest or passion. Wouldn't it be such a beautiful world if we could suspend our judgements about other people and how we believe we should be, both as an individual and in relation to others. The girl who looks at the other girl up and down wouldn't do this and just talk to the person as a unique person. The man, who looks and judges the other man's car, evaluates their job or intelligence before they speak would just not consider this and simply speak to a person. A person to person communication with no judgements, evaluations or criticisms.

- **Praising, agreeing, paying compliments**

Would you say that praising is the same as judging? Is praising just favourable judging, and is paying a person a compliment much the same? This style of communication may motivate others, it may build confidence and highlight positive attributes, comments, beliefs or values and generate good will between people.

This would be from a person who has no ulterior motive, the person who wants to encourage with no other motive may be like the soil in which a seed is planted, the soil just offers nutrients and a stable base, and the seed grows and becomes a plant from this supportive ground. However it is also a means of coercion and manipulation, the man who is only interested in the attractiveness of his partner may only give compliments in this area, and the manipulative effects would be the belief of the woman that *he is only interested in me if I am pretty* and so she may creatively adjust to this introjection by focusing on her looks and appearance. Praise as a means of communication at places or work may be a manipulation so that the staff get a reward if they can achieve certain targets. The football coach who praises his team for playing well has the intention of them winning. When used in this way the way in purpose of the praise may be similar to asking the person to jump through a hoop, the praise or the compliment is the carrot dangling in front. Is the person offering the compliment taking a superior stance? I remember I was taking part in an organised walk across Morecambe Bay and there was a father whose son was struggling to walk in the soft sand, he was offering praise saying "come on son, you're doing great" as words on encouragement, though I noticed that there was a certain urgency and pressure in his voice, as the child slipped further and further behind the group the father shifted from being encouraging and praising to criticising and name calling, saying "come on then you're holding everybody up" and "dig in you girl, you're making me look stupid" the father's praise initially had been for manipulative purposes as he didn't want to be embarrassed by his son who was finding it difficult walking on that terrain.

Praising and paying compliments from this position may be an indicator of the person's own values or beliefs, that is to say *if you are more like me, or do something that I admire then I will offer you a compliment, or praise you* and in this it may be seen as also an introjection that the person creatively adjusts too. I recall a person who had low self-esteem and a lack of belief in herself, she had met a man who had a passion for tattoos and started to coax her to get some herself, he would offer praise and compliments say that she would look great with a sleeve tattoo and although hesitant she eventually acquiesced and got a tattoo and her upper arm, the man was full of praise for this and said it looked great, the last time I heard of this lady she had both arms tattooed. I often wonder if this lady actually wanted the tattoos or if she was fitting in to what her partner wanted, and he was communicating through praise and compliments as a means of manipulation.

As I am interested in this field I have lost count of the amount of times I have heard a man offer a compliment to a lady he is interested in, in fact I am sure there a few books on this and one of the tactics I recall is to give a negative compliment which isn't what the girl is expecting, as she is expecting him to flirt with her or charm her, and this is still a means of manipulation.

Another aspect of his style of communication is the person who attempts to court favour from the other person, to get on the person's good side. If the person has adjusted to this from many introjections so that he thinks he is only of worth if the other person likes him, this style of communication may result (such as becoming a people pleaser) however, the person who is manipulative may pretend to be this way, to get on the person's good side by offering compliments and praise, as well as agreeing with the other person, even if they secretly disagree. The term "buttering someone up" is apt here for this style of communication. The person may ask questions (that they already know the answer to) in an attempt to make the other person feel good, they may show an interest in the other person with the ulterior motive to have their needs met. They may choose a topic of conversation that they know is favourable to the other person and pretend to listen intently as the person rattles on and on. I knew a person who worked in sales, he was hopeless at his job and couldn't achieve his targets so he showed an interest in the supervisors and managers at the business where he worked and asked them questions about their weekend, how their partners and children were (while making a mental note for future conversations where he could ask further questions related to them) and where they were going on holiday this year. When it came to his appraisal the managers said that although he was down on his targets they liked him and didn't put much pressure on him. I have seen this style of communication in other people in sales roles who attempt to know their customers and show an interest, not because of a genuine interest in the other, but so that it will meaning getting a sale or to form a *working relationship* for future sales or business from that person.

- **Humour**

There are many reasons why a person would communicate through the use of humour and while this may be exhaustive I will explore which ways I have observed the use and purpose of humour in others as well as my own reflections.

I have found that in some abusive relationships the dominant person in that relationship may use humour to diminish the self-esteem or confidence in their partner or children if he views them as a threat to his dominance, this form of relating to others may also involve name calling or labelling the other person, often said in a humorous way, saying "what's the matter, can't you take a joke?" if they are hurt by his words. I am reminded of a man who entered into a relationship with a lady who had a number of children, the eldest being a boy around 16 years old. The man was gently controlling the younger children through giving the gifts as a form of manipulation so they would respond to his control, but the oldest boy didn't respond to this and so the name calling began, he would call him girls names and criticise him for his interests (he liked playing guitar in his room) as he didn't view them as being masculine. He said to the mother that something was wrong with him and that he would try to get him involved in more masculine sports and so began taking him to football games on occasions, but the boy was reticent at doing this and preferred doing is own thing. The man became more aggressive in his use of humour calling him weak and girly, he would try to have some rough and tumble games with the boy, that always seemed to end in the boy getting hurt, which the man then said "there's nothing wrong with you" and "i am only joking around" to the boy and continue using what he called *banter* with the boy, but was in actual fact just a way for the man to be continually sarcastic to the boy, in an effort to diminish his self-esteem, so he could assert his dominance in this new family. As I recall the mother became aware of man's methods and the relationship ended. This was his style of contact when in relation to another he view as a threat, competition or the another (the boy) didn't do what he wanted.

Other ways in abusive relationships in which humour may be used is that the person being abused (such as the wife) may continually become the butt of the joke when they are with friends, which may seem funny at the time but is a manipulative attempt to again dominate the other and reinforce the dominant position of the abuser. I had a neighbour once who communicated in this style, no matter what her husband did around the house it was never good enough and she seemed to take delight in putting him down in front of other people, I am aware of some of the field conditions (from Field Theory) that may have precluded this, that she would cherry pick incidents that she could use to humiliate her husband and in a sense put them in the bank ready to withdraw at the right time and with the right audience.

A person may have learnt to tell jokes to ingratiate himself to the other person, much like people pleasing, he can gauge what is funny in that group and start telling jokes. I have noticed this in certain people, some people will tell a joke or do something funny and then quickly scan the room to see if this is accepted or approved of, that is to say if the audience start laughing. The use of humour may not be limited to telling jokes to be funny, a colleague at a previous job used to make sexual references to get people to laugh, and I noticed that the same scanning the room for the reaction was also there. I noticed that as time went on and he endeavoured to gain the same reaction that his references would become more graphic and depraved sexually.

People may tell jokes or use humour as a means of acceptance and to gain popularity or to be liked. In the example above of the abusive husband and the wife who was the butt of his jokes, this man may have been trying to get people to like him, to be popular or a means of acceptance, the wife then is not seen as a person who has feelings, but an object or a thing to use to achieve this end. If he first used his wife to make a joke and the others frowned at this then he may use another person for the same reaction. The introjection and creative adjustment that drive this may be *I must be liked, I have to be accepted, I have to win* I include I have to win as an introjection as the person may construe that if he succeeds in getting other people to like him then in means he has won, and the satisfaction from knowing that he has won, particularly if it means he used humour to dominate other people.

This is another use of humour I have found, as a person can use humour to be aggressive as a means of control. I remember I was working in a team and the way they talked was with a very vicious and attacking humour masked as banter, I observed as they all picked at each other, and it seemed to be a competition who could be the most cutting and derogatory to the other, but in a humorous manner. This type of humour may mean that again the person has to highlight faults that the other has made, or put in the bank or reserve some joke to be used if they are attacked in a humorous way be the other. I have found that this type of interaction is like verbal sparring, and if the creative adjustment or introjection drives this the person may purposefully talk to others this way to avoid a more intimate or personal way or talking. He is always attacking the other and putting them on the defensive so no real meaningful contact is made. In this way the person uses humour to avoid contact, but also directs the other to the style of contact that is preferred.

Humour can then be used to avoid meaningful contact with the other person, for example if the other person has gone through a difficult period and the other person doesn't want to talk about it or to enquire as to how the other person they may use a joke or other form of humour to avoid the topic. Humour may also have the purpose (as in people pleasing) to be able to build a rapport with the other person to be able to gain information, as in the case of the salesperson whose goal is to make a sale, he may use humour (after gauging what type of humour is acceptable to the person) in an attempt to manipulate him so he feels more comfortable and relaxed, the salesperson is therefore likeable and seen as friendly.

As mentioned previously in the cliché section, this is also a way in which some people talk, for as long as I can remember men have used clichéd humour to interact with each other, in fact if I am honest as I was brought up in a household with no father I always found this way of talking to be difficult, to talk in a superficial humorous way, I always wanted to know the other person and talk to them, but talking to men who used superficial humour was difficult for me, and even now, even though I work in a team of mainly men it is still something that is difficult. I don't have to talk this way as I prefer a more authentic and genuine way of relating, but it is interesting to see men use this form of relating to communicate with each other. This for me is another introjection, to communicate in a light hearted and humorous way with other men.

A person may also use humour to give out information but still save their self-concept, and this may be an example of where the person may feel judged by the other, and feel they have to give a humorous reason as to why they can't do something. This also happens I have found when a person asks another on a date, they may appear to use humour to mask that they want to go out with the other person, and if she or he says no then it can be written off as just being a joke, or light-heartedly saying that it didn't really matter anyway what the other person said. For the person to save their self-concept on more serious matters then the use of humour may serve to alleviate feelings of shame or inadequacy. A colleague in a previous job had been trying for some time to progress in the organisation and try as hard as he could he couldn't pass the test that was required, even though he studied relentlessly he couldn't succeed, and so this was rationalised to say that it was the organisation's loss, and that he was a more practical person anyway! Humour then has the purpose of saving face (which would mean that the person feels that he is being judged by others) and to cope with the embarrassment of failing the test.

I am aware that the use of humour is indeed a list that could go on and on, and the many beneficial aspects of humour. The use of humour though, as a creative adjustment from many introjections is something that I am particularly interested in, as the person may have adjusted to use humour for a variety of purposes, to gain attention, approval, worth or recognition, to deflect attention from an area that causes embarrassment, guilt or shame, using humour as a means to control groups, to diffuse difficult situations, to be able to vent frustration in an acceptable way, to be able to attack other people that the person doesn't like, to use people as the object of humour, to use humour to not be bullied, to be able to get information, to be liked, to avoid the other's concern or problem or to attract the other with the use of intelligent or witty humour. What is fascinating to me is that when humour is used as a medium or a tool then much like the other areas here, it may serve to make safe contact with the other person, and in that the avoidance of meaningful contact with the other. The person who feels they have to be liked by another person may use humour to gain acceptance, instead taking a risk and simply being himself and not to play a role to gain recognition, success or popularity. Such is how people may exist, that they cannot be themselves, but feel that have to play a role to be accepted.

- **Questions**

The use, meaning and purpose of questions has always interested me, does the person take a passive role in how and why they ask questions, do they have to take an aggressive position in asking questions to elicit a method in which to gain a reply and therefore information. Is there a more assertive attitude to the other when asking questions, as the person realises that the person has a right to answer if they wish, and there are no manipulations present that drives the questions, just an enquiry or interest toward the other person.

There was a girl who had made plans on the day she was meant to meet her mother after school for dinner, as her parents had separated her father was a very manipulative and controlling man who had promised the daughter that he would treat the daughter to her most favourite meal on the day that her mother had arranged to take her daughter into town. The daughter could have said "mum, I've changed my mind and am going to dad's instead as he has promised me my favourite meal" but she realised that this would have caused her to explain why she had made this choice after making arrangements with her mother, so therefore the easiest thing to do was to phrase a question that meant her mother would have to take responsibility for her daughter's decision to cancel, the daughter asked the leading question to her mother "where are we going today after school?" the mother replied saying "anywhere you like, we can go into town or anywhere else you'd like" this interrupted the leading question that the daughter had asked so couldn't justifiably say that she didn't want to go to a place that wasn't arranged yet, so she asked the leading question of "so, what are we having for dinner then?" and the mother replied that it was up to her, but that they could go into town if she liked to McDonald's (her favourite place to eat) that her mother took her as a treat, or anywhere else that she liked. The daughter then said "it doesn't matter then as that sounds boring, I am going to dad's instead for dinner" it didn't matter what the mother had said or where she was going, the daughter had phrased her questions so as to give a viable reason to not see her mother after school, and that there was a shift in responsibility as the daughter was implying that she wasn't going because her mum's open ended suggestion sounded boring. This enabled the daughter to go to her father's house guilt free and the decision to cancel her arranged time with her mother. There is also the creative adjustment from the daughter of being exposed to the controlling father, and viewing the other person (the mother) as an object to blame, and to not consider the consequences of her decisions, in that her mother was feeling sad and confused as to why her daughter would act this way towards her.

The purpose of the question then was to hook support from her environment, she couldn't or wouldn't accept responsibility for her decision and the question to her mum transferred responsibility and gave an excuse based on the answer.

The use of questions can fulfil a message being sent to the other, and is an easy way to make a statement, such as the parent asking their child the question "what do you think you are doing?" then waiting for the reply before stating what it is the parent believes the child is doing.

Questions can also be used to bully someone to get the person to answer before they proceed to criticise behaviour or answers. The initial answer then becomes redundant and rhetoric, as it has no bearing on the person asking the question.

After a gruelling incident at work in which we rescued three people a senior manager arrived to critically assess the incident, as well as the actions and decision making process of the manager to ascertain if he followed procedures. The incident fell outside procedures though the manager's decision making skills were exemplary, he had managed a team that had rescued people from a flat fire in extenuating circumstances. The assessing manager arrived and walked around the incident actively looking for faults or omissions. He approached my manager and asked to speak to him, he then asked "where areas of operational procedure do you believe you have got wrong or left out here?" and "what do you think you could have done better?" The assessing manager already had his answer prepared, as it was his intention to critique my manager towards a negative outcome, and whatever my manager gave in reply had no bearing at all on the outcome. The purpose of question was much like the previous example with the daughter who already had the answer planned. The daughter was looking for an answer as an excuse or reason for her to not attend, and the assessing manager had his answer planned, though the question and the phasing of the question had the purpose of putting pressure on the manager as he listed areas that were missed or omitted, before disregarding the answer to state his own findings. He may have also be quite adept at using clarifying questions so he could get a precise detail of the person's actions, not for his own knowledge, but to apply more pressure.

I have found that questions can also be used to elicit information, such as a teacher asking if the student has gained a knowledge or understanding of the subject taught, or a police officer asking a question to ascertain the whereabouts of a suspect or to try to determine the truth. This is a functional purpose of a question, though I am more interested in the purpose of a question and how a person may use questions as a result of introjections and creative adjustments in life.

Imagine the person who is passive in relation to others, their question may be to source the view of the other before stating their own, and then when knowing the other's opinion may filter their response so an not to antagonise the person. (people-pleasing or walking on eggshells) I recall a person who grew up with a very arrogant and self-important parent, the introjected message of *you are not important* or *I am more important than you* resulted in him putting himself in a more passive role and he would gain attention and worth by becoming an expert at listening and asking questions to the arrogant and self-centred parent, his purpose of asking questions was to draw the attention of the parent and he would listen as the parent talked for hours about herself, as the parent talked the child would listen intently to the themes and patterns of the story and knew which topics to focus on, he was also adept at clarification questions, to find out in detail the topics that the person was talking about. The person who is passive and prefers not to have attention focused on them (though this may be passive aggressive as the person controls the conversation) may also use this kind of open ended question so that the attention is never placed on them. The person answering the question may believe that the person is really interested in them, and that they are a good listener, but in actuality the person is just an object that subject to the passive person's manipulation by using questions to focus attention away from himself. The person then may have become very adept at asking open ended questions such as "how did it go?" "How do you feel about the relationship?" "Tell me about it" "what was your experience of that?"

The purpose of the open ended question is to place few limitations on how the person can reply, generally opened ended questions has a how, what, when, who, which or where factor (but omitting the why question as this may be a closed, probing or directed question) The person may answer the open ended question in a number of ways. I have found that some people who work in a sales environment are quite proficient in the use of open ended questions, but much like a funnel this is a means of manipulation as the questions become more specific and then culminating in the topic that the salesperson had originally wanted to talk about (which would be guiding the person to a topic resulting in a sale) I have found a similar theme in abusive and controlling relationships as the dominant person asks an open ended question such as "where would you like to go on holiday this year?" and whatever the person's reply is the dominant person's question may then be "that sounds good, but I am thinking about us going away in the caravan, how does that sound to you?"

Of course this is another open ended question, as the person can answer any way they want, but the dominant partner has informed his intentions to the partner in the first part of the dialogue, and though it transfers from a conversation about where to go on holiday to a preplanned holiday that the husband wanted to go on regardless of the partner's answer. He can then feel justified in going to the place he has decided perhaps be saying "well I asked her, and she said yes" though he is omitting exactly how she came to say yes.

The person who has creatively adjusted to be a problem solver, or is searching for a role (such a the masculine man who has difficulty showing emotions) may encounter a person and ask probing questions as they search for a role and what they can do, this is a manner in which a person can avoid the concern of the other person but still offer support, such as a person who is pregnant and having labour pains, the partner feels uneasy about this and offers practical support instead by asking questions to highlight an area in which he can help, but in an area that creates the least anxiety for himself. He can't offer much emotional support to a woman with the pains of labour, but he can drive the car to the hospital or make a cup of tea.

The person who asks the question at the beginning of the conversation, but has the motivation to take over to their own topic regardless of the answer, may as a simple question such as "how are you?" then steer the conversation to their own area. If the person talked about their own interests first then they may appear selfish, but by talking about the other person first, before taking over the person is manipulating the other, he just doesn't want to appear selfish and so pretends to listen for a while until he gets his chance to take over.

The person may hook the environment for support by manipulation, during the initial question of "how are you?" then the person gives a closed answer such as "fine" the person may ask "how's the kids?" or "how's it

87

going?" as the person moves from area to area as then try to manipulate the other to disclose information that they can reply to and carry on the conversation. The purpose of this is so that the person asking the question can have a talk *about* the other person, and that they do not to disclose anything about themselves. The use of clarifying questions may be used here as well, as the person focuses on the other to gain more detail, as the person elaborates on any given topic.

Closed questions have the purpose to elicit information and the way in which it is asked can only be answered in a minimum number of ways. For example, when moving into my old house a number of years ago, my old neighbours asked a number of closed questions, such as where are you from?, "what do you do?", "do you drink?", "do you have any children?" and after I had knew them for some time I asked why they had asked some many questions when I first moved in, they replied saying that their previous neighbour was very noisy and used to play loud music, so they were concerned if this was my intention as well. This for me was a passive frame of questions as they were gaining information from their use of questions to allay their concerns, when if they were assertive they may have enquired that as their previous neighbour was loud they were concerned if I would be the same, and if they were aggressive they may have told me "our last neighbour was loud, and we're fed up with up, so you'd better not be" or passive aggressive in saying that they has young baby, and if I was planning on having any parties, this type of question also gives information as they have just told me they have a young baby before asking me my intention. This last example could also be viewed as leading as they are leading me to an answer.

Leading questions have the purpose of guiding the person to few possible responses, and is a favourite I have found in salespersons and people who control others, people who are dominant, aggressive or passive aggressive may use this style when in communicating with others as they direct the conversation. I knew a person who would ask leading questions in which she would guide people to sensitive emotional areas of their life for in her words "to have a good cry" she would join them in their tears and then offer to be supportive to the person. Her use of questioning had the final purpose of giving her a role in that relationship, she was manipulating and guiding the other to an emotionally based reply or conversation with which to have a role (and therefore give self-concept meaning and a purpose, that she was a supportive and caring person) It is worth noting here that a person can use leading questions to gain information so they can judge, agree, form an alliance, send solutions, criticise or judge, to be able to praise or pay compliments, to warn or to evaluate the other person. This again has the purpose of giving their self-concept, or way of relating to others meaning. If the person has a need to be negative, to feel down or depressed then they may ask questions, either closed, probing or leading which may serve to filter or distort what they hear so they can be negative. They may ask questions about the difficult parts of a person's life so they both can feel down.

Questions may also serve the similar purpose of avoiding the other's concerns if they *must* be positive and upbeat, so if they encounter a person who is feeling down they may elicit questions that avoid this and only focus on the positive aspects of the person's story, this may have the benefit of offering support and being upbeat, but if the person feels they must be positive (that they have creatively adjusted to this from a number of introjections) then the person is manipulating the other away from an area that may cause anxiety. If the person finds it easier to be angry, judging and critical as opposed to calm and understanding, he may guide the conversation so that he can be angry and critical, particularly if the person's topic of concern is something that the person can be justifiably angry against. For example, the woman who believes that men are perpetrators, or wholly dominant, abusive and controlling may associate with women who share these views, or work in a setting where they encounter women who have been abused by men.(To substantiate their own view) This would still be a manipulation of the environment, as much like the question the person is deciding the ground (as in leading the person to an area or topic in which she can vent her anger) so that she can get justifiably be angry towards men.

A person whose intention it is to put another person under pressure may ask a series of questions to gain a reply, I have noticed this in abusive relationships when the abusive partner asks a series of questions to put pressure on the other, this also has the effect of confusing the person. A further type of question in this area is when the abusive partner denies saying something and says "you're wrong, are you sure I said that, you must be wrong" and the person may begin to doubt whether are sure something was said or an occurrence actually happened.

Much like humour, this could be an exhaustive list as to the use and purpose of asking question, but as I see it the use of the question for the purposes of giving meaning to a self-concept or from a style of contact from a number of creative adjustments and introjections. The person with the aggressive way of being may use more I statements such as I think, or in a question form as "don't you think?" or ask probing questions to gain information, they may even use self disclosure and tell the other person information about themselves, before asking questions, the purpose being to try to manipulate the other person to feel like he can be trusted, or that the person likes him and so he is more likely to answer the questions. I have experienced this before when a person tried to ask me questions about a female friend that I thought was very personal, so when I didn't answer then he disclosed information about himself and tried to appear more friendly and warm, before asking me the same questions, I suspected what he was doing, so I still didn't give him the information he wanted. The passive (or passive aggressive) person may ask questions to deflect attention, to probe to gain information so they feel more comfortable, to be able to focus the attention in more detail towards the other person (such as knowing the children's names etc.) to not disclose information about themselves to highlight a belief (that people are only interested in talking about themselves and have no interest in other people) (from the introjection of *people only care about themselves, people aren't interested in me, I am not interesting, I am more superior as I can guide conversations)* or to ask leading questions that imply something, then when the other person starts to talk about this, or answer the hidden message then the passive aggressive person may begin to talk about it. The person may also state a rhetorical question, the purpose being not to gain an answer but to state a thought or opinion, but phrase this as a question. The person asking questions may be seeking agreement, but this would be manipulative as he is choosing people who he knows will agree with his questions and therefore feel justified in his position and way of relating to the world. The person who is aggressive may ask questions that are also leading as it serves to create hostility or aggression in the other person, then when the other person bites and responds in the manner which the person wants them to (whether that is person getting angry, getting emotional, becoming passive, becoming defiant etc.) then the objective of the question has succeeded and the person has been manipulated to serve the needs of the person asking the question. In all these occurrences I have seen of people who are passive, passive aggressive or aggressive the use of questions can serve to gain support from their environment, and as such people around them.

Another way that relates to the use of questions is when the person who is assertive and respects the rights of the person to be a unique individual, the question then has a different meaning and purpose, there may be a genuine and authentic interest in the other person and the person has an enquiry or a sense of wonder about the other and is interested to know more about their life, the person who respects the individual also may ask questions, not because they have to offer advice or make suggestion that only serve to satisfy a need such as a desire to appear to be caring and supportive, but because the person actually is caring and supportive and they are genuinely concerned and the question "how are you?" has a special meaning as this person has a genuine concern for the welfare of the other person. The person then may begin by saying what they are feeling or experiencing before asking how the person, such as "as you sighed there you seemed like you are carrying a heavy weight and I am wondering how you are?" the question is used, not for manipulation, to guide the person towards an answer, but with a caring and inclusive belief towards the well-being of another person.

- **Statements/Other ways of relating to others verbally**

It is not the purpose of this book to include all the ways in which a person verbally makes contact with another, but to highlight that a person may creatively adjust to communicate in a certain way, I think a person can either be competitive or collaborative with another person, to either view the person as an object to judge, order or compare, to satisfy their needs or to reinforce the person's own view of their self, or in a dialogic or assertive sense, that the person is a unique individual with their own right to exist the way they choose. Other ways that a person may verbally communicate with the other may include; Shaming, name calling, ridiculing, through the use of silence, shunning or ostracising, interpreting, gossiping, analysing, diagnosing, reassuring, lying, hiding feelings, pleasing others, rescuing, playing sick or helpless, playing the sage, playing stupid, creating dramas, filtering, consoling, supporting, by unnecessary probing or interrogating, guiding, through submission, obedience or compliance, or through distracting, diverting, escaping, whining or complaining. The person may excessively explain or they may withdraw, regress or retaliate through the spoken word. The person may do any of these from an aggressive, passive aggressive or passive perspective, so for example the person may withdraw from the other person so as to punish them (for example the son who punishes his mother by not letting her see him at Christmas) Which could be viewed as aggressive or passive aggressive if he makes an excuse such as "i am working and don't have the time to see you" the passive person who withdraws may do so because of a fear of confrontation.

The person who reassures the other, may do so in a passive aggressive manner, as reassuring the person may have a pay-off in a different setting such as "yes I had to sit with her and listen to her as she was talking about her problems" the person has no interest in the person who they are listening too, but uses it to gain recognition when the person uses this to gain attention or so that someone else thinks better of them, such as, "isn't he great, sitting and listening to that poor woman talk about her problems, he must be so caring."

The person may be passive if the other is telling them a hard luck story (trying to manipulate their environment to gain attention) and the other *feels* they have to offer reassurance the other person. In the first example I am often wary if a person discloses that they have helped another person or assisted them in some way, are they telling me for recognition, attention or a sense of worth? I have noticed as well that some people often go into a type of whining or complaining way of talking, inviting the other person or group they are with to offer reassurance or support to themselves, such as "i am weak and helpless and the world is against me, please listen to me". Is the purpose then to tell the story to get support or attention? From that, if this a part of their self-concept, that this is their outlook (if the person habitually relates or interacts with the other person in this manner) I remember a few years ago, upon meeting a person for the first time he told me about his alcoholic father and how had to take care of him, to get up early to see him before work, then go after work to make sure he was ok. Was the person crying for help, or was he trying to gain support from people around him. I often wonder about that, and since this was the first thing he said upon meeting me I believe he was trying to manipulate me to offer reassurance, and the benefits of this disclosure meant that the other people on his team (of whom he had disclosed this to as well) took it easy on him and let him do less work. Was the purpose then for himself to be seen as a martyr, to be selfless, or was he telling everybody so that they would feel sorry for him, and that he could be lazy at work, as the team made excuses for him, or was he at the end of his tether and needed a respite from care from his father? If that was the case, what were the introjections that meant he felt he had to look after his father in this way? Was this a generational introjection as the father was playing sick or helpless to gain support from his environment, and now the son was using the same game, to play helpless (that he *had* to help his sick father) and use that to get support from his environment. I am aware that this person could have chosen any area to talk about, but instead he chose his duties to his sick father instead of any other topic. He was therefore filtering what he spoke about (with the associated paralanguage to reinforce how difficult it was for him) and the judgement that if the person didn't offer reassurance or support then it meant that the person was cold or uncaring. I noticed something else that when he was talking about his role with his father he talked a certain way that suggested he was helpless, however, a few minutes later he would be laughing and joking. There was a certain incongruence (falseness) that made me suspect that because of this shift in how he related to people that it was a game to gain support recognition or attention.

The examples at the beginning of this section may fall into different categories, whether the person may judge the other, whether they offer a remedy or solution or whether they avoid the other person and their problems, concerns, issues or just topics of conversation.

The husband who is self-centred and uncaring to his wife may call his wife names if she gets emotional when they argue (judging) he may tell her to stop crying (ordering) or that he will leave (threatening) and then, when she cannot stop being emotional he may walk out to go to the pub (escaping, withdrawal) The argument may have been caused by the man as he knows that if he starts an argument he can get what he wants as his wife will give in as she gets emotional and just wants it to end. The man may use the argument to get his needs and his desires met, be that to go to the pub, what type of sofa to get, complaints of not getting enough sex or where there are going on holiday. The may also be plan to the man's actions as he knows that as the wife does not enjoy the arguments that she will walk on eggshells around him, and to give him what he wants. Alternatively the woman who routinely gets emotional and cries may use this to get her own needs met, as she has found that if she cries then it diverts the attention away from something else or a way to escape from responsibility, that her partner will take care of her, or perform duties that he knows she will become overwhelmed at and become emotional.

I am aware that the way in which a person speaks and relates to others could be an endless subject, and as I have said before in this chapter, for myself, it's not so much that they communicate this way, but how it is that they communicate this way, how it would be easier or more preferable to divert attention from someone else to talk about their self (hijacking the story) than to listen to the person, do they start to talk about the person's job for example then take over to tell the person about their new job. If they guide in this manner it may create less anxiety than to just tell the other person they have a new job, but, it is easier then to invite the other person to talk about the subject they would like to talk about then when the door is open then then can take over for the real reason they have started the conversation, to talk about themselves.

Other areas of the contact functions, how a person interacts, influences and communicates with their environment is with non-verbal communication and paralanguage. I will no go into too much detail in the following examples, and mention them mainly to give you an indicator of just how a person can communicate or make contact.

- **Paralanguage**

As I see it paralanguage is the term used to describe the non-verbal messages that accompany the spoken word. Paralanguage is integral to how a person communicates and the contact functions. Imagine a person talking about seeing a new film "i saw that film and it was great!" and it could be said in a positive manner, and another person could say the exact same thing in a sarcastic negative way. Facial expression, speech rate tone, emotional state, volume and the focus or stress on individual words. The passive or non-assertive person may speak in a certain way so as to appear boring to the other person, if they do not enjoy attention focused towards them. A different person who thrives on the attention of others person may say the same words as the first person but with passion and conviction. I am thinking about two pastors who present the same sermon to their congregation, one says the sermon with an enlivened attitude as he love of his faith is conveyed through his words and his actions, he talks in a loud and commanding voice, highlighting the phrases that have meaning and pausing so his words can be considered he speaks with great fluency, and the other is merely saying the words in a quiet, bland and droning way. The first pastor may appear strong and confident and the second pensive, bored and timid.

Communication through paralanguage isn't always intentional, and may be interpreted wrongly. I recently watched a television programme in which a person joining a group spoke in a loud and confident voice, the group he was speaking too believed that he was arrogant and so took a dislike to him. The person was speaking in that manner as he was nervous and was talking that way to mask his feelings, which perhaps may have been a creative adjustment from the fear or being judged, a fear to show vulnerability or a belief that he should appear confident and outgoing to be liked or approved of by others.

- **Facial Expression**

Facial expressions can convey much about the person's beliefs, what they are experiencing, their expectations, thoughts and moods. The term "putting on a brave face" is an example here as the person may mask or hide their feelings or thoughts (perhaps the result from an introjection or creative adjustment) or the person may outwardly appear happy and smiling when the person may actually be feeling stressed or anxious. A lady I knew would always smile when talking to her friends, as she never wanted them to know the difficulties she was experiencing in her marriage, she didn't want them to think she had problems with her husband, for the fear of how they would judge her. Facial expressions may be authentic or for the purpose of hiding thoughts and feelings, or even for the purpose of manipulation (if the person appears to look confused and puzzled as he attempts to discredit or discount someone) so expressions may include frowning, sneering, puzzlement, disgust, anger, lying, joyous, open, irritated contempt, fear, sadness, grimacing, frustration, surprise, confusion or smiling, there may be a varying degree of intensity due to the strength of the feelings, or the feelings that the person is attempting to portray. A simple smile can express an enormous amount of information, a false smile may have an aggressive or passive meaning to this, as the person is superficial or unassertive. Facial expressions may have a positive, neutral or negative meaning to them, the person may have a natural and lively intensity when hearing good news or solemnly or intently when listening to a person talk about something that is difficult. There may also be micro expressions as different parts of the face convey different messages such as a look of surprise as the persons eyebrows are raised as the person smiles in a convincing manner. The facial expression may be a way to manipulate the other, as the person may smile or frown to encourage or discourage the other person's behaviour. Micro expressions may also mean that the person may react authentically for a moment (like a flash of truth) before the person puts their mask on, and the face that they would like to portray to others.

- **Movement/Gesture/Body Language**

Body movements may originate from a creative adjustment or introjection, leaning towards a person may be a indicator that they are interested in what the other is saying or doing, they may lean away if they are not interested in the other, or wish to distance themselves. The person may also have an open posture or closed posture. I notice sometimes on breakfast television that the two presenters on many occasions are almost stuck in an open and leaning posture towards each other, perhaps to present an image of warmth and familiarity. Movements may also have an aggressive, assertive, passive or non-assertive meaning to them, the person slumping in a meeting may be attempting to be passive and to hide from other, another person may be slumping being passive aggressive and their posture indicates they are not interested in what the other has to say. The person who is intimated by the other may approach him with pensive and quick movements, the person affected by anxiety in crowded places may rush through treating the crowded place as an assault course to overcome. The person who is tall but doesn't wish to attract attention may move with a stoop, in an attempt to make themselves smaller. The person who has adjusted to the belief that he is important may make an entrance into a room by walking slowing and noticeably, so that other people are aware that he has entered. The woman who has been in an abusive relationship may walk with her head down and almost scurry as she does everything to not draw attention to herself. The person who has no confidence in his self may move in a clumsy manner and the woman who believes that she has to gain the attention of others to be of worth may enter a restaurant or bar and sit in a manner that attracts others, she may scan the room, not to look around her, but to look at who is looking at her.

A person's posture and body positioning may convey the person's thoughts, beliefs and feelings, and in this respect may be contextual or situational. The beautiful woman who sits in such a way in a bar to attract other people may be found slumped in front of the sofa as she, in that safe environment no longer feels the need to try to gain the attention of others for her own worth, or to sustain her self-concept.

Gestures and movements go hand in hand and gestures normally have the purpose of conveying a message to the other and are an important aspect of paralanguage. While again, it is not the intention of this book to list all postures, aspects of body language and gestures, merely to highlight that these may be the result of an introjection of creative adjustment (and will be explored further in chapter 2) for example, the person who is getting bored listening to the other may look at his watch (his watch would be a prop in this case) as a indicator to the other person that he is getting bored and would like to end the conversation. He could say "i know you are talking, however I am late for a meeting" but because of his beliefs about himself and in relation to the other person is creates less anxiety to look at his watch, which is a gesture that has the same message (that he wants the conversation to end) Gestures may also include rubbing eyes, stroking one's hair or a part of the body to convey a message, shrugging shoulders, making a fist, pointing a finger and anything that conveys a non-verbal message.

- **Props**

Props are an important factor in the contact functions, and as the name implies, it is an object, role, person, people or affiliation to a group that a person uses to give their self meaning or as a means to be seen a certain way by another. I know a person who is involved in a certain aspect of charity work that involves rescuing people in distress. Although he is a very self-centred person he wants to be seen as caring and helpful, and usually discloses that he is a member of this charity to other people when they first meet and wears clothing with the rescue logo in view, to be seen to be a nice guy. He is therefore using the charitable organisation to been seen in a good light by other people and this is a prop for him. Props may be associated with other contact functions such as appearance, and the person may wear fashionable clothing to appear to be popular, attractive, to be included (maybe to stay away from the feelings of anxiety of what it means to not be included) or to appear youthful and trendy.

Men who want to be seen with a pretty woman on their arm may be using the woman as a prop, as it means that they may be of worth or popular if they can have a beautiful woman as a partner. People who have a need to gain the attention, notoriety or recognition of others may use the internet as a prop, to have *likes* or people *following* them so they can gain a sense of worth or achievement (as in I have 100000 views on my You-Tube video so it means I am popular) I knew a manager once who used to bully his staff so they would work harder and exceed the organisational targets, and in that he used other people to look good to senior management. A person may name drop famous people they know but not as a means of normal conversation, but in an intentional manner that has the purpose of appearing special to the person they are talking too. An animal can be a prop also I believe, as when a person has an aggressive dog on a leash to indicate that he is not to be messed with, or conversely, I was listening to the radio one day recently and an older lady said that she used to go walking alone in the morning, but felt that she was being looked at by people (a little old lady out walking by herself) so she got a small dog to accompany her when walking, this way she felt that she wasn't walking alone, but was walking a dog. She noticed that more people said good morning to her after this. When the person uses another person, group or object to gain attention, to fit in or recognition they are *using* the other for their own benefit. For the man who *has* to have a beautiful woman on his arm the woman inevitable becomes an object to satisfy the man's idea of his self-concept. This man though, may alternatively be using the prop (a beautiful woman) so he may feel insecure around her and has to chase after her as he may have the introjection of *you can't be happy* or *you are not special* so he continually chases after his beautiful partner so as to reinforce that he is never a special person.

The person who has these beliefs doesn't even have to meet a beautiful woman, he may meet an average person and spoil her and focus all his attention onto her, the purpose being to put himself second to the other person. The prop then has the purpose of sustaining his idea of himself. What may happen in this case is that the man who uses the beautiful woman as a object to give his self-meaning, or to gain attention or recognition may search for another woman if his *beautiful* woman gains weight or has children. Since he is objectifying her and she no longer fits into what is important to him, he may look elsewhere. A similar situation may be for a woman to meet a man who is rich or successful (this is often viewed in the way she speaks, as she may describe him to her friends as to what he does for a job, such as "this is Mark and he is a Solicitor") so if the man loses his job, or isn't so successful then she may look for someone else, or someone better. A prop may also take the form of a present to a person, in that they may be generous and buy the other gifts. The purpose of the gift is not to show feelings of love or gratitude, but to display their wealth or generosity, or to appear to be a loving person, when the gift is used as a token, as an object. As I write this I am aware of the person who has done something wrong and presents his partner with a gift, is he using the gift as a prop to convey his apology? Props can be anything, a scar, a pair of crutches (to convey that the person is ill or sick) a car, or the woman who has a low self-worth and has many boyfriends may use each man as a prop, or an object, she may speak and relate to them in a manner in which they will eventually leave, and thus reinforce her believe of low self-worth.

- **Listening**

A few years ago I was attending a course, and after the break on the very first evening the woman sat in the circle and began to tell those on the course that she had heard a person making a comment that was derogatory and making fun of her, and, since no-one had intervened, stopped or questioned him meant that we were just as bad a him. She went on a bit of a rant about values and ethics and one of the other students on the course asked her what she had actually heard, she replied saying that the man had made a comment about her and her background, implying that she was stupid. The lady then asked the accused man what he had actually said, and he replied saying that he was talking about the course and how each person may have been experiencing it, as we all came from different backgrounds and may have had a different view of what the course offered. The lady asked the woman if this is what she heard and she said no, however other people on the course spoke and concurred that this was what the man had said. It became apparent that what the man had said wasn't what she had heard. It later transpired that she had always had a type of selective listening, in which she had become very sensitive to how others viewed her, and she distorted what the other had said to create an argument. The argument had the purpose of keeping others at a distance and as she became more aware of her self she realised that she listened to others in a judging manner and would cherry pick what the person had said to be able to attack them. The style of listening had originated from somewhere and she realised that she had a sense of inferiority introjected from her earlier years and listened for any time that reinforced this belief. She had therefore creatively adjusted her way of hearing to be highly selective to anything she could take offence to.

In this section I will focus on the different types of listening from a creative adjustment perspective. As with other sections this is not meant to be a complete list of listening, but to highlight (as in the example above) that how and why we listen can give meaning to our self-concept.

When a person is being assertive and engaged in active listening this normally involves putting their own concerns to one side to be able to focus on what the other person is saying. Active listening not only involves listening to the words, but also in the way they are said (paralanguage) and trying as much as possible to understand their meaning. Active listening means being able to bracket your own assumptions, concerns, attitudes, ideas and values, to be able to focus on the other person. Active listening also involves empathy, respect, acceptance and being genuine. The person who is active listening may ask questions for greater clarification of what the other person is saying, as this type of questioning may encourage exploration for the person, to focus attention and may help people to disclose information about their self. Active listening may also involve reflecting back the person's feelings, to be able to *tune into* the person's point of view and how they experience their world and to have a non-judging acceptance of the other person.

However due to the nature of creative adjustment from many introjections this type of listening I have found is very rare, though it can be developed. I have found that people listen in different ways, and these include:

Pretend listening; the involves pretending to listen, I am visualising a person who is pretending to take an active interest in the other person but really they have an ulterior motive, be that an intention to appear concerned, to sell something, to ask a favour or a request or to use the person in some way for their own gain. The person who pretends to listen is putting on a false face to manipulate the other.

Ego driven listeners; this type of listener like the initial example at the beginning of this section may highlight an area of what the other person is saying so they can shift the topic to their self, the person may manipulate by asking a question to the other that may initially show an interest, however the real intention is to shift the focus to a topic that they can take over and dominate. A person who is very passive may appear that they are interested in what the other person is saying, as they may get a sense of worth from this.

Judging listening; this involves listening in a judging manner to criticise the other person, they may be attentive and ask exploratory questions, however has the purpose of gaining information about the other person, to decide if they are right or wrong. This type of listener may gain information to be able to attack or ambush the other person. The person may also listen in a judging manner to be able to offer praise and reassurance to the other person, not because they are authentic, but to manipulate the other for their own benefit.

Distorted listening; as the person experiences the world from their own view of their self, so it may be that they listen from that position. The person who is sexist or a misogynist may filter what they have heard to reinforce that opinion or view, so if there is a car accident involving a woman they may immediately conclude that it was her fault.. This is also the case for people who have a low or high self-esteem, they will filter what they are hearing to give that belief meaning (Field Theory)

Diagnosing/problem solving/advice giving listening; this type of listener listens and highlights an area so to be able to diagnose, offer a solution, analyse the problem or issue, they may listen to problem solve or to be able to offer advice. This type of listener may also offer guidance or try to order the other person towards a remedy of outcome.

Using humour; here the person listens to be able to avoid the other person's concerns, and highlights something humorous that has the purpose to not focus on the other person, but to turn it into a joke or witty interpretation.

Stereotype listening; this is similar to distorted listening as the person filters what the other person is saying. For example, a manager may listen more intently to a senior manager than to a subordinate. A dominant and abusive husband may listen to what his wife is saying, then quickly disregard it as it challenges his own beliefs of women.

Defensive listening; this type of listener is fine-tuned to filter comments or questions from others (much like judging listening) and re-frame them as personal attacks.

Negative/Positive listening; like filtered listening this type of listener focuses on the negative or positive areas of what the person is talking about, for example if the person has recently started a new relationship the person who sees the world through negative eyes may make a comment about fidelity and how a previous partner cheated on her, or they may only focus on the positive parts of a person's story, whatever that reason may be.

Listening to help: this type of listening is looking for a reason to help the other person, and may be adept at asking questions to elicit an area that they can help with. The person who is a *do gooder* who has to help regardless of the helpee's best interests may fall into this.

Argumentative listening; the person listens for an area to begin an argument or disagreement. I have seen this in people who harbour prejudices towards others and listens for any area to disagree. I once knew a woman who was "against all men for the thousands of years of oppression against woman" and no matter what I said she would listen intently to try to create a disagreement. Some people may engage this way to create a distance between themselves to the other, as forming a close relationship may create anxiety.

Self-centred listeners; these type of listeners only look for agreement with their own opinions or views. This type of listening is monological as the person only interest is their self, and all means of relating to the other only has their own benefit as a goal.

Dual listening; this type of listener is only pretend listening, although unlike pretending to be interested this person may be watching television or looking at their smart phone or computer, only showing a half interest in what the other person is saying

Distracting listening; this type of listener tries to avoid the other person's concern and may change topics to something more agreeable to him, for example instead of talking about something the person is concerned about he may divert the topic to another area she had disclosed, one that he would prefer to talk about.

Competitive listening; as with previous examples this type of listener is sensitive to any area where he exists in comparison (such as if the person speaking is talking about learning to cook or buying a new car) the listener may downplay, distort, challenge, undermine, discount or dismiss the other person. The person who utilises the way of speaking (needing to win, hating to lose) may listen in this manner.

Evaluative listening; the listener who evaluates others only listens from the position of how they see the world (just as with judging listening) and their self -concept or self-image. As example would be a person who is listening (but from a self-centred position) to another who is telling them about going on a run of about 10 miles, the person's response may be "you must be crazy to run that far" the person listening and making that evaluative statement is only seeing the person from the own perspective or self-concept. A person who is a marathon runner who has the same type of listening style may say "is that all?" this type of listener may judge and evaluate others from their own position. This person does not actually see the other person as a unique individual, but forms an opinion from their own self. The person making this type of statement says more about themselves than about the other, for example the mother who evaluates and judges another mother and labels her as crazy for studying at college as well as being a mother is only highlighting her own values.

To conclude this section on listening I would like to say that due to the nature of introjections and creative adjustment we inevitably listen to others from our own position, which may have an assertive, aggressive or passive purpose. If we can understand how we listen to others, whether that is waiting for a chance to jump in to state our own thoughts, or if we listen more to some people than to others (such as the person who is attentive and listens for hours to the beautiful woman as she discloses her woes but disregards his wife as she tries to talk to him when he returns home) the means and purpose of how and why we listen can provide a valuable insight into how we view our self and how we relate to others from that position.

- **Looking**

I was in a shop the other day and the person working at the till seemed like she had been working there all day, I noticed that she wasn't looking at her customers while sending their goods over the scanner, it seemed that she was gazing at them blankly, there was no change in how she was looking, it seemed like she was looking past them and not focusing on them at all or paying any attention. I have noticed a similar look in other people who work in a customer facing role, such as paramedics, nurses, police and security staff, there is no sense of connection from the person to the other. Perhaps it indicates boredom or the person doesn't have the energy to focus intently on each individual?

A person may look in different ways, such as rolling eyes, shifty eyes, evil eyes, looking at a person with daggers, soft eyes, staring, gazing, looking away, lack of eye contact, a look of boredom, blankness, fear, disgust, intimacy, disapproval or to antagonise or as a sign of happiness or sadness.

- **Makeup, Jewellery, Tattoos, Perfume, Bodification**

Have you ever noticed that a lot of women have a fear of going out in public with no
make-up on? From a creative adjustment point of view I think this is interesting, as the person has had to adjust themselves so to be acceptable to others. Also, what level of makeup is she wearing and in what situation, I know a lady who felt she had to wear make-up just to go to the corner shop, and also some women who wear make-up to visit the gym. Is the person using make-up as a prop and wearing it to convey a message or to show a belonging to a particular group, or to attract attention? Is there a meaning to the make-up in that it acts as a barrier from the world, or that the person is "putting on a face" to the world. Does the make-up attract attention, deflect attention (the person is manipulating the other to focus on one aspect of their self and in doing so the person can talk about her make-up or beauty, and this deflects attention from other areas of her life that she doesn't want the other to know about or talk about. Makeup may also be a measure of creative adjustment as the person may believe that to attract a person they have to look alluring by wearing make-up to look good (as well as wearing sexually provocative clothing and flirting) the woman is adjusting herself to her idea of what a man finds attractive. In that, the use of make-up may be included in the same group of non-verbal communication as jewellery, false nails, perfume, aftershave, tattoos and bodification. When this creative adjustment becomes part of the self-concept and is integrated into how the person views their self, then it can become its own goal. For example the person may have begun to wear make-up and perfume as she believes that to look good she has to utilise these (as well as looking healthy and fit) and they become so incorporated into her sense of self that to not wear these means to create anxiety.
I have noticed a recent trend with sleeve and neck tattoos and I do wonder sometimes if the person decides to get a tattoo because of an authentic reason, or a belief that as they are currently fashionable then to fit in the person feels that this is an option. Does the person get a tattoo because of this message that sleeve tattoos are cool or trendy or because of the person's beliefs and values? When I was a child a family member was covered in tattoos from his time in prison, and I do wonder that if he had become a teacher instead of a criminal would he have had a body covered

in tattoos, or did he introject the beliefs of those around him, and that tattoos were masculine and the thing to do to prove your worth in that environment? I do think now that some people only get tattoos to fit in, as a measure to be included, especially in niche groups. In this the use of bodification as the person identifies with a certain group and integrates the values of that group. Tattoos and bodification may also be a means of non-verbal communication as they may convey a message. I remember a person who had a facial tattoo and wondered why he couldn't get a job, he had the belief that he could be any way he wanted and that the employer had to accept him. He was judging the company based on his values, instead of recognising that he appearance may have conflicted with the company appearance policy. His tattoo may have been appropriate if he worked in a tattoo parlour, but was deemed inappropriate for work in other fields. The introjections *don't fit in, you'll never be a success, other people have to fit in to what I want, I am special* and so some of these may be a driver for this as his use of tattoos and other bodification may be a block to him being a success, as he can blame not getting a job on his innate self-destructiveness, but by blaming the world for not accepting him, the other may be an expectation that people have to share his view of the world. The purpose of the tattoo may have had the ulterior purpose to make sure that he never succeeds, and that he could then justifiably blame others for his not succeeding or being successful.

There is also a measure of how people creatively adjust to the values of a family, a group or a society, and if they steer away from those values that the fault lies in them? If I have a different work ethic and values to my family and decide to go to university and these challenge the introjected belief that men in the family always get manual jobs. Who is to say that a person with a tattoo on his face is any less competent that a person who does not, all it shows is the belief that a person is not going with the commonly held beliefs and values of that group or society, and is viewed with disdain, as well as being judged and criticised. Is this not growth though? The person may be pushing the boundaries (if he is authentic) as living his life to his own free will and choices, instead of accepting the commonly held values of that society.

The use of tattoos, make-up, jewellery, or bodification may be another way of hooking the environment for support by manipulating the other, the person who had the tattoo may do so to fit it to the larger group or to be accepted, the man with expensive necklace, bracelet or watch is conveying the non-verbal message that he is financially successful (use of props) and is sign of his view of himself in relation to other people.

- **Appearance, Dress, Clothing**

I remember watching a programme and it was about a man who viewed himself as very important, he had all the props to give this meaning, a fast car, designer watch and was impeccably dressed in very expensive clothing, I believe he was wearing a designer suit and everybody around him was treating him the way in which he expected to be treated, as a very important person. He had visited a business conference and arrived in his very expensive car and strutted into the conference, he had been hoping to meet the head of a global company to ask about a partnership of a business idea (association with a successful person, used as a prop) and when he encountered the leader of the global company (who was worth billions) he noticed that the global head was wearing jeans and t-shirt and was actually quite scruffy, the global head ignored the person as he walked past him and went about his business, leaving the man very embarrassed (as he had a camera crew following him and had just been snubbed) and rationalised that the global head was just busy. This was a good example I thought as the person had the idea of himself as being very important and dressed as such (even talking to the camera and stating the price of each article of clothing) however, this belief was not shared by everybody, and when it wasn't (by the head of the global company) he quickly made an excuse as to why he didn't stop and give him attention.
A person's dress and appearance can speak volumes, and in that occasion the use of clothing (as well as his body movements, use of language, way of looking and other props such as expensive jewellery) was an indicator of his economic level and social position, as well as his level of success and social background. Unlike the global leader who may have originated from a similar background the man wanted other people to be aware just how important he was. Clothing as a means of non-verbal communication can convey much, and is a strong indicator of our values and background, as well as how we would like to be seen. I know a person who spends most of his available income on expensive clothing for him and his children, so that they appeared to be "well off" to the people who looked at him. This level of introjection can be generational as his children may feel that they have to wear expensive clothing to be confirmed by another, or to feel of

worth. I am amazed sometimes as I look at young children wearing expensive sports clothing, though it is not for the child's benefit, but for the parent who feels they have to, or wants to dress their children in the expensive clothing as they may be in an unspoken comparison with others. I remember once a friend *had to* wear expensive clothing anywhere he went, and I asked if he could wear my old walking jumper to go shopping, initially he said yes that this was no problem, but realised that he couldn't when approaching the store, he realised that if he wore this type of branded clothing that he would be acceptable to other people, and if he wore this old walking jumper that no-one would notice him and he would feel that he would just be a normal person. There is the other side to the coin for this as I often wear outdoor and athletic clothing and a person I knew on a self-awareness course asked if I could wear trousers, shirt and tie to the next session and I said yes of course. I realised that this would be difficult as I associated this way of dress with men who were feminine and helpless (probably an introjection from my life in Belfast in that only men who worked in offices wore this clothing, and as such weren't that masculine or tough) when compared to the men in my area who were rough. I put the shirt, trousers and tie on and it felt strange, that somehow I was emasculated and less masculine, and it did feel uneasy to wear these clothes that evening on the course because of the association and meaning I had inferred on them. I also realise that I was not as casual in my relations to others, and was more formal and professional (as this was also the introjection I had of people who wore this type of clothing) I realised that I wore my outdoor and athletic clothing not only to affirm to myself that I was masculine, and in that the clothing sustained my self-concept and self-image. This is true when people who identify with a particular group wear clothing associated with that group, almost as a sense of belonging. A person who is in a motorcycle club doesn't necessarily have to wear a jacket with his club emblazoned on the back, but it fits his identity. The lady who has to wear feminine clothing may do so to affirm her femininity and sexuality. It is only when we become something that we are not I think can we notice just how much our clothing meant to us. The person I mentioned in the previous chapter who was dressed like a clown and decided to wear normal clothing realised that when he wore the clown type clothing people noticed him, but when wearing normal clothing he just blended in, as he had the introjection to be special and to not be noticed wearing normal clothing made him feel uneasy, as the self-concept and self-image of himself was no longer sustained. Clothing then is a representation of how we see ourselves, or how we want to be seen, and in some respects may be similar to the use of wearing make-up, as the person puts on a face to another person, sometimes perhaps to create a favourable impression. Although if the person has the intention of keeping a distance from people the appearance and clothing (as well as facial expressions and use of language) may have that effect. Different social groups may have a similar way of dress (an introjection resulting in the creative adjustment of the person who adapts their appearance to be part of that group) and I have noticed that the adverts for clothing, jewellery, hair products and make-up often try to associate their product to a well-known celebrity or model in an attempt for people to copy them, or to affirm that the product is used and worn by people who are popular, special or in the public eye. Clothing may be used as a statement as to who we are or the person we wish to portray, does the woman who wears revealing clothing on a night out do so because she feels that men are only interested in her in a sexual way and she is conforming to that, is there media pressure (from the advertising of models in scantily clad clothing) to dress that way (an introjection) or is she part of a social group where this type of clothing is considered normal? Is she normally flamboyant and is trying to gain the attention of the people by wearing revealing clothing, or is she not that confident and feels that she has to wear this type of clothing as it is less anxious to fit into other people's ideas as to what is appropriate rather that follow her own idea? The only person who knows the truth is the woman, and this is why I try to not judge a person or to make inferences based on their style of dress. The woman who has been involved in an abusive relationship with a controlling man creatively adjust to this and dress in such a way as to not attract any attention to herself, as she know if she does then her partner will accuse her of leading men on and call her derogatory names, so in an effort to dissuade that possibility she dresses in a bland way, almost to try to be invisible to others, if the man is controlling and want to show her off to other men (used as a prop) he may persuade her to wear revealing clothing, and when men look at his wife it, he is aware of this as it means that he receives a confirmation that he is of worth, as men desire his wife. I feel that the way a person dresses and their appearance can signify a message about their self to those around them, how they want to be seen, as well as how they feel about their self. The person may have the introjection to *be a good boy* or *you always have to look your best* and as the person adjusts to this belief about how to be a person, it may affect their appearance and dress. There are many introjections from the media and from clothing manufacturers, who spend vast amounts of money on advertising (often with their logos on the clothing as an affirmation to those wearing them, and also for free advertising) to try to get the person to wear their clothing. The person who rejects this media message and wears clothing to not fit into this message is still adjusting their appearance to be the antithesis of a mainstream media message, and may also be a creative adjustment, to *go against* the media driven message as to how to be a person.

- **Hair, Facial Hair**

From a creative adjustment perspective a person's hair can say much and just as with appearance and dress is part of the package of how the person presents their self to others, as well as affirming their own identity or self-concept. My older neighbour as well as my grandfather used to wear cream in their hair as in their day this was a fashionable application to a person's hair, I remember both used to wear their hair in a swept back fashion, such was the power of this introjection and the integration in the self-concept these men still has the same hair style in their later life. Interestingly, their style of dress was pretty similar as well, and wearing trousers and shirt seemed to be common place. I was walking past a barber shop the other day and observed a different style of hairstyle, in the lines that are cut into a person's hair, different cultures have different attitudes to differing styles. There is a man I know who has a dyed mohawk, and I do wonder why he would have this style, he behaves in a manner that suggests that he enjoys drawing attention to his self, and like much about a person's dress, this hairstyle may draw attention, to keep people at a distance, to indicate an affiliation to a group or as a mask to deflect attention from another area of their self (this is true of a lady I know who preferred men to look at her breasts rather than her stomach, and as such she displayed her breasts by wearing revealing clothes)
When I was younger there was a local skinhead gang in my area and one of the requisites for joining this gang was to have your hair shaved, so to become part of this group a person had to creatively adjust to this requirement, this isn't a world away from some reality television programmes that are popular now and revolves around wealthy

housewives and their lives. Just like the skinheads there are values that the housewives adhere to, such as having their hair neatly groomed (usually at a very expensive hair salon, and has the benefit that they can disclose to others that the use such an expensive place) as well as wearing designer clothes and shoes. This is such a powerful introjection, as the message is *if you want to be part of our group you must follow these values* and just as in this section, a person's hair is an indicator of this, as the person creatively adjusts to this requirement, to receive recognition, approval or acceptance. Hair may also indicate a level of adjustment as the person becomes something that is valued (from the introjection perhaps of *I can't be accepted for who I am, so I have to adjust myself to be liked*) as I noticed that some women change their styles and colours as fashion changes. The use of hair extensions means that a person can usually adjust to anything.

I recently saw a woman who had grew her hair down to her waist, and I was wondering what would it for a man to have a similar style, would it indicate an anarchical belief or an introjection? There is also the person who sees his self as masculine and has a very short haircut to indicate this. Also, the man who has an image of his self and this is thrown into disarray as he begins to lose his hair by going bald. In the old days, some men would have comb-overs or wear a wig to protect their image and vanity, though so many men I have seen nowadays have hair replacement surgery to feel more confident or for some other reason. Some men who are losing their hair resort to wearing baseball caps or hats, or grow facial hair to compensate for their hair loss, while other men who begin to lose their hair as they get older, but whom are in denial that they are ageing may also experience depression or anxiety. Another person whose well-being is relational upon other people and how they are viewed may *look* to what the person is looking at when they are speaking, and if the person looks towards the man's hair loss then the person's self-esteem and confidence may be affected. I have seen some men who are losing their hair and cut their hair in styles to hide this, and I do wonder if this is relational to how they want to be viewed by others, or if the truth is a challenge to their self-image and how they view their self.

Sometimes facial hair can be grown to compensate for hair loss, I have seen many men who grow beards or stubble because of this, though in recent years I have noticed that (just as with sleeve tattoos) beards are becoming fashionable. As such I have noticed that many men have begun to grow beards, and much like a person's need to conform to be accepted or fit in the person grows a beard. I was out walking and came across some men rock climbing, I noticed that it seemed that to indulge in this hobby meant to wear clothes of a certain style (shirt and shorts) and have a beard. I do wonder about this superficiality, and if the person engages in this sport and dresses this way, or like the skinheads they adapt their self to fit into a particular group; the sport, the haircut and facial hair, the appearance and clothing as well as the equipment used may all be props, to gain acceptance and a sense of belonging. I think that this could be used for any sport or past time, with reference to facial hair this could be used for people who try to fit in to a alternative group (such as hippies or environmentalists) bikers or those involved in extreme sports. I do wonder if the person would have a style of hair or grow facial hair if they were not part of a group that gave a meaning to this, or if they were not influenced by popular fashion? Is the person being authentic, creatively adjusting to the introjections of others?

Women's hair loss may have a special meaning, as men's hair loss can be seen as more acceptable as it is more common. I knew a lady who suffered from alopecia and had large patches of bald hair, she at first tried a wig then began wearing a hat to cover this up. I do think sometimes of the introjected values that she had assimilated and how this medical condition caused issues as it challenged her view of her self as well as her beliefs as to how others would view or judge her. What does it matter if a woman has hair or not, but because of the societal view of women and so much emphasis placed on image (and the introjected and assimilated beliefs) this can affect the person's self-image in a negative way. On a personal note, I noticed I was losing my hair about 5 years ago, this did cause some anxiety for me as I still brushed my hair back like my grandfather, and I thought about what to do. I called to a local store and bought a some hair clippers and decided to shave it, it was difficult at first, but as time passed I am more accepting of this and now it doesn't bother me, except when my aunts and cousins from Northern Ireland looked at me when they were visiting, and the first thing they said was "where's your hair?" (Asking a question to have a joke, or to manage their own shock or surprise as they focused the attention away from themselves) and I replied that it was having a shower but should be finished soon.

- **Body**

How the person makes contact with others through the use of their body can be an important Contact Function, and as I see it is integral to how a person speaks, their appearance, props, and may give a meaning to their use of speaking, such as ordering, advising, dominating, threatening, either in an aggressive or passivity manner. I used to go to the gym, and I would observe many people who would become physically fit and muscular, not because of an authentic interest, but because of the introjected ideas of what is attractive, which way to be a person, to be competitive (being stronger, bigger or fitter than the other) or for the fear of not fitting in. So many people may *buy into* this idea of how to be a person, by being slim, muscular, fit or athletic, it may also necessarily mean that anyone who does not fit into this *image* or introjection may be viewed in a judging or critical manner. The man who is overweight and working out in the gym may be looked at less favourably or in a critical judging manner by a person who has integrated the introjection that men should be muscular or athletic, or that someone who is has an athletic physique is better than the other (which after all is just one characteristic of the many facets of a person's being) I remember I was watching television and a celebrity said he worked out just to look good in a suit, and also other reality programmes where this introjected idea of how to be a person is assimilated to both men and women as they strive for a muscular and toned body. This is a thin red line, for if the person's self-worth is based on their body (or is in competition with others based on their fitness level or physique) and they gain weight or have an injury, their self-image or introjected self-concept is challenged and so then a crisis may follow.

As I mentioned in chapter 1, growing up in a rough area meant being fit and strong, and my use of my body meant that I could survive there, by being tough. If I didn't go to boxing, lift weights and train to be physically fit then I would not be able to protect myself, and so this was a creative adjustment to my environment. The girl who feels she has to be slim and pretty to be accepted (or confirmed) by others has to adjust herself this ideal, and as the self-concept becomes and the girl regulates to this, then this becomes it own goal. The yoga teacher, the body builder or the dancer may have become this after the many introjections as to how to be a person.

Imagine the man who views himself as hard and so lifts weights and builds a strong and muscular body. He may use this to dominate or threaten others, or to be noticed or gain attention (I often wonder why men wear such tight t-shirts) he may have a low self-esteem and this is a way for him to gain a sense of worth, or he may view himself as superior and becoming muscular and athletic (which is often combined with wearing fashionable clothes, getting tattoos and hairstyle or facial hair to become a total introjected package) When I see a person who displayed their self this way, I often think if this way of being is authentic or is it just to fulfil an introjected image, or a creative adjustment. Of course as there are many benefits to being athletic or muscular this may be rationalised in statements by the person such as "i enjoy being in shape" or "I like being healthy" or with secondary gain (endorphins released by exercise) however when the person can't be that, and they *must* or *should* be that way, this is an indicator of an introjected belief. Contrastingly, the person who believes they are weak and helpless or have very little self-worth may outside their awareness adapt their body to their own image of who they think they are, so the person who believes they are worthless may gain weight and not take care of their body, which when judging themselves against the introjected ideal as to how to be a person (athletic and fit) may be another to reinforce their own negative self-image (and a manipulation of their self)

I have often wondered about people who adjust their body as they become older, or when younger and feel they have to have plastic surgery to fit in with others, to appear youthful or to be judged favourably by others (I am reminded of the quote "when you let others be your judge, they become your master) and isn't there a massive introjection against the effects of ageing, or to have a beautiful, symmetrical or proportioned face or body. So much energy and effort to look good, or from a fear of looking old. Most older actors and actresses I have observed have had some level of plastic surgery, as this industry sustains this introjection, and the person feels they have to adjust to this requirement to work in that industry, this would be the same for people working in the fitness industry, as a person may feel that have to look fit to work in that field. I knew a young woman a few years ago who felt she has to get breast implants to feel good about herself (to be judged favourably by others) and I do wonder why we can't be accepted as individuals without the being judged by other people.

As well as the people who endeavour or become driven to develop or adapt their body to fit in to an introjected idea of what a person should be, and what is attractive or desirable by others (which forms the self-concept,

113

identity and self-image) is the person who is antithetical to this, the man who through many introjections creatively adjusts to this and becomes weak and feeble, the woman who has been sexually abused and creatively adjusts to a person who is not desirable and becomes overweight or believes that she is only of worth in that manner and communicates her sexuality through her body (and appearance and way of speaking) or the person who is overweight and views her self as less worth because of the introjected idea. The media has long offered introjections about what is attractive or appealing about a person's body, and when a person assimilates this into their idea of who they are, it becomes an invisible judge as they try to live to their assimilated expectations, as well as the expectations of others. The person's environment may also offer this, as with myself and becoming capable and strong, or with the person who dominates others with their use of their body (such as becoming muscular to be able to threaten or bully others) or though their acquaintances, as with a woman who feels she has to look good and adjust her body to do the same.

- **Appropriateness**

This style of the Contact Functions, is the appropriateness of the style of contact to the other, and largely relates to the appropriateness of the occasion, and in their appearance and actions. A person wouldn't wear a bikini to a court and if she did, there would be a reason for this, such as to create attention towards herself, naivety or to undermine her self or self-sabotage and similarly a person may create some discerning looks if he was swearing in the presence of children. The man may view this as normal though, due to his own introjections as to what is appropriate is each situation. The same could be said for behaviour as the attention seeking person who may speak loudly and tell jokes in a situation such as a funeral, the purpose of speaking loudly isn't part of their normal way of relating, but is artificial as it serves a purpose. The person though may not know about manners or dignity (from a lack of beneficial introjections about how to behave in different occasions) or may choose to ignore or retaliate against those values, to show that he doesn't care what people think, or that he may be insensitive to others, he may also be self-centred and unaware of the impact he has on others. This could be at any event or situation, the woman may wear a low cut top or revealing clothes to a sombre occasion, or the man may make offensive gestures and behaviour when in the presence of others. I recently heard of a man who when his daughter was speaking to her friend on the phone started to shout obscenities towards the daughter's friend, the man did not consider the impact of his behaviour towards his daughter and was inappropriate for occasion, however, as he was arrogant and self-centred, this was not a concern for him. #

- **Sex**

Although this has a functional as well as pleasurable purpose, it may also I believe be part of the contact functions, and is often used in conjunction with facial expression, looking, speaking, use of props, being passive, submissive, assertive, aggressive, passive aggressive, appearance, movement and use of make-up, jewellery and touching. A person who communicates through sex may be acutely aware of how to arouse others in a sexual manner to get their needs met, they may wear revealing clothes and speak in a sexually provocative language, they may always try to look attractive and know just how to talk to other people. I noticed once a lady who was talking to a man and asking for some assistance with her car, she was laughing at his jokes and would touch him on his arm as she laughed, as she was being outgoing and playful, his body position became passive, it seemed that she was melting in his presence as she became pleasing and submissive. The woman had a flat tyre on her car and the man bought into the game she was playing and duly changed her tyre for her, she kept showing an interest in him until he had finished and just as he was hoping that she would follow on her flirtatious behaviour she thanked him and then drove off, she had used her behaviour in a sexual manner to get her needs met.

I knew a man who was very promiscuous and had slept with a large number of women, his mother was a very dominant and controlling woman and he had adjusted to survive in that world by keeping his mother happy, he would clean the house and did whatever she said, but she always complained about him and criticised him yet he was always doing small things to keep her happy. He was very sensitive to her moods and was aware of what he could do to alleviate her criticism, and would buy her gifts and listened to her, agreeing with her views and beliefs. In that household the mother was the person in charge and everyone had to live by her rules (to please her) to survive. I noticed that later he took this introjection and transferred it to other women and when they approached him sexually he gave them what they wanted and have sex with them. This had a bad effect on his relationships with a woman who became his girlfriend, because as he put himself second to others he would have sex with any woman who made it clear that this is what they wanted. He would flirt and behave in a sexually suggestive way as he carried on this pattern of pleasing others, and seemed to take a pride in his appearance, though this was not for his own self-esteem, but a further aspect of how he pleased women. He had a dedicated fitness plan and as such had a very athletic body, though this was for the same purpose and when he spoke to women, it was always in a very charming, but helpless manner, as if he was trying to make the woman feel sorry for him and to mother him.

This is true I believe of some women, as there is a powerful introjection that a woman has to be attractive to men, as well as offer sexually charged behaviour, and though this is only a small part of a person, some women highlight and accentuate this in their relations with men, perhaps from the many introjections about the needs and desires of men. I do wonder if a woman does this, what other aspects of her self has atrophied. If a person uses sex to communicate she may make her self more physically attractive, and may know just how to act when in relation with others to evoke sexual feelings. Other ways to communicate with that person may not be developed and I am thinking of a person who has spends their time looking attractive to others or to bolster their self-esteem, but finds it difficult to speak or engage in conversation, or to focus their attention on the other. Sex can also be used to dominate others as well as a means of comparison or competition. I am thinking of some people who sleep with others, and that as well as the pleasurable feelings that sex offers there is also the purpose to tell others about their experiences with a sexual partner, as well as the number they have had sex with, as a sense of worth, approval or confirmation from others.

Some women who are passive and have a poor self-worth but yet crave affection, may believe that men are just interested in them for sex, may behave in a sexually arousing manner as they act in a way that they believe that the other wants them to act. This may also have the purpose of persecuting the other, the person may have that belief that men are only interested in them for sex, then fulfil this perceived desire, and so when the man does have sex with them then can feel justified in saying that men only want sex, which may reinforce the belief of their poor self-worth. Part of this may involve selecting men (outside their awareness) that will fulfil this expectation, instead of choosing to enter a relationship with a man who will offer them respect, warmth and understanding.

A person who is resistant for some reason to become emotionally close with others may offer sex instead, as it offers physical closeness without emotional intimacy. The person who has this fear may steer the other towards a sexual relationship, and on a slightly different perspective a person who has an awareness that the other is interested in him may hint at a relationship and leads the woman on to be able to have sex with her, the man then, after fulfilling his needs may sabotage the relationship or deny that he ever intended for the relationship to develop. The person may also treat the other as an object to fulfil his sexual needs, and instead of viewing the other as a unique person, they are seen just as a thing to use. Using sex as a contact function may arise out of a need to please others, or a safe way to please one's self. The man who has become promiscuous because of a need to please others may become rigid in this idea of his self, and he may (outside his awareness) sabotage relationships so that he can continue this behaviour as this initial creative adjustment and introjection become part of his self-concept. Such a person may have many ways of speaking, and may become charming and use flattery when in relation with women. Sex may also offer immediate gratification to some, as well as stave off the effects of, or the fear of loneliness. If the person creatively adjusts to view the other as a means to satisfy their own needs they may choose partners who will readily engage in immediate sexual relations, or choose people who have a low self-esteem or self-worth and by the means of flattery or a charming disposition the person can engage with them sexually (a person with a low self-esteem may feel a need to please others to gain recognition, and if the others' *currency* is sex, then the person may engage in that type of behaviour)

- **Touch**

A further part of this use of the body and the contact functions is the use of touch, and may communicate many non-verbal messages. As with the previous section does the person touch the other in a suggestive, sexual, sensitive manner, does the use of touch suggest closeness, warmth and friendship or is it more aggressively motivated, as for example the person uses a handshake with a tight grip to convey the message that they are dominant. Does the man who is aggressive hold his partner by the arm as a symbol of ownership and dominance, does the woman hold her husband's hand, not out of love, but as a sign to others that he belongs to her. The use of touch is a very complex area and for each person the meaning can be different. If a man touches his partner is a suggestive manner, is this through dominance or through a respectful show of warmth and love. If a person accidentally bumps into another person, is there an aggressive purpose to this, or is the person passively making contact with the other person (as happened to me in my younger years as a girl bumped into me by accident, but actually had the intention of trying to talk to me) There may also be a lack of touch and physical contact from some people, as they have creatively adjusted from an environment when touching others and physical closeness was something that never occurred, the person may also become overly tactile as they search for the physical closeness that was negligent in earlier years. As we shall examine in chapter 2 and the self-concept, some people adjust to have their own purpose for physical contact with others, and how touch can be an important and complex area of the contact functions.

- **Voice (including Silence)**

I remember the old saying "it's not what you say, it's how you say it" and consider the use of the person's voice. On occasions when listening to a person I try to filter out the content and focus on the person's voice and how they are speaking (as aspect of the paralanguage) Such ways may include: Tone of voice, speech rate, enunciation, accent, the syntax (if the person use "I" a lot as they speak this may be an indicator of their view of their self as being important) Is the person putting on a voice to try to manipulate the other, to sound understanding, considerate, empathetic, or conversely trying to sound like they are in charge or being dominant. Does the person speak in a low droning voice or a whining voice, or are they positive and upbeat, this may be for a number of reasons, for if they speak in an upbeat and positive manner this may have the purpose to avoid the other person's concerns, or to guide them to a more positive topic of conversation, or the person may appear lively and fun to draw attention to themselves. Similarly the person who speaks in a very low and depressing tone may be guiding the other to a more negative outlook. Is the person's voice loud (which may indicate a need to be heard) or soft and quiet, is their speech hesitant or full of ums and ahs. Do they speak with a lot of emotion in their voice, or is their speech dull and lifeless. Do they mumble, whisper or tail of at the end of speaking. Does the person speak in an educated voice, or do they use common slang and swear. Is the person direct, sharp or vague, do they speak with conviction, fluency and passion, or with an *i don't care* attitude. Does they focus or place an emphasis on a particular word or is the syntax of how they speak geared towards directing the person, to steer the conversation. Does the person speak louder or quieter as the conversation evolves with the other, so they may speak louder and with enthusiasm when talking about their self, and quieter and with little interest when the other speaks. I once worked with a person who would start talking in the group in a shouting voice, this had the benefit of immediately drawing attention to himself, then his voice lowered once he had gotten that attention. Does the person stress certain words and do they time their interruption of the other, or do they pause to let the other person interject with their own opinions (the person who leads conversations at offer little pauses so that the other can't speak, this isn't a conversation I believe, but one person using the other person as a sounding board to express their views)

These ways of speaking may exist in relation to other people, the person who speaks with a normal speech rate may increase their speed if they are feeling pressured by the other (an increase in anxiety) the person with the loud commanding voice may talk quietly and hesitantly when talking to his wife or employer, then mutter afterwards, the person who has had to adjust to living in a large busy family may talk louder to be noticed in that environment, then this is carried on to other situation with the belief *to be noticed I have to be loud.*

How a person speaks as a contact function exists in conjunction with the other contact functions, the person who strives to be noticed will talk in a manner that they will be noticed, the person who believes they are not worth anyone's attention may speak in a low droning voice to bore the other person, the person looking to be rescued, or to sabotage relationships may talk in a whining and pleading voice. How a person speaks can offer a door of understanding to how the person views their self and may have an aggressive, passive, passive aggressive, assertive or non-assertive meaning to them, if the person identifies with some areas of polarities then the way they speak may also be influenced by this.

Silence and not speaking is also a contact function, is the person being silent when in relation to another as they listen intently to the other person and contemplate and consider the other's words, or is the silence an indicator or passivity or passive aggression as the person sits and says nothing, or aggressive and they give the other the silent treatment. Silence may also mean the person is clamming up as they feel pressure from the other (to answer, explain or for an opinion) and may indicate embarrassment or the person asking the question is touching on a sensitive or emotional subject. Some people may try to fill silences to avoid feeling uncomfortable, and a person who is silent may be manipulating the other so that they fill the void. Silence may also mean that the person is being quiet and expecting a question from the other as to how they are, then they may answer with vague of ambiguous answers that only elicit to draw more attention towards their self. I have observed two people sitting in silence as if in silent competition with each other with the *i am not going to speak first* attitude. Silence can also be a sign of withdrawal from a group or person, or that the person has a deeper more significant meaning to the other person and the silence suggests warmth, understanding and emotional depth. Silence and other contact functions may also suggest where they are, such as the person sitting silently and looking out the window, or using a prop to enable them to be silent, such as looking at their phone or book. Silence has a particular meaning to each person, and may be an indicator of the creative adjustments of introjections that form the self-concept and self-image. If the person steps outside their self-concept and feelings of anxiety or crisis emerge then silence is a way of withdrawing, manipulation or to fulfil a need.

- **Non-verbal Noises**

Non-verbal noises may accompany other contact functions and include:
Gasping: Which may indicate surprise, disgust or shock.
Sighing: When used in conversation it may indicate sympathy, boredom or sadness. It may also indicate the person intends to say something, but is holding this in (especially from a passive or non-assertive person) It may also mean that the person is dismayed or expressing sadness.
Coughing: This may be used to gain a person's attention, as a means of control (if used to indicate a person's behaviour is unwanted or inappropriate) or to express frustration, anger or disapproval.

Such other non-verbal noises may include ums and ahs, splutters, growling, snarling, giggling, sneering, huffing and puffing, breathing heavy or tutting as each situation emerges, From an introjective or creative adjustment perspective for example the person may have found it easier to sigh than to state an opinion (since the person is sighing for a reason) or the person may sneer and huff and puff as a way or threatening, dominating or bulling the other person. The silent judge may tut when observing someone's behaviour.

As we leave the contact functions and move onto Polarities and Assertion I would like to say that the way in which a person relates to and interacts with other people may be outside their awareness, the person rarely chooses to exhibit a way of talking, listening, the use of props or any of the other contact functions This purpose of this book is not to list all functions, but to note that through creative adjustment and introjection we may limit the ways in which we communicate with others, and how our self-concept can become a fixed way of relating to others. I have purposefully avoided including experiments in this section as each contact function can have a separate meaning to each individual. The only person who knows the truth about you and how you speak, dress, listen, props you have or use, the purpose of questions and so on is you. This is part of the discovery of who you are as a person, and I welcome you to consider how you may express yourself in each of these areas.

Polarities

In a person who has an integrated sense of self they may be able to respond from two opposing polarities, or two opposites, as an example hate or love. Through the process of introjection and creative adjustment just as with the contact functions the person may integrate one of the opposing polarities and this may become fixed or rigid and this limits how the person may respond or interact. In a healthy fully functioning person they can respond flexibly to a situation, such as whether to be considerate to others or inconsiderate, however the person (through creative adjustment and introjection) who is fixed in a response such as a person who is arrogant and self-centre may place his own interests as a priority, and therefore is inconsiderate to others, that is unless it suits his interests. That is to say, the person may appear to be concerned or considerate about or toward others (such as the person who volunteers for a charity) but it may only for the purpose of directing attention towards himself. His actions may only be for the purpose of gaining recognition or achievement instead of a genuine interest or concern for the other. This process of owning a polarity and the subsequent atrophy of the opposing polarity can influence how the person develops their self-concept, it may be easier for a man to be angry and negative than calm and happy. The opposite still exists in the person but is outside their awareness, projected onto others or disowned. This may also be situational or relational, the woman who has been the victim in an abusive relationship with a man may become resentful and bitter towards other men, yet is kind and accepting towards women. The man who is dominant toward people he views as less important may become subservient to those who in his idea are more important.

The person who is able to encapsulate both polarities may be able to respond freely from both sides, a person who is normally happy and friendly if encountering a situation in which they are threatened will be able to become aggressive and defensive, and in that can react to situations with a greater authenticity. The person who feels they *have* to be happy or friendly (if this is part of their self-concept) may have difficulty in exhibiting behaviours that are part of the opposite polarity. As an example the man who believes that to be a man he has to be responsible, strong and tough may have difficulty in showing any type of area that would be the opposite to these qualities, such as being weak and vulnerable. If this person can no longer be strong and responsible then anxiety or a crisis may ensue. This would be true also for the person who has been involved in an abusive relationship, if the person integrates the introjection that the other person is in charge, especially in important decisions they may believe (or creatively adjust) to this, and think they are incapable, to not be responsible or even to think for their self. This may have repercussions if they have the courage to end this relationship and these beliefs are introjected into who they believe they are, and this may limit the possibilities of what they could become after leaving this relationship, which would mean to inhabit the opposing polarity of responsibility and making decisions for her self.

Of course, the other person in this abusive relationship may feel that have to be in charge, to be responsible, to make important decisions or to be in control of the other person. There may be a manipulation of the other person so that they creatively adjust to become a person that they can control, so that they can be the controller, and be in charge. Each of these persons in this relationship who have incorporated each side of this polarity and each display different aspects of the contact functions in the way they relate to each other, as well as their style of contact with the assertion spectrum.

There many polarities that can encapsulate many areas, such as;

happy – sad
genuine – in-genuine
maturity – immaturity
love – hate
responsibility – irresponsibility
truthful – deceitful
calm – angry
positive – negative
kindness – cruelty
weak - strong
ordered – chaotic
narcissism - empathetic
honesty – dishonesty
weaknesses – strength
exploiting – helping
sensitive – insensitive
hope – despair
vulnerable – invulnerable
caring – uncaring/selfish
simple – complex
confused – clear
thoughtless – thoughtful
warm – cold
polite – impolite

As a person develops through introjections and creative adjustments so they assimilate different areas of a certain polarity, a person who has introjected the belief that they must be *a good girl* may become a person who is well-mannered, polite, caring, helping and honest, and any time the other sides of these are touched then this may challenge the self-concept, if they are ever uncaring, tell lies or selfish then guilt or anxiety may be a result, there may be times however when it is necessary to be selfish, or to be uncaring towards others, or to tell lies.

The opposites still exist but may be denied, or displaced or projected onto others. When a person can incorporate both aspects of a polarity then they may be able to stretch their self-concept and begin to be able to be authentic or real, the person isn't nice caring to others because of an introjection as to how to be a person, but because they choose to be. The man who never allows himself to show any weakness or vulnerability can never be genuinely strong, as he only strong as a result of the fear of being weak. Being weak to him may also mean that he cannot own his emotions or display his feelings to others. He may talk and relate to others in a way that exemplifies his strength. When he can be flexible and be both strong and weak then he can respond to situations with realness and authenticity. When we can respond from both sides we can become centred instead of living in one side of that polarity. The person who may exhibit both sides of a polarity in different situations, as in the woman who is aggressive towards men but nurturing towards other women is not being genuine, but is an example of a contact boundary shift. When she can gain an awareness of how she exists and realise that this shift is occurring and she is responding to each gender from opposite polarities, and, if she chooses to become experiential and experiments with becoming nurturing towards men or she stands up for herself against women then an anxiety may occur as she reaches the boundary of her self-concept (the impasse) and the meaning she may place on an individual based on their gender. (For another person this could be colour, ethnicity, religion, sexual identity or socio-economic status)

The person who identifies with one side of a polarity may be attracted to others who inhabit the other side of this, the person who fears to draw attention to their self may become enamoured by people who are show-offs, extroverts or are narcissistic. The person who feels they can never do anything wrong or to be honest may watch programmes about criminals or other people who break the law, the man who is afraid to be masculine may watch action films with strong male lead actors. I look at the media and how some people are attracted to people who are self destructive and this may be a source of attraction, I do wonder if the person finds this self destructive person actually appealing, or if they are resistant to touching their own capacity to be anarchic or to live a less ordered life.

As we leave this section on polarities I would like to say that a person through introjection and creative adjustment may identify with one side of a polarity or shift incongruently through both polarities (such as acceptance or intolerance) with different people or groups based on their own beliefs, and as there can be hundreds of polarities this can be a complex area, the greater awareness a person has of how they exist, and how these polarities affect their contact functions and how they relate to others, as well as their beliefs about their self. Although this is an ideal, when we can integrate these polarities we can live our life with greater flexibility and authenticity.

Assertion

In this final section of this chapter I would like to talk about assertion and how it relates to the process of introjection and creative adjustment. There are many books and information on assertion so the purpose of this section is not to go into detail but to highlight each part of the assertion spectrum. I think the easiest way to see how a person relates to others is in the way they speak, have you noticed how some people engage in conversation? Some people actively or aggressively direct conversations towards a topic or goal and disregard the other unless they are in agreement. The person may use questions, gain knowledge (to use in conversation to manipulate the other) or form arguments that has the purpose of leading the other towards their own perspective, some people may state their views or opinions with little regard for the other person, or purposefully create dissent or arguments. (Aggression) Some people ask questions, play a role (such as playing sick, being helpless or the victim, the persecutor or the rescuer) or use some other prop to direct the conversation towards the topic or area the person has the intention of discussing about (passive aggression) If the person is passive or submissive they may follow the other person as they talk, or talk about the topics that is favourable. Whether the person is in conversation with an individual or group they may restrict their own values or thoughts unless they are the same as the other, and if the other person or group is speaking with for example negativity or positivity then the person may adapt their style or outlook to imitate this, the person may also give a view that is easily ignored or discounted, which would also have the purpose of reinforcing their own self-image or self-concept. Although this may be passive or submissive this may also be aggressive or passive aggressive. I am imagining a person who is looking to ingratiate himself in to his employer so as to progress, or a child trying to achieve a sense of worth of worth or confirmation from their parent, although on the surface they both appear compliant or submissive they do in fact have an objective and are covertly trying to survive or to achieve within the *rules* of the authoritative person or group. Although the person may appear submissive or compliant this may be a role they are playing to actively influence the group, such as a person who joins a group and initially have the intention to be liked and so appears to be the "nice guy" and slowly as he asserts himself in that group he becomes more and more aggressive and dominant, until his goal is achieved and people have adjusted to his leadership or dominance. I have noticed this also in some abusive relationships, although the person initially appears like the nice guy (being assertive, submissive or passive in the relationship) when the really have the intention of becoming dominant in that relationship. The aggressive person manipulates the other by *appearing* to be something else, something that is more agreeable or desirable when they have a deeper intention, and in my view this is an example of being passive aggressive.

When a person displays assertiveness they are respecting the other person's values, needs and feelings, they may actively listen to the other and try not to lead, criticise or judge the other, and respect the other person as an individual. Being assertive also means being able to stand up for yourself and to be treated fairly and equally. Assertiveness means standing up for yourself, but also considering the rights of the other person. In conversation this may mean that a person doesn't take another person's comments that they don't agree with personally, and don't try to form an argument against that view, as the person has a right to have whatever opinions they want. The assertive person has a right to their own opinions or beliefs and is not the judge of others. The assertive person has an acceptance of others, and does not have to give reasons for their own opinion, change of opinion or if they make a mistake. I think importantly the person has a respect and an acceptance of their self, as well as an acceptance of the other person.

I think though that assertion is something that is difficult to attain, but is something that a person can strive towards.

Being aggressive means putting one's own needs first, or violating the rights of the other person to put their own needs first. Other people's rights and opinions have less meaning or not as important. Assertion means respecting your own rights and well-being as well as the rights and well-being of the other. Passivity means putting other's needs before your own, passivity also means that you avoiding standing up for yourself, or that you state your opinions so weakly that they are easily dismissed. Passivity may mean that you hold back with your thoughts and what you would like to say, then either regress into your own world or withdraw and talk to yourself, or displace or vent your frustrations at something or someone else. I often imagine the process of holding back with expressing feelings is like putting each item into a bag you have to carry, putting one item in the bag isn't too bad, but over time the bag becomes heavier and heavier as you hold back and eventually you may become bitter and resentful to others, explode in a passive rage, become depressed or collapse in an emotional crisis. Being passive means that you may not have the belief in your own abilities to overcome problems or issues that arise, and by this may mean that others are more capable, more intelligent, better or more superior than you. Conversely the person who is aggressive may believe himself the opposite, that he is more superior than others, that other people have to listen to him and that his views are more important. The aggressive person who believes himself to be inferior to others may actively give this meaning, as he creates a life for himself where he is inferior to others. The passive person may fear taking ownership of their life, such as living their life by their own choices, and instead looks to others for guidance, influence or control, this may mean living within the rules or confines of a group, role, organisation, society, religion or within the safety of an intimate relationship with a partner. The passive person may feel they are nothing if they cannot fulfil for example the role of mother and so cling onto this, or the person who has been in a role such as a teacher, police officer or nurse and may feel that without the meaning and purpose that this role gave them they are nothing. The same could be said for a person entering retirement and feels that if they are *not productive* then they are not of worth or value (however, what the person accepts as what is productive or unproductive could be an introjection and the person creatively adjusts to this) The passive person who integrates and assimilates religious *rules* may feel guilt or shame if they break or cannot follow these. (This would be different than the assertive person who feels that they are attracted to a certain religion or duty because it mirrors their own values and beliefs)

The aggressive person through his fear of not having a choice may mean he dominates and influences others, as this reduces his dependence, he may also have a need to control others also because of the fear of what it means to not be noticed or not have the affection, approval or attention of others, and endeavour to have their voice heard, this may mean entering into a role or relationship to give this meaning, such as a manager, parent, or other authoritarian role or position that offers control or influence over others. The passive or passive aggressive person may have a fear of success, responsibility or maturity and as such manipulates their environment (or is manipulated from their environment) so they avoid this. They may feel that success, responsibility or maturity is something that is difficult or impossible to attain.

The person may creatively adjust from many introjections, the child being told continuously that he is special or to not consider other's feelings or opinions may believe that he is more special than others and treat others as servants or disregard their opinions or rights. Is this person passive or aggressive? They have passively introjected the idea of who they are, as well as how to value other people, in this example as inferior. The person then after having this self-image or self-concept may aggressively manipulate their self and their environment to give this self meaning (Field Theory)

Creative adjustment can occur at any point through a person's life from a multitude of influences or introjections, but has the effect, just as with the contact functions and polarities or restricting how we make contact and interact with our world.

All this influences restrict how we see ourselves so it affects our self-image and the formation of our self-concept, this self-concept after all is just a number of composite beliefs that can become fixed, certain parts of our self are highlighted or owned, and other parts are switched off, which as the symbol above shows can only narrow how we see ourselves or believe our self to be, as well as how we interact with the world around us.

In the next chapter we shall see how this self-concept is given purpose and meaning. The person normally isn't aware of the many facets of their behaviour or contact functions, what polarities they identify with, or where their behaviour lies within the assertion spectrum, the person is just existing within their world, the person is just living.

*

First learn the meaning of what you say, and then speak

Epictetus

Chapter 1b

A Word on a Field

The need organises the field

Of all the theories that I have encountered, Field Theory is one of the most difficult to explain or to talk about, but is integral to how a person interacts with and influences their world or their environment, and how their world or environment influences the person. This chapter will not be a complete explanation of Field Theory, but rather I will try to highlight the areas that are pertinent to this book.

This chapter is based on the work of a person called Kurt Lewin (1890-1947) who developed the theory in physics and was highly influential in the field of social psychology and group dynamics. He is the author of the formula B = f (P,E) which in relation to the person means that behaviour is a function of person in an environment.

Each person will interact with their environment in a different manner and will give their own meaning to this. The person who works in a busy bakery will have a different meaning to the bakery and may see it as a job that involves working in a hot environment and dealing with irate customers. Another person may see the bakery as part of their routine, she may be at college and calls into the bakery every day for her lunch and looks forward to getting her favourite snack. A person who is very health conscious may actively avoid the bakery as he believes that it is full of fatty food. The bakery remains the same, but all these people ascribe their own meaning onto this. Although it is not part of this book the term is called phenomenology and as I see it means the subjective view that each person takes of the world around them, as well as their self.

When the term *field* is used it is meant to mean literally everything, every object, situation and relationship (Joyce, Sills 2010 p 28) and relates to how the person interacts with their world, as well as how the person's world influences the person. Yontef (1993 p294) states that there is not a correct or true field theory, there are many differing and equally valid field theories. He lists 5 characteristics of Fields and these are:

1. A field is a systematic web of relationships
2. A field is continuous in space and time
3. Everything is of a field
4. Phenomena are determined by the whole field
5. The field is a unitary whole: everything affects everything else

As the web is a systematic web of relationship, everything is of a field, everything affects everything else and the field is continuous we shall see that with the application of introjections and creative adjustments that a person's field will be influenced by their previous experiences. As the field is a whole so if there is a change in one aspect, then there will be a change in all areas. As I write this I am imaging the person who has creatively adjusted to survive in an abusive relationship, her view of her self may be that she has a low self-worth (the introjection from her abusive partner) and her view of her environment will be based on that, and she may sustain it and give this self-belief meaning through her contact functions, polarities and how she relates to people on the assertion spectrum. She may passively interact with others, or be resistant to stating her opinion, and instead ask for advice of guidance from other people. This way of relating to others sustains her view of herself and gives it meaning, that others are more capable, which therefore means she is less capable. As the field is continuous and a systematic web of relationships, the way in which she views her self in the here and now (based on her previous experiences) influences how she is *seen* by others and also how she sees her self. As everything affects everything else people may treat her the way in which confirms her view of her self. In this there is a two way street happening here, the person's idea of who she is influence how she is treated by others. Any positive attribute that a person may say to this this woman may be denied, defected or rationalised as she rigidly sticks to this idea of herself. The man who has the belief that he should be responsible and in charge (from his own introjections) may create a world in which he can be responsible and in charge, he may find a partner that needs help, or he may manipulate her to achieve this end. He may talk in a manner that gives this meaning and aggressively direct relationships where this view of his self has meaning. The same may be said of the woman who believes that she is entitled to being supported by others (from an introjection perhaps of being spoiled or pampered by her parents, and who catered to her every whim) and this may direct how she interacts with her environment. She

131

may become a manager and view that her subordinates have to cater to her demands, or play helpless or sick so that people take care of her. She may become unemployed for a long period of time and try to claim extra sickness benefit for being ill or sick, and convince others that she is ill. She may believe that the government has an obligation to take care of her and become resentful and aggressive when they challenge her. She may have found a man to play this role with, and he works and takes care of her, while she has her *problems* and cannot possibly work. The need that arises from the many creative adjustments and introjections through life can organise the field, and as the field is a systematic web of relationships, the field is continuous and everything affects everything else then the need can organise that field (the person's world) to fulfil it and give it a purpose and meaning. As everything if of a field and in the person's environment how the person *sees, hears, speaks, listens* and the other contact functions, polarities and means of assertion will be based on the belief that the person holds about their self and their world. As I was walking down the street recently I encountered a family with whom it was obvious that they had just arrived in the U.K from a foreign country and they seemed to be familiarising themselves with the town in which I was working. I thought to myself the experiences of the family and what they had gone through in their home country, the parents decision to leave that country to travel somewhere for a better life that may mean they could live and be free from persecution, their journey to this country and how living here may be for them. I was thinking that I hoped that they would be able to settle here and wished them well in this new home. As I walked I overheard two people talking in a very derogatory manner about this family, about how there were "too many of them over here" "a drain on our society" and that "they should clear off back to where they came from" I considered then that how they saw this family was different than how I saw this family, we both saw the same people, but ascribed our own meaning onto it based on our different beliefs, values, ways of thinking and experiences.

With this applied to Field Theory, this person's outlook and beliefs will have a impact on how they exist within their field or environment. As phenomena are determined by the whole field so it is that we put our own meaning and beliefs onto each phenomenon. The result from myself of seeing that family was a belief that people was one of acceptance and a wonder about their journey to this country. I felt enlivened by this experience. The two people who had their judging attitude seemed like they were resentful and angry. Therefore the field is a unitary whole, everything affects everything else.

As a person organises the perception of their field and how they relate, then so if there is a fixed attitude about their self so it has an impact on their self and there is a manipulate of their environment or field to give this meaning, the person who has a distrust of others or finds close or personal relationships difficult may interpret questions from others as intrusive or remarks or statements by others as insensitive or damaging (the person may also manipulate their self to invite these remarks to fulfil the need to create a distance from others) the person may behave in a manner that means that the other avoids a close or personal relationship with them. Yontef (p289) States that so*me people construct a self that has harmony and continuity while flexibly adapting to their current field* this is what I view as a healthy self-concept and may grow with the experiences of their world. The person who has a fixed way of seeing their self and their world may *have no flexibility and only a limited capacity to grow by being transformed by the interaction in the field Yontef* (p289)

As we have seen in chapter 1 and 1a the process of introjection and creative adjustment invites this fixed way of being in the world, with rigid views, beliefs, attitudes and means of interacting with others, and as everything affects everything else in the field, so this fixed way of being can have a negative effect on the person's life and how they exist. However, as everything affects everything else in the field, when there is growth in one part, then the whole field changes. The woman who has ended an abusive relationship and decides to enrol on a assertiveness class and reduces being passive in relationships may forever alter her belief of her self, her view of others, and how others interact with her. Previously she may never have thought she was capable of being assertive, as through the function of creative adjustment this had the purpose of not believing she was capable of anything, and accepted that "this is just the way I am" but, when she challenged her self-concept, when she challenges her idea of herself, then growth is possible, and can be enlightening and almost magical as the person takes charge of their life.

Field Theory is an intricate and complex area and I invite the reader to read further on the subject if it takes your interest. To understand yourself is not to understand yourself in isolation, but to consider your self in relation to others. How you relate and interact with others, how you associate with some people and not others and what this means to how you view yourself. Field means everything in your world, what car you drive or even if you drive (the subjective meaning of what a car means in your world) the clothes you wear, way you speak, way you hear, what your job is and all the other aspects of aspects of a person's life and how you exist.

As we leave this chapter we will move onto the self-concept and the impasse, and how creative adjustments and introjections form the self-concept, comprising of the contact functions, polarities and level of assertion, which has an impact on your field, and how you exist in your world.

*

Chapter 2

The Self-Concept and the Impasse

The soul becomes dyed by the colour of its thoughts.

Marcus Aurelius

A few years ago when i first had the idea of writing this book, i had the visual image of what has become this book. I have been writing notes on this area for years, from my own contemplation, awareness and reflections of my self in relation to others as well as by being observant of others and how they relate in their world, writing ideas about the self-concept, where it evolves, how it becomes and how it is sustained and given meaning. Also what we may become if we can gain an awareness of who we are and for want of a better term to *stretch the self-concept,* to inhabit that ground beyond the impasse, the area that creates anxiety, to challenge the many introjections and understand how we have creatively adjusted as we journey in our life, how it is we see the world a certain way or talk to some people one way and to another people another way, or towards our general beliefs about our life and how we should exist.

I believe that if we inhabit or become a role or label, then it is likely that those we come into contact with will be seen as a role or label as well. If our self is an object that is a culmination of many introjections then those we come into contact with will also be seen as objects, and that these objects may be subject to our own introjected beliefs and values. As a child in my home country the attitude of people who were of a different religion and lived across the divide weren't really seen by people from my own area as people, but as objects to throw stones at, to call them derogatory names and labels and to march down their road even though it antagonised them because many people in my community believed they had a right to do this. Fortunately I didn't buy into the introjects that caused these beliefs as my aunt had changed religions because she married a man from the other religion and moved to that other side, we would go other there for Sunday dinner, and as a child i saw that those other people were just the same as myself. I see this now in the place where i live with people of different ethnicities being labelled (as well as people from those different ethnicities labelling people who are indigenous to this country or other ethnicities) being called names and other forms of prejudicial behaviour. I wonder about this in the context of the world, and in the many areas where there is conflict and persecution, how the people who live in an area are labelled because being of a certain religion, sexuality, nationality or ethnicity and this acts as a means of persecution which may mean diminished human rights, or prejudicial stereotyping. If a person sees another as a label then how can they see the person as a whole person who is more that in which they judge the other. Can there really be dialogue within the spirit of inclusion between people who see their self merely as roles and the identity of the person that becomes that role (made up of introjections and creative adjustments) if one person who has this stance attempts to negotiate with the other from this monological view then how can there be an understanding of the other. There is no search for how the person comes to believe how and the way they exist and the implications of this into their own self-concept, and the way they interact and relate to others. People can become labels or objects based on the beliefs of the other, all that a person is and how they exist is reduced to their gender, ethnicity or some other characteristic. The person's beliefs are invariably part of their own self-concept.

I have heard with disbelief people who talk of inclusion and holism in one sentence, yet in the next are only *seeing* me based on only my gender and the colour of my skin, the person who talks this way, and only pretends to be inclusive often I believe have a hidden agenda, to highlight an (in their own view) an inequality, or to distort the world or discount part of the other to give meaning to their beliefs or their values (which would be a manipulation of the environment) Such is the strength of their self-concept and the rationalisation as the person searches for meaning and purpose, but in doing so creates labels for others. I am no longer Michael, a person who exists and is an unique individual with many different characteristics, beliefs, attitudes and values, I am now just white and male, and this view of me (as an object) only serves the purpose of prejudice and discrimination. I don't believe this is world away of a person from an immigrant trying to enter this country for a better life and is viewed in a negative way by others, an abused housewife or a person who is living under control of an abusive husband or persecution in another country of a person who is a different religion, nationality or ethnicity. They are all stripped of everything that makes them a unique individual who exists and only the parts that give meaning to the other is seen and judged on by the other, based on the beliefs and values that form part of their own self-concept.

Imagine a child who only has the purpose of being someone's son or daughter. The father has the self-concept of being a provider, to look after someone and to able to protect. As the child grows older the father's image of himself is still the same and rather than try to encourage self responsibility in the child and for the child to become a mature and responsible adult (which would make the father's role redundant and therefore create anxiety as he cannot fulfil his self-concept) he becomes an object for the father, the child grows up to rely on his father to provide for him with any issues or problems being rectified by the him. The father is always there to pay for unpaid bills, to talk to organisations or businesses on behalf of the child and to offer guidance or advice to the child. The child's self-concept is forming also based on the introjections from his father and he may creatively adjust to this, and have little belief in his own ability to overcome his own issues or problems, or seek the confirmation or approval of his father before making any decisions.

The author and psychotherapist Fritz Perls, devised the 5 layer model, and for me this is a means to explore the self-concept. As I have hopefully illustrated in the previous chapters, that how we may exist may be a composite of many different introjections and creative adjustments leading to how we make contact with our self and the world around us through the use of the contact functions, polarities, assertion and the zones of awareness. This is given meaning by the function of field theory, as we continually influence the world, as well as be influenced by our world.

The 5 layers starts with the cliché layer, this is what can be considered behaviour that is socially acceptable, (or acceptable within a role) making chit-chat or small talk and the clichés that is involved in conversation, such as "how are you?" "How was the holiday?" "What job do you do?" other social niceties and greetings. Just as with my neighbours in the previous chapter some people exist this way in their relation to others.

The next layer is the role-playing layer, the individual fulfils the role, such as father, mother, teacher, nurse, doctor. The man who through a series of introjections adjusts to a person he thinks he should be, he may work out at the gym and adjusts his appearance to be a clichéd idea of what he believes is attractive to women or how to be a man. He may meet a person, who he finds attractive, but she is also playing a role (the pretty girl) and although this is simplified, it has the purpose to show that a person can meet another not as people, but as roles. Other examples can be the helper who needs a person to rescue, the manager who needs a person to manage, the person who is *sick* and needs a person to take care of them, or the person who has to feel bitter and resentful, and whatever situation the person enters this is the outcome himself.

These first two layers is where I see the self-concept inhabiting, for the person isn't being an authentic individual free to make their own choices, but through the many creative adjustments and introjections.

Part of this role-playing also involves the use of playing games or fulfilling a need through the manipulation of the environment. If a person believes they are a certain way, or has a need that is to be fulfilled then, as with regard to field theory and *the need organises the field* so there is a manipulation of the environment for this to be achieved, if the person's self-concept is to win and never to lose then the person may adapt their self (manipulation of self) and put their self into a position so that they rarely lose. (Such as becoming a solicitor, consultant, police office or other authoritative figure) There is a phenomenological field here also, if the person has to win, and their idea of winning is to be more ill than the other, then a manipulation of the self or the environment may occur. I remember a few years ago I was on a self-awareness course I noticed that when any person talked to the group about some difficulty they had endured the same person replied to each of them disclosing a problem that was worse, she seemed to be in a silent competition to make sure she was the worse off. You may see it yourself, some people always seem to tell a story that is worse than the others, and additionally there is no real desire to get better. It seems that for some people this is way to win. It would seem that these people keep these old wounds from healing, because of the benefit of having that wound. This would be true of a person who once diagnosed with a certain condition clings on to it and uses it to remain ill, rather than another person who when diagnosed with an illness looks for ways to develop and grow in spite of the illness that affects them. A way of manipulation of the self and environment may be the person who gains a lot of knowledge or becomes qualified in a certain area, then gains employment or in a role that supports this. The purpose of this would be to be able not only to prove themselves right, but also to prove other's wrong. The person may rationalise and say they are being professional or to be competent, but the need to be this way is not to know one's job and to be proficient at it, but to be better than others. The person who has endured an abusive relationship with a person who has a need to win, or doesn't like losing may try and use others (another example of manipulation of the environment) to achieve this, the person may try to use the against them, they may try to alienate the child from the parent (while saying to others that they are trying their best to help the other parent see the child) or use coercion or play helpless or the victim to get the child to take their side. The person may also use gossip and other tactics to try to influence other people's opinions of the parent. In each of these the person is viewed in a competitive manner for the person to win against and the others, such as the parent, the child and the recipients of the gossip are only objects to achieve this objective, to win. As we shall explore further in this chapter on the self-concept, the are many ways in which a person can influence their world to fulfil a need, and configure how they see their world to reduce anxiety.

The third layer is called the impasse, it's that feeling of anxiety or fear when a person tries, encounters a situation or becomes something that isn't them or is new for them, so for instance the person who has to win as part of their self-concept may feel anxious at the thought of losing. The person who is passive and does something that is *not them* such as standing up for themselves may feel anxious at the thought. The person who prides himself on his ability to help other people may feel anxious if they encounter a situation in which they feel they have to ask for help. The person who judges others and puts themselves into a situation where they can give advice or guidance may feel uneasy if they have to ask another person for advice or guidance. The man who rarely speaks and prefers to listen to others, but encounters a situation in which they must speak out may feel uneasy at doing this. The man who has controlled and emotionally abused his wife may feel anxious if he becomes very ill and his wife now has authority and responsibility in the home, or if they separate and she applies for a legal order barring his contact with her, before applying for a divorce (knowing that he is now powerless to influence her) The woman who adjusted to a self where she plays helpless and vulnerable and manipulates others to take care of her may feel anxious if she takes responsibility for her self and forges her own path in life. In all these examples the areas of chapter 1a (contact functions, zones of awareness, assertion and polarities) give meaning to this idea of their self, and as I see it then the impasse is at the outer edge of the self-concept, where the *me* becomes the *not me*.

If we look at the symbol above, as I have previously said the first section is creative adjustment and introjection, leading as the symbol narrows into the areas of Chapter 1a (Contact Functions, Polarities and Assertion) Field Theory encompasses all areas of this symbol as it is always active as to how the person interacts with their environment.

The self-concept is second section, of all the possibilities of how we could be a person, the process of creative adjustment and introjection restricts us and how we form our self-image, our self-concept or identity. The purpose of field theory is to give this image or concept meaning. As I see it the impasse is the long outer borders of the second section (which borders onto an area that is unexplored or a void, and possibly frightening or anxiety provoking) and the closer we get to this edge the more anxious we become as we border on the divide between the *me* and the *not me*. There is some comfort in the cliché and role-playing layer. It is easier for a person to say "this is just who I am" and live their life within these boundaries rather than ask the question "what could I be?" as that would involve pushing the self-concept and perhaps to gain an awareness of what their self-concept means to them. (Such as "if I stay the same and am aggressive or monological, then I can be selfish and get my needs met, but if I listen to others, and consider and respect them then I can no longer bully or manipulate people to get my needs met)

There may also be the existential anxiety here, as the person asks "if I am not this, then what am I?" The more we head to the edge of the unknown or the *not me* the greater the anxiety. The purpose of games to fulfil the need of the person can also keep the person from the anxiety of the *not me*. Imagine the child who dislikes the mother's new partner because he believes that he will not get as much attention and instead of reacting to this is an assertive manner, such as telling his mother his thoughts and feelings (which may create its own anxiety if he has to talk about his feelings) about her new relationship he plays games, tell lies and manipulates to try to create tension and to hopefully end the relationship. If the relationship ends then the child may believe he will receive attention. This belief that he *should* get his mother's undivided attention, or that his mother has to do what he says (that he is superior) may have originated from many introjections, or adjustments following the separation of his mother from his father, or observing and copying the way in which the father behaved towards the mother.

There are many games to fulfil a need or to keep the person away from the impasse and I believe that the closer we get to impasse has the benefit of knowing where our self-concept boundaries are, when we have a knowledge and awareness of the boundary we can see what the self-concept means to the person, how it has originated, how it is maintained and what happens if the self-concept is challenged or threatened.

The fourth area of the five layer model is called the implosive layer is when the person goes beyond the impasse and touches on the *not me* the person begins to freeze as they are no longer on their comfort zone (which is why the role of manipulation and games has the purpose to take the person away from the impasse and entering the implosive layer, and to stay in the boundary of the self-concept) The lady from a previous chapter who dressed in a manner both to get attention and restrict relationships, and talked in an esoteric language to keep herself away from relationships with others, yet attracted others due to her style of dress and props, placing her apart from others. This lady when dressing in normal clothes and trying to talk in an everyday language may have touched on the implosive layer. As she discovered what her way of being meant to her as well as feeling anxiety when these methods and games were not being used, this lady was creating a safe emergency, she was experientially trying what it was like to *not be me* to gain an awareness what it meant to *be me*, and how she maintained the *me* (or the self-concept) and to feel that uneasiness as took a step over the impasse.

Another person may have the belief they are confident, self-assured and can handle or overcome any difficulty, and then when an event or incident occurs and they cannot overcome this, then panic may ensure, this may touch on the implosive layer and so they freeze, and may experience many of the effects of a traumatic reaction, such as increased heart rate, sweating, trembling, nausea, emotional numbing or feeling spaced out, anxiety and dizziness. Their self-concept, their idea of their self is challenged and the person may find themselves unable to respond. They may enter a period of denial, rationalisation, deflection or distortion to save their idea of who they are. It is not so much the event that was traumatic, but the beliefs that they ascribe to their self were challenged. I remember once reading about a person who had the belief that they *should* be able to walk anywhere, regardless of the area and time of day. He believed that if anything were to happen to him then he would be able to defend himself, so one night he was walking home about 2am from a night out and got assaulted by some men who jumped out of a car and beat him up. He was in shock and denial and looked to blame other people for this, and suffered from the reactions of trauma. His view of life and how he believed it should be did not mirror reality, instead he was putting his beliefs onto the world, and suffered the consequences when the world didn't exist according to his expectations. During the assault he was saying that he just froze and didn't know how to react, I think at this he was indicating that he had entered the implosive layer. If he was more pragmatic and knew that he was walking home through a deprived part or town at 2am he may have been on guard or open to the possibility of his heightened risk to something bad happening. However his own beliefs about his view of his self and the world were decimated when these men assaulted him. Although this is not part of this book I think it explains how we see something as traumatic, and also how we experience trauma. If I have integrated into my self-concept that I can do anything, am invincible and fearless, then if i get lost at the top of a mountain it may become traumatic (entering the implosive layer) when I discover as the snow falls down, the temperature drops and i can't retrace my steps to safety that I am ill-prepared and without a means to contact the emergency services. I may begin to panic due to the realisation that I am not invincible and can handle anything, and that instead I am vulnerable and incapable to help myself in that environment. I think the implosive is when we are firmly in the *not me* area, and this may be identified as beyond the blue section on the symbol, in a void where there is nothing.

The fifth layer is the explosive or authentic layer, when we can drop the roles, labels and games and to be real, free from the need of approval, recognition or affection, and to not manipulate the environment to get our needs met, to be able to view the other not as an object, thing or label, but as a person. I will write more about this in the following chapter but the way I see the first four layers is something that we do or how we exist that is from the many introjections and creative adjustments and the ensuing development of the contact functions, resistances, polarities, zones of awareness and assertion. For the purposes of this book, I will describe in more detail the fourth and fifth areas in Chapter 3, which is the third section on the symbol. As I see it when a person enters the implosive layer this is definite step outside the self-concept, and may be when the person encounters a situation in which their idea of their self can no longer be sustained or is attacked from the outside world that doesn't have to adhere to the person's own self-beliefs. I see more the search for authenticity a gradual process (which is why the third section grows slowly from the second section) as he person explores how and why they exist, and in that is a discovery of being.

We will explore this layer more fully in chapter 3 but will say that when a person can have relationships with others in the spirit of dialogue and with authenticity they are not contained by the view of who they are, and the many constructs that make up their self, but with the freedom not to interact with others from the narrow limitation of the contact functions, they may be able to be flexible and inhabit both polarities depending on the situation, and can react to events with authenticity and assertiveness in the assertion spectrum. This may also mean being able to embrace the feelings that were so long held at bay through manipulation, denial, rationalisation or distortion to give the self-concept meaning, and an integration of the disowned parts of the person.

What is the self-concept if not a collection of beliefs as to who we are as a person, the way in which we organise how we see our world is based on this, the child who has learned from childhood that he is not accepted the way he is as other people tell him to change to be normal or to fit in may develop a belief that he is unacceptable, and to gain affection or to be of worth must adapt to what the other wants. A child who believes that he is always right and is never wrong may integrate into his self-concept the belief about himself that he may give advice to others, but cannot accept any criticism from others. If this belief is rigid then he may listen for any sign of a person judging him, or to manipulate his environment to interact with others who do as he says, and wouldn't challenge his dominance.

I don't belief that we are born with a self-concept, or an image of who we are, the child doesn't have a sense of self, it just exists with realness and authenticity, as the child grows, it now only develops a self that fits with its own beliefs, but also the belief of how others see it, and develops with both the positive and negative messages that a person receives. The person who has taken the message that one must be work and be of value, may view this as positive, but when they retire they may view their self as having little value to society, there may also be the fear of growing old, and what growing old (within the phenomenological values of that society) means to the person. Part of this belief of the self-concept may involve how we view ourselves in relation to other people, as well as how we view our self in relation to our own belief as to how we think we should be. Does the man feel that he must not be inferior to men who have more money or success than he, or of a higher status? Does he believe that he must support his family by being financially successful? So in an effort to not enter touch the impasse he views being financially successful as a goal of his life or he develops a career in which he is superior to other people, Then he would view other as he views his self, that a person is only of worth if they have a career and a focus towards achieving money. The same would be for a women who believes that to be an attractive person she must be slim and pretty and manipulates her self to achieve this, she judges her self on how others view her and so engages in social media, showing images to promote this belief, her worth is determined not on her own self-belief, but of how others view her, she blocks other aspects of her self and only focuses on her looks and appearance, while other attributes are neglected.

The wife who has integrated into her self-concept the belief that she is of value only if she takes care of others may cause anxiety if she puts her self first, and may feel guilt or shame if she decides to go to college or develops an interest. As the self-concept develops from the many introjections we see the world from the point of view, so it is not really case of seeing is believing, but believing is seeing. We see the world based on our own beliefs.

Zinker spoke of the self-concept and said in the healthy self-concept the person is aware of the many opposing forces within himself. He is willing to see himself in a multitude of "contradictory ways. He experiences relationships between a variety of inner parts. He described the pathological self-concept as seeing himself in a unilateral stereotypical manner. He is always this and never that. He lacks fluidity and broadness of self-perception. (1978 p198-199)

The housewife who rigidly sticks to the belief that she must be of value to others finds it difficult to take care of her self, the girl who has to be pretty and slim could never put on weight or go shopping with no make-up or not taking care of her appearance. The man driven by financial success may find it difficult to give up his job, take a less well-paying job and lead a less materialistic and money driven life. It is the rigidity of the many creative adjustments and introjections that help to create our view of our self, and we see and interact with the world based on those fixed beliefs as to who we are. I believe that this stuckness in our view of our self may also be stuckness in how we view other people, do we see people as unique individuals or see them with the same beliefs that we see our self, or do we place expectations or *shoulds* onto how we believe others *should be*.

Many styles of relating to others begin to make sense, when the person gains an awareness of the meaning of each event, and begins to discover just how it is they see the situation, understanding the values and demands that maintains this rigidity. Then the person has their own existential choice, do I keep on *seeing* my self and the world this way, or do I explore other ways of being. To explore these other ways of being may mean touching on the impasse and the growth of the person's self-concept.

I think the person who has an idea of their self and who they should be may guard against any challenge to this, the person who feels lonely may not acknowledge these feelings and instead drink or take drugs, have promiscuous sex, engage in affairs or develop an interest such as fitness training, running or joining a social group. Doing any of these wouldn't necessarily be something negative, but the reasons that drive this has the purpose to reduce the anxiety of feeling lonely.

I remember once meeting a person who was from a different country and had settled here in the England. She had the view that she was very intelligent and self-assured, and that people should come to her to socialise, rather than she go to people, She began though to feel the pangs of loneliness as these beliefs impacted on her relationships. These feelings of loneliness went against her beliefs of her self, and so, instead of exploring the meaning of these feelings and how they related to her view of her self, she decided to join a group that had the purpose of speaking in her own language. She had joined the group not to engage with others because of a shared interest, but to put a plaster on the feelings of loneliness. I do wonder about this, what happens when the self-concept chapter is challenged, and how some people may have a low tolerance to the feelings of anxiety if the *me* cannot be sustained.

Another person I once knew found being single difficult and as such so she would go from relationship to relationship with men, she had an awareness that she didn't like being alone, but instead of staying with these feelings to a greater awareness of how she existed she would casually meet a man (the man here represented a manipulation of the environment as he was viewed as an object that only served the purpose of reducing the woman's anxiety) and start a relationship, he contact functions adapted so as to make this easy, her appearance, way of speaking, props and her submissive behaviour meant that she could always entice a man. I believe that she had a fear of self responsibility and the maturity that accompanies this, it was easier for a man to take care of her, rather than take care of her self. There were many introjections that lead to this aspect of her self-concept, her father had always been an authoritative man who always had the reins in all aspects of the house, and her mother was submissive to her father. She introjected the idea that a woman needs a man to take care of her, and cannot exist alone. Another woman may have adjusted to go against this idea and actively become independent of a man's (perceived) authority and distance her self from intimate relationships, or enter into a relationship with a man adjusting her listening, seeing or hearing like a radar to identify any point in which she became less independent or that her partner was taking control. Instead of being passive this lady may aggressively distance herself from equality or mutuality and the way she spoke, such as saying things like "i don't need any man to take care of me and he knows it" although her drive for saying this and being this way would be based on the introjections and creative adjustments from earlier in her life.

The man who views his self as being a little worth and a certain *need* see the world so it means that his poor self-esteem is never questioned may guard against any behaviour that would mean he can put down that role (a person who is one down when compared to others) and begin to live in a equal way with others, his *other people are better than me* introjection may manifest itself in his job, his failing relationships with others, which may be self-sabotaged and in his outlook, which only serve to further give meaning (field theory) He may have an awareness that he has a talent for maths, art, science, the law or some other field, but his negative self-talk stops him frim developing these and being a success, he may also discount all these attributes as they do not fit in with his idea of who he is. Through the manipulation of his self his focus on the negative keeps his attention and reinforces his self-belief. If this person was the editor of a newspaper, he may find that doom and gloom inhabit the top stories and any positive story in tucked away near the back page.

So it is that through field theory the person who has a belief about their self may find a person or group, or *see* the world in such a way to give this self meaning. The person who dislikes authority may transfer this onto the police and distort their role, to be only one of control, instead of public protection. The child who has been involved in an abusive relationship with his step-father may rationalise ways to avoid any close contact with his mother's warm and understanding new partner, as he has creatively adjusted to view men with distrust, aggression and fear then it would create anxiety if he were to respond to the mother's new partner with an openness and authenticity, which would be beyond the impasse and implosive. Instead it may be easier, or less anxiety provoking to distort any actions done by the new partner to be able to be this way, or play games to invite the mother's boyfriend to get angry, and therefore he is justified in creating a distance, or, he may simply lie, to try to get his mother to separate from the man. All these stem from a fear to be something he is not. The self-concept then may carry many scars in the creative adjusts from which it is formed.

This would also be true of a person who is single and may have an aversion towards a relationship for many reasons, it may be a fear of maturity, a fear of intimacy, a fear to let go of one's youth, (as they may associate being in a relationship with getting old) a fear to be committed to one person or a fear to be emotionally vulnerable. The person may have developed impossibly high standards of what they look for in a partner, so they can justifiably say to others "i just can't find anyone who is right for me" and, if they meet a person who does tick all the boxes then they may say that "it just doesn't feel right" as their final get out. This person may enter into relationships, but he does so knowing that it won't develop, or outside his awareness sabotages the relationship so that it does not continue. He may have relationships that have no depth, just as with the stone skimming on the surface he maintains his role-playing and games to keep it light and superficial. If he forms a relationship with another person, his contact functions and zones of awareness may alert him through his sensing that the relationship is getting more intimate and therefore more anxious (approaching the impasse) and again through the use of the contact functions he may end it. He may have some stories to justify to himself for ending the relationship, such as blame a difficult childhood or other traumatic event that takes away his own responsibility for his actions He passes on his self-responsibility onto an incident or event, such as "i am sorry but I just can't see you any more, I had it difficult growing up and can't commit to people" as a viable and believable means to end it. Shortly afterwards though he may be back out there and looking for his next relationship and so the cycle continues. Also, as the self-concept can be very complex he may begin and end these relationships to be able to punish himself, or to make women fall for him, then by ending it and hurting them he is punishing women. He may alternatively distort how he sees the world and believes that it is women who have the problem, and he is only trying to meet someone nice. Although his actions are obvious to others the ways in which he *sees* his self and others may mean that this truth is ignored or denied, so it stays outside his awareness. If he meets a woman who has the same fears of intimacy and emotional closeness, then the two may enter a relationship that is without connection, and lacks authentic emotional contact.

I have noticed that of all the ways that a person may make contact with the world around them, such as sensing, feeling, thinking and intuition the person may creatively adjust to only develop one of two areas of contact, and then exist in the world from this way if being. Before I became interested in this field I used to be very analytical and responded to events from my head, I would logically analyse a situation and break it down into its component parts, in fact I put together an acronym to help with this, and called it P.A.C.C (based on reading many books by Edward de Bono) which stood for:

Plus, Minus, Interesting.
Alternative, Possibilities, Choices
Consider all Factors
Consequence and Sequence

I invite you to use it for yourself, and can be a useful tool to use to understand a situation or problem and its likely development. Prior to becoming interested in this field I would regularly take things apart, such as my car and motorcycle as well as being keen to complete DIY projects. I was interesting in the causality of things and events as well as a desire to know how things worked.

Later in life when I was embarking on this path of self-awareness I realised that *thinking* for me was my safe ground, my preferred way of relating to the world around me. I remember a few years ago on a self-awareness course the tutor invited a stranger into the room and asked us to write down all the thoughts we had about her without her speaking (an experiment on how we judged others) I was still firmly in my head then and analysed all the details and interesting points that I noticed about her. When the tutor went around the room asking what people thought of her, some said she looked like a granny, some said she looked warm and another said she lived in a terraced house. When it came to my turn to state my own thoughts and observations I went into a long list and said that she had previously been a keen runner, but had stopped that now and enjoyed walking and gardening. I said she felt lonely sometimes but she put on a brave face in front of others, that she drove a medium sized car and had been married before but no longer was, she had a dog that was medium sized, probably a Golden Retriever or Labrador and had a love of reading. The woman, the tutor and the other people on the course were amazed at my inferences, which was simply based on being observant. The tutor asked how I picked up on all this and I replied "i am analytical" it was only much afterwards that this was an indicator of my dependence on my analytical thinking skills, and the other parts, the feeling, the sensing and the intuition had not developed. On the same course I would offer reflections to what the person was feeling and their underlying emotions, but I wasn't necessarily being empathetic, instead of using affective empathy (feeling the feeling) I was using cognitive empathy (thinking the feeling) as well as analytical skills to understand the person.

As I became more self-aware I started to wonder where this almost dependence on thinking originated and what was it like to live in the here and now. As I grew up over in Belfast as a child there were many introjections as to how to be a person, and in that world men were rough, tough and rarely let an emotions out. Also I had It quite difficult growing up and I think I *switched off* the feeling and sensing side of me because of the trauma I endured as a child. I realised that I wasn't a total robot though as I could express feelings and feel feelings when in relation to people I trusted, and it was then I considered that I could show feelings when I was in safe relationship. I therefore developed my thinking and analytical skills not because it was innate, but because of the avoidance of what feeling and sensing meant to me, as well as my beliefs of my self as well as other people. I rarely felt the cold, and when people said it's so cold today, i would reply "is it?" and also I would rush down my dinner and bypassed the taste and smell of the food, as I thought it were only energy so I could engage in fitness training. I later learned that real strength lies in the strength to be vulnerable, to touch the uneasy feelings of what it meant to be *not me* which meant sensing and feeling. Through the manipulation of my self and my environment the way I saw my self had an impact on how I saw the world, and my actions invited other people to see me this way as well, for example I didn't say to the tutor "i have difficulty feeling my emotions and so have developed and refined my thinking and analytical skills" I merely said "I am analytical" By labelling myself this way I was inviting the others to view myself in the same manner, and by them following this image of myself so it was that it reinforced my idea of myself. (Field Theory) How I saw, how I listened, the props I had (by always reading books) and the way I spoke (contact functions) also gave this self-meaning and purpose. In reality though I was in my safe zone and leaving that meant touching the impasse and the anxious feeling in my stomach if I left that secure harbour.

I would like to suggest the following experiment.

Awareness Experiment – Living in Your Shoes

The purpose of this experiment is much like the previous experiment in chapter 1 (The Shirt) but instead I would like you to remove your shoes off and place them in front. Now, get a pen and paper, and draw a figure of you in the middle of the page. I would like you to think about what it would be like if a person has to wear your shoes for a week, to be everything you are, whether this is at work, at home or with friends. I'd like you to write around the figure all the qualities and characteristics about yourself. Do you generally listen to others, speak more, put other people before yourself or expect others to fit in to what you would like to do? Do you manage or advise people and solve their problems, taking on responsibility for others, either because you have to or because of your situation, or do you let other people take the initiative and tell you what to do. Are you passive in conversation or do you lead, do you hold back with opinions or do you speak and invite the other person to respond to you? Look at your clothes and ask yourself if you wear named brands or do you have the idea that if it fits it's ok, do you wear sports clothing, fashion clothing, bland clothing or clothes that attract attention or approval as well as how often you buy yourself clothes? Think about your own beliefs about yourself and ask if you view yourself as equal to others, superior to others or inferior. Do you believe in yourself or is your feelings about yourself dependant on what other people say about you? Consider if you have to get dressed up or care about your appearance before you go out. What type of car do you drive and consider what this car means to you. Does it mean that you are important, part of a group (as in a bike or camper van club) or is it just a vehicle to get to work.

After you have written these down I would like you to think about your own identity, image or self-concept and if this is person dependant, that is to say, do you switch or shift into different parts of your being if you talk to different people, and if so, what is it about the other person that you can feel yourself switching or shifting? Is it based on the person's financial success, is it the authority, do they appear more educated, do you become compliant or passive, do you ingratiate yourself, in the sense that they are more important than you, or, are you more superior to them based on the qualities or values that are important to you?

If you do switch (and most of us do I believe until we start to become more authentic) then record the types of people you switch to. (Such as the headmaster, the mother-in-law, the boss, the teacher, the beautician, the solicitor or the police officer, or the person who is popular)

Now after writing all these down I'd like you to consider your own image of your self, and if what you have wrote is accurate. I'd like you now to revisit chapter 1a and consider if you are assertive, passive, aggressive or passive aggressive. If you shift then ask yourself what people do you shift with, are you passive or aggressive with your partner then the opposite with your boss or friends. Of all the qualities you have written down which ones are polarities, such as happy, strong, kind, responsible, sad, positive, negative, warm and so on. With the contact functions in mind I'd like you to consider which way you speak to people, which was you listen, what the purpose of questions means to you, if you work out or keep in shape, your appearance, dress or clothing or if you have tattoos or wear jewellery and what this means to you.

I think by now you may have a good idea of how you see yourself, and I would like you to think about how you influence others to react to you. If you are negative and sad, or always feeling low, do you steer the conversation towards negative aspects of the person, or do you self-disclose to guide the conversation. If you have to be strong and responsible or in charge how do you make it so that this is possible, that is to say, have you chosen a partner who is weak and irresponsible so you can be strong, or do you cherry pick the any part of the other to highlight a weakness. How do you speak and interact with others so the self-concept has a purpose that is to say, if you have a need how is it fulfilled by you view of yourself in relation to others. If you have a need to be noticed, to be special, how do you dress, what props do you use to direct attention towards your self. Contrastingly, if you have a desire or a need to not be the centre of attention how do you do so to enable this, for example, this belief affect your hygiene so by only having a shower once a week people avoid you, or do you dress in drab clothing or a poor conversationalist. Put simply, when writing all the qualities and characteristic about yourself, what is it you do, who is it you are that gives this need or desire a meaning and purpose? If you have the view that you are not that special how is it that you create a world in which you are indeed not that special. If you believe that life is a burden or that life is hell how do you see the world that gives this view a meaning?

I remember once I knew a person who had a very negative view of herself, and as I was talking to her she showed me her diary. The first three pages were full of negative writing that reflected her thoughts, and on the fourth page was her happiness at seeing her daughter who lived away from home. He negative view of her self influenced her actions, as she wrote about all the bad stories or experiences first, (or how it was that she construed experiences as bad or negative) before including the positive experience about her daughter, and so I asked her what would have meant to her to put a positive story first, and she realised that her image of her self was contaminating her actions, how she experienced events and how she organised her world.

As the need organises the field so it is that the self-concept or the self-image is fulfilled. The self-concept is very sneaky though and with regards to holism no part of a person's life is any less important than any other part. I would like you to consider that if like myself and my direction towards thinking as a preference on how to relate to others as well as my self, then so it is that the goal to communicate a certain way will mean that there may be a resistance towards other areas of communication, that is to say, as the lady communicated in a negative manner then the possibility of positive communication was switched off or restricted.

I knew a person who said that she was a *feeling* person and didn't believe in reading books as she gained her knowledge solely from her experiences. It became apparent that she had a fear of looking stupid in front of others, and felt intimidated by people whom she considered learned or academic and steered away from reading books so as not to give an opinion or to engage in conversation or debate with others. In her view, as she focused on feelings she could never be challenged, as a feeling is neither right nor wrong, it just it. Her contact functions developed so that her sensing and feeling skills were advanced, though it was only this way because of her fear and anxiety of what thinking meant. The self-concept in an effort to give itself meaning can create goals so that it can survive, the lady who relied on feelings could have worked in a field that gave this a meaning and purpose, just as I could have be drawn to a role in which my analytical thinking skills were given a meaning. Please consider for yourself your own goals or life path and how the qualities you have listed are given a meaning and purpose, both in how you see yourself and in your relationships with others. As we will touch on this later in this book I wonder if you could retain your notes of this experiment.

Another measure of the self-concept is how we creatively adjust to circumstances, and there are no hard and fast rules as to how a person creatively adjusts. I came across two sisters while ago who had a mother that was very distant, selfish and viewed herself as being more important that anyone else in the household. She didn't express her feelings to her daughters, or was she warm or caring towards them. The two sisters adjusted in different ways, the first sister seemed to love being in a warm and loving relationship, and actively created situations in which she could cuddle on the sofa with her partner, saying such things as "let's stay in tonight and watch a film" (manipulation of the environment to get her needs met) as she knew that this would inevitably mean that they would have a warm embrace that evening. The other sister eventually, after a series of failed relationships in which she was called cold or unfeeling by her then partners married a very affectionate man. She was very distant emotionally, and kept her husband at arm's length, rationalising to her self that she wasn't a *touchy feely* type of person. As she had integrated the belief into her self-concept *I am unlovable* physical contact scared her, she denied these feelings as she rationalised this into the "i am not touchy feely" as a means of avoidance or denial. For as physical contact caused her anxiety, as it touched her impasse or into the implosive layer so it was she constructed her field to avoid this anxiety of what touch from others meant. I often wonder why she didn't find a partner who was just as ambivalent about touch as she, and she could have met a man who was cold and unfeeling, and perhaps she was so used to keeping partners at bay she gained a sense of worth from knowing they wanted physical contact, yet she still avoided this. Her husband, although he was kind and understanding was also highly compliant and passive in relation to other people (from his own creative adjustments and introjections) and though he was a tactile person he restricted this part of his self, so as to *fit into* the world of the sister.

Writing this reminds me of another person I knew, he had been involved in a long marriage with a woman who was similar to one above, and as creative adjustment can be a continual process through life, that after he and his partner separated he found it very difficult to express feelings of love and affection to any woman he met. He had been in a loveless marriage for a number of years, and that expressive part of his self had atrophied or died away, as it had become redundant in that relationship. When he decided to start dating again he felt that it was difficult for him to show his feelings, or to respond to any other woman in a loving way, such as when if a woman he was dating displayed emotion or any type of closeness he would freeze. This was how this man had creatively adjusted to the long term partner. As the need organises the field so it was that he desired closeness and sexual intimacy with a woman, but not anything that was emotional, so he manipulated his environment to only engage on a superficial level and became promiscuous, and enjoyed the safe contact of only transient sexual partners. His manipulation of his self gave this a meaning, he would wear props to attract women, his manner of talking and listening only skipped on the surface of intimacy (though he would promise the world to any prospective sexual partner) and he became sensitive to what women would engage in a sexual relationship, when he did find a women, he had a number of ways to make this possible, he would manipulate his self by working out at the gym in an effort to become physically desirable, wear fashionable clothes and expensive aftershaves, he would become charming and entertaining, give gifts, flowers and send regular texts (the use of props) to remind the woman he was thinking of her. In reality the man was manipulating the woman, to fool her and to lure her in so as to get his needs met. Then after this happened he became distant and if the woman *bought into* his trap he would eventually become insulting to make the woman stop contact. I have seen this many times with both sexes, as they seem to creatively adjust after a damaging relationship and wish to avoid emotional closeness. Their style of dress changes, as does their way of speaking, and it seems that have closed down their emotional side to focus only on physical relationships. This creative adjustment though becomes its own introjection, the fear of vulnerability, the fear of relationships becomes an introjection (such as *I will get hurt if I become emotionally close*) and the person adjusts from that. If the person tried to become emotionally attached again he would realise that he would be touching the impasse, and would have to endure feelings of anxiety of he allowed his self to feel emotions again. Of all the reasons of why a person would sabotage relationships (and I am sure we will cover some more ways in this book) the fear of   emotions, and the feelings of anxiety is one of them, they may say things like "i am sorry it just doesn't feel right when we are together" or the person may create arguments or tension so the relationship fails, the person may also engage in behaviour that will mean the relationship will fail, such as having an affair, becoming aggressive, self-destructive, helpless or weak. The purpose being to manipulate the other to end the relationship, or to be able to give a good reason as to why it isn't working between them both. The underlying reason though I believe is the fear of being loved, being emotionally close or vulnerable, or indeed a need or desire to not be loved, the fear or anxiety guides and influences the person. Also, if the person has introjected the belief *you'll never be happy* or any other introjection that means the person will be unfulfilled in their life may have the implication that relationships will end as this belief becomes a need of the person.

The purposes of starting a relationship would perhaps become an inexhaustible list, though I have noticed one of these recently, although I was going to talk about the need for affection later this reminds me of a person who engaged in a relationship, not because of a desire to know the other person, but because of a need to feel the affection from the other person. This man was only of value if another person wanted him and was affectionate towards him. He had creatively adjusted to this need by talking in a helpless way, almost in a defenceless and unguarded manner. He seemed to play the *little boy lost* role (manipulation of self) and playing this role meant that he was trying to hook a person, or lure a person (manipulation of environment) to look after him, to love him and to show him affection. Now, as this desire was his primary need, then it meant that it didn't matter who it was that fulfilled this need, the other person was just an object to fulfil this, and to maintain his self-concept. He was very good at playing this game with his way of relating to others and how he made statements or asked questions exemplified this. I believe that in effect he was pushing his responsibility onto another person, to look after him. The impasse for his self was responsibility and maturity, as well as what it meant to not receive the affection of another person. Outwardly he seemed to lead a very successful life, had a career and had been to university, however emotionally he was immature, selfish and childish. I noticed that his partners thought they were special to him, but, when there was any difficulty in the relationship, or if the person got fed up looking after this man and an argument erupted he would end the relationship and move on to someone new (his rescission of responsibility and the need for affection meant that he didn't care about other people's feelings) leaving the other person heartbroken. As the other person was just an object that fulfilled his need he found another object to gratify him. The lure for any woman he enticed was the role of *little boy lost* (evoking the maternal feelings of a woman perhaps) and also materialistic appeal of the successful financially solvent person with the professional career. (Which may have been a prop for the woman, as she received a sense of worth or approval from her friends for being in a relationship with this man)

As a person's self-concept can affect all the parts of a person's life so it is that how a person creatively adjusts from one area can affect another, imagine the man who has entered into a relationship with another person who has the need to be in charge or to dominate, and if they cannot get their own way then they become moody, sulky of spiteful. The man then may begin to *walk on eggshells* around his partner for fear of upsetting her, as he knows the consequences, and so in that relationship he may become passive. This passivity may become mirrored in other relationships, for instance with his boss at work who is seen as an authority figure (which would be similar to his wife) he may become passive in that relationship also. If the boss has become a manager to be able to tell people what to do, and becomes moody or sulky if he encounters problems, then the man may remain silent if he has any problems or requests, to avoid upsetting the manager further. Just like the wife the manager is affecting other people in how they interact with them, and invite the other to adjust to them. Maybe you have seen this before, how some people become angry or unapproachable and other people give them a wide berth, if this person is in a relationship or in a position of authority it also has the impact of people being wary of how to raise issues. I think this type of behaviour can be a form of coercion, the manager or wife enforces their rule by their behaviour, and if the man has experience of this with his partner, his feelings may be evoked if he encounters a manager who behaves the same way, and he may become passive and *walk on eggshells* around any person who exhibits that behaviour. If the initial creative adjustment or introjection has been integrated into the person's self-concept then to challenge any person that displays this controlling behaviour may mean they touch the impasse and therefore the anxiety of the *not me*.

I have seen this with some people who have endured abusive relationships, if the person has the courage to end this and leave the abusive partner then unless they have an awareness of the partner's tactics of control they may discover themselves going silent or passive if the person they are talking to displays aspects of the abusers way of control and dominance. Of course I write here that the person may become silent or passive, but another person may become aggressive if they sense that another person is behaving in the same way as the abuser, and retaliate *as if* they actually were that person. A similar vein of this would be the man who has integrated the introjection that *listen to your elders or be respectful to your parents* and the man when encountering an elderly person or someone older than him may become the little boy again, and offer little argument or disagreement to the older person.

The person who has integrated into their self-concept the belief that they must *live up to* the expectations of another instead of just simply existing, may try to placate that person through their career, partner, children or outlook. I remember knowing a person who seemed to live up to the expectations of his father, on the surface he seemed to be a very driven and motivated person, his girlfriend was very attractive and his children were well mannered and polite, it all seemed to be for the purpose to show to his father *look dad, look how well I have done.* As the person creatively adjusted to the need to fulfil his father's expectations he put his own desires second, so if he did put his self first then it meant feeling feelings of guilt (as it went against his beliefs as he *should* be living his life) The person I knew started to take drugs to be able to fulfil these expectations, and in effect he was burning the candle at both ends to try to make his father proud of him. As this person had spent their whole life trying to gain recognition or approval from his father so it was that there was resentment as well, as nothing that he done was good enough for him. I once listened to how his father spoke to him, and he criticised the son and what he had done, the son then tried to justify his actions. It seemed like the father had set the bar for the son, yet the son couldn't quite make it as the father was always moving that bar just a little higher. I often wonder if the introjected message was *you're not good enough as you are* and the son aimed higher and higher trying to gain approval, affection or recognition from his father. I think that this relationship is similar to the previous example as the person, whether that is the partner, the manager or the father is expecting the other to live to their standards or expectations, as the person adjusts to live within the *rules* of that relationship. This adjustment may have implications for how the person views their self in relation to the other. The example of the son trying to live up to the father's expectations created a person who adjusted their whole life to look good in front of the father, and though he has developed a drug problem as he tried to look good to the other. His father never knew of this as his son believed that if his father knew then it would mean that he wouldn't be liked. The son was then trying to please his father for affection, he became the *good boy* so he would be liked by his dad, and integrated these beliefs into his role in life. The impasse for this person would be challenging his father, in effect to become the *not me,* becoming assertive or risking any behaviour that had the repercussion of his father not liking him. This was not the same I believe as when his father criticised him and the son explained to him his actions, to justify his behaviour or thoughts. The passive person in any relationship may feel the need to justify or explain their actions, reasoning or decisions, and then look to the other for their agreement. The assertive person may disclose their reasons for a decision but it not disclosed looking for agreement or acknowledgement, that is to say, the assertive person's sense of worth or value of their self is not affected if the person agrees or disagrees with them. The man above lived so as to please his father, and the impasse for him would be to *not please* his father, such would be the move from *me* the self-concept to the *not me* as the person moved towards the impasse into the explosive layer.

Going back to the man who tried to live up to the expectation of his critical father, I often wonder if the use of drugs had different reasons, was it to secretly rebel against his rules as to how to be a person (such as the good boy who secretly behaves naughtily when his parents aren't looking) or as a temporary release from the pressure to live to what his father wanted him to be, or to enable him to burn the candle at both ends so as to maintain his lifestyle and therefore his father's approval. I was aware that this man had a type of dual existence, on one side was this dutiful son trying the best he could so his father would acknowledge him, and on the other was a person who would associate with people who were involved in the drug lifestyle. I wonder if both sides to this man were artificial, that they were the repercussions of adjusting to his life, and how he felt he had to hide this secret side. The message as well to this person was *don't be you, be the way I want you to be* as the son put on a face to his father that meant being the good husband, the good dad, the provider to his family and to feel the pressure to have a career. If as a creative adjustment the person has learnt to hide what he sees as undesirable aspects of his self (which may evoke feelings of shame) then it may mean that there is a self that is inauthentic, as the person struggles to live behind a role, or a false self. Is this the consequence of developing a belief of your self that is only of worth if you fulfil the demands, rules or expectations of another person? If the person's self-esteem or confidence is not based on their self, but on how others see them, and this creates its own pressure, to live up to this image, or this false self.

For this person it was easier, or less anxiety producing to fit in to what other people wanted him to be, rather than to risk not being accepted by significant people, be that a partner, a manager or a parent. The person conforms to another person's rules as to how to be a person (an introjection) and creatively adjusts to these rules.

The role such as *the good boy (or girl)* can have many implications, as the term *good* isn't necessarily something that is positive or beneficial, but by something that is valued or appreciated within the subjective framework. If a person is born in deprived circumstances he may believe that it is *good* to be able to be able to fight or to swear or shout to be heard, another person may believe that it is *good* (within in the values of a particular group or family) to not work, or to become part of a particular profession, such as belonging to a family of teachers. With myself I creatively adjusted to believe that good meant to be strong and protective, and also to never lie and to do the right thing. I also believed that it was important to be a good role model to my younger siblings. Was I always this way? Not always as sometimes I wasn't that strong and made some mistakes, I even told a lie or two to protect some of my friends who were in trouble. I rationalised this though as I made excuses as to why I should be able to lie (as a justification to go against my introjected values) and to be sometimes be weak. If was as if I had the image of the person I was, and I had to give an excuse, or to keep it secret if I couldn't live up this.

As I have touched on these areas a few times in this book I would like to give a brief explanation as to how a person may resist contact, or resist awareness. I hasten to add though that the person isn't resisting with an awareness they are resisting, but the means of resistance has the purpose of enabling or supporting the self-concept. There is a difference between *your truth* and *the truth* as the person sees their world from their own truth. If the person's truth is that they are important and that their needs come first then anger, bitterness or resentment may be a consequence if this do not happen. The person may then adjust from this position and becoming resentful towards the inequalities of life which may become a goal, as the person rationalises their own need that isn't being met, and may therefore project this onto the world or to a cause.

There are different ways in which a person may resist anything that would challenge their self-concept, or to keep this possibility outside of their awareness.

The following is a collection of what I see as resistance or forms of creative adjustment, these are a collection of Psychoanalytic Defence Mechanisms, my own thoughts, areas of CBT and aspects of Joseph Zinker's Contact Cycle.

- **Desensitisation**

In this area of resistance the person may desensitise their self from bodily emotions. The person who is lonely may be cut off from their feelings because experiencing their loneliness may be too difficult for that person. This process of creative adjustment may mean that this is necessary for the person to be able to exist. The person who is being bullied may desensitise their self from the feelings that are being evoked. The woman who has been emotionally abused in a damaging relationship may desensitise her self from the feelings of anger and resentment, as she has the belief that this is all that she is worthy of. The person who has the image of their self as being kind and caring may have desensitised their self to the opposing polarity feelings of selfishness, and deny that they are sometimes this way. This may then be projected onto another person, a group or an organisation. As an introjection the process of desensitisation may emerge if the child has developed in a household where for example they are treated as special and to not consider others may desensitise their self from the feelings of empathy, compassion or sympathy. The sales person who has a target to meet may desensitise their self in that they are using the person to achieve that target, and from this they are treating the person as an object. Through the process of creative adjustment the person may become desensitised to feeling some feelings, but to be able to feel other feelings, the may be able to feel sympathy for one person, but be unable to feel the same feelings for another person, such as for example the person who may be able to feel feelings of sorrow for a person of their own ethnicity, religion or sexual identity but are resistant to feeling the same feelings of someone else who may be an object for blame or anger. Also, if the person has had a difficult childhood from a negligent parent who may creatively adjust from this and if they regularly went without meals the person may desensitise their self from the feelings of hunger. If the child integrates this into their self-concept they may not know or only vaguely aware when they are hungry.

- **Deflection**

The purpose of deflection is to turn away from direct contact with a person, experience or feeling. The person who has integrated into their self-concept that they are unworthy may deflect any attention of care from another person (as they may believe that are not worthy of this) The person who feels they are superior to others may deflect any attention that may portray them as weak. The person who wishes to avoid a certain topic may deflect the focus of the conversation (a manipulation of the environment) onto a more agreeable or less sensitive area or subject. The person who has a resistance to speaking (perhaps through series of creative adjustments) may have a preference for listening, and as such deflects the meeting with another person to one in which they can listen. The person with the self-concept may deflect anything that challenges this.

- **Projection**

The purpose of projection may be as a way of disowning parts of one's self onto others, or to project parts of his self onto other people or situations. The person whose self-concept has developed to only feel negativity in situations may project the opposing polarity onto others. The person who is truthful and honest may project this onto others and believe that they also have the same value. The person who i mentioned previously and thought he could walk through a dangerous part of town may have been projecting his values onto others, and as such he would be safe. The person who has a belief that they must be good may project the opposing polarity onto others (that other people can be bad) as well as a person projecting their beliefs onto another, as with the person who is having extra-marital affairs and believing his partner is doing the same. A person may also project their own abilities onto another person, believing that another can do the same, the person who is sexually attracted to the other may project this onto the other and believe that the person is attracted to them, they may interpret or distort any behaviour to reinforce this belief. Also, if the person has a poor self-esteem or negative self thoughts they may project this onto the other, and interpret any behaviour from the other to also reinforce their own belief about their self. Another aspect of projection is when a person may *see* people as difficult to get on with as a reason not to develop relationships, however it may actually be their own self that is difficult and people may avoid developing any type of relationship with that person. It is easier to see the problem as being the other person that to take responsibility for their own self. The person who wants to deceive of cheat others may be looking for the same in the motivations of other people. Projection in the person who is passive and avoids being aggressive may place this onto another, they may become the victim or be helpless to entice the other person to become aggressive for them instead, such as a person who because of their own self-belief they cannot be take a stand against an abusive partner, so they tell another person their story, who stands up for them instead (manipulation of the environment) and may feel quite justified in feeling aggressive or assertive towards the controlling partner. The person though merely serves as an object for a projection of what cannot be felt or acknowledged in the other person.

- **Introjection**

Although chapter one covers introjection this is also a means of resistance as it may be easier, more preferable or through a series of creative adjustments to follow an introjection, and to actively seek an introjection from their environment. If the person has integrated into their self-concept the belief that they cannot make their own decisions or feel that they do not have the ability to make a choice they may then seek out an introjection, such as asking a person what they think they should do, if the person encounters a problem or issue in which they must make a decision this would be tantamount to touching the impasse and anxiety may ensue at this. By seeking an introjection as to how to be a person, the person is *following the herd* as independent thought and actions may be alien to that person. The *shoulds* are alive in this area of resistance, as the person seeking an introjection may only be focused on what they *should* do in any situation, such as what they should wear, what job they should have, what to find attractive in a partner or what type of car to drive. Some people live their whole life through the belief of how they *should* be, or creatively adjust to a position in their life where they feel they have to accept introjections, such as with a person who enters into a relationship that is abusive and her self-esteem is diminished, as she relies on the other person to tell her what to do. In the work environment the person who is the employee and works in a disciplined job may ask a superior what they should do before any decisions are made. If the person works in a job in which they have a manager who directs others through giving orders, this style of management may have the effect that his subordinates do not think for themselves, and rely on their ordering manager to tell them what to do (an introjection)

- **Retroflection**

Retroflection is a process in which the individual turns back against himself what he would like to do to someone else, or he does to himself what he would like someone else to do to him. If the person has a self-concept in which they are passive or submissive and want to criticise someone else but as they feel they are not justified in doing so then this is not possibly and so may be turned around towards their self, resulting in becoming self-critical. If a person has introjected the idea that they are of less value that another person, and their worth as a person depends on how others view them, or their self-concept is based on the affection or approval of another then if they do express feelings of frustration and resentment towards the other then it would jeopardise their own sense of worth, so these feelings (if they are not displaced, suppressed, denied, rationalised or avoided) are turned inward (if they view their self as less important) and they become their own critic, with the outcome that they resent their self. If the person wants to harm someone else, or feels that his is only deserving of a person's punishment (from many introjections) then this may be retroflected and instead it becomes self-harm. This self-harm may become a physical harm, a constant self-judging attitude or the person may harm their self through the use of drugs, alcohol or behaviour that is dangerous, it may also mean that they make relationships or careers fail as they commit to being self-destructive.

The person who believes that other people are cruel and insensitive, and feels that he is justified in avoiding or distancing himself from other people may begin to feel the lack of a warm touch or soft words, and this may be retroflected back towards himself, he may indulge in a kind of self -love as he pampers his self, this self-love is not a self-care that is based on his own belief that he is worthy of this, but on the belief that he cannot access this from other people and so he must love himself. The person who becomes highly adept at looking after himself, fixing problems and rarely asks people for help may be retroflecting his desire for other people to support him and look after him, but if his beliefs are such that people cannot be trusted, he may become his own source of support. If this becomes it own introjection this person may creatively adjust to this and being their own source of support can become part of their self-concept. As I walk down the street I can sometimes hear people walking past me talking to themselves, and I do wonder to myself if this is another form of retroflection, the person want to speak to someone else, but because of their own beliefs this may be difficult and so they resort to a kind of self support and begin talking to their self. The person who is lonely but feels the anxiety of talking to others may use this form of self talk to reduce the feelings of loneliness.

- **Rumination**

I have found that this type of resistance may be found in a person who has a *fixed* way of seeing the world and hangs on to an event because of the benefits it brings to the person. The person who wishes to feel justified in feeling angry towards another person may *hang onto* one incident to create this feeling, they may discount or discard anything that would challenge this, so as to maintain their view. For example a child who feels that their parent has never offered them support may ruminate on a single incident that from their perspective the parent did not support them, and anything the parent does to apologise or explain will be ignored, as it is a reason for the child (in their mind) to become angry or to withdraw from the parent. The child who has become selfish and self-centred may view any action in which they do not get what they want as their parent not supporting them, they may become stuck in this belief (from an introjection that people *must* do what I want them to) and resent the parent for the single time they did not fulfil the child's demands. I have seen people who have become stuck and ruminate on an incident for years, and I do wonder that by becoming fixed in a certain belief may provide a justification to alienate their self or to provide an object to resent. For example a person who is involved in a bad relationship may ruminate on the belief that his partner never loved him (through the distortion of events) and as such keeps his distance from any new relationship. By doing so he does not risk entering a relationship again. Rumination can also be a means in which the person can fulfil a need, so if a person has a need to be pessimistic or negative, he may look upon a single occurrence repeatedly to have this belief or view. Rumination then can become a rationalisation, a deflection or a displacement to avoid feeling feelings of maturity, responsibility or forgiveness. These may create anxiety so the creative adjustment may be to manipulate their self or environment to avoid this, and instead to hook onto feelings or anger, resentment or negativity depending on the need being fulfilled.

- **Transference**

Put simply. Transference is the passing on of an emotion, value, feeling, emotion, fear, attitude, belief or response from one person to another person or object, so the feelings you feel towards one person may be transferred onto a person, object or group.
I first became aware of this when I felt that I was being protective towards younger women than myself, and realised that I was it was the transference of the protective feelings I had felt towards my younger sister growing up, in this it became a monological relationship as I was not seeing the younger woman as a unique person, but transferred on her the protective feelings I had towards my younger sister. From a different perspective and

with respect to field theory there was also the possibility that I transferred these feelings onto younger women, so it would enable me to become protective, which would fulfil the need on my self-concept as I had the integral belief that as a person I *should* be protective of others.

Another example would be the person who resents his parents as they are an authority figure, and transfers this onto other people who are in an authoritative position. Transference can be positive or negative on whether the person develops good or hostile feelings towards the person, so if a woman has endured an emotionally abusive relationship she may project those hostile thoughts and beliefs onto all men, even if the man is not guilty of any wrong-doing.

Transference may be a part of the self-concept if the person has a role or a need to be fulfilled they may transfer thoughts, beliefs and feelings onto others, so the person who *sees* his self as a dad may project the image of his daughter onto others so that he can have a parental role with them. In that I believe this indicates a manipulation of the environment, the other person serves to fulfil a need in the person.

Transference may be an indicator of a fixed way of relating to others from the person's past from a creative adjustment or introjection which are transferred onto a new situation or person. The man who is fairly well adjusted and has a healthy self-concept may find himself being quiet and sullen when he encounters a man who reminds him of his dominant father, as he is transferring the image of his father onto this man he may regress back to that difficult time, and may sweat, stammer, be lost for words and hesitant, his heart beat may rise and he may look for an exit. For that moment his transference took him back to his earlier traumatic years. Transference may originate in a long forgotten creative adjustment that becomes alive if the right conditions are present, so if another person gets angry at them, or conversely nice and considerate it may evoke the same feelings that were present as a small child.

As the nature of transference is to transfer thoughts, beliefs and feelings onto a person this has the meaning I believe that it is monological, the person is not seen as a unique individual but as an object to place those thoughts and beliefs onto. As an example on a previous course I had enrolled on one of the other students was ambivalent to being in the same study group as myself, as she felt that I was intimidating. It later transpired that I had reminded her of her grandfather who was a very authoritative man because I had the same job, and as such she transferred all those feelings she had of him then onto me. By her monological instead of dialogical view she was treating me as a blank canvas so she could paint her feelings and beliefs of her grandfather onto me, and that is I believe monological. Transference occurs in many areas of a person's life, a person who I once knew who was very kind and supportive had a bald head I am often more friendly and open to people who also have a bald head, it is the same with people who have a Scottish accent as I have fond memories of Scottish people in my home country, so if I meet a Scottish person all the thoughts and feelings I have are transferred onto that person, this is still monological as I am missing the person and putting onto him the thoughts I had of all the friendly Scottish people I had met as a child. Although this may be seen as positive, it may be a form of prejudice, as I am pre-judging him on my previous experiences, so if my experiences of Scottish people were unsavoury or filled with anger I may transfer these feelings onto a person instead, through creative adjustment or an introjection. If these thought are integrated into my self-concept then I may behave in a discriminatory manner towards these people.

- **Confluence**

Confluence is when *me* becomes a *we.* The person who is in confluence leads to a loss of their own self. Confluence is the lack of separation between their self and the other. The person may drift from relationship to relationship as there is an anxiety if they are alone (based on their own self-beliefs) and so prefers to be part of a relationship. Abusive partners may try to create a confluence with their abused partner, to create this dependency. The abusive partner may initially appear to be helpful, offering to take over the *responsibility* of paying the bills and managing the house. The purpose being is so to diminish the confidence of the other and to create an atmosphere of dependency, the abused person feels they need the other as their own self-confidence has eroded to an extent that they now feel they *need* their abusive partner. The person who fears being alone may develop an strong belief in a religion or become part of a group. There may be little distinction between who they are as a person and the group or religion then belong to, the person may become enveloped by the beliefs and the values of the other, which can also be an introjection and so a purpose for creative adjustment. A person may also become confluent with their role or career, and this may be true of what has been considered vocational occupations such a member of the church, a police officer, counsellor, nurse or firefighter. If the person integrates all the values of what it means to in that role and sees little differentiation between their self and their occupation, then it may be a sign of a confluent relationship, that it easier to identify their self with as a role rather than as a unique individual. This may become an existential crisis if the person (who has become part of something to give a meaning and purpose to their life) suddenly becomes made redundant or retires. The abused wife may resist becoming single (and justify or rationalise her reasons for staying with her abusive partner) for the fear of being a *me* again.

Confluent relationships have an unequal aspect to them, just as with the person who lives to follow the rules of a religion, it is the religion who is in charge and the person may feel feelings of guilt or shame if they cannot follow the requirements or what it means to follow that religion. The abused housewife who lives within the rules of the abusive partner may face the consequences if she becomes more confident and plans to enrol at a college for example, this may be faced by a retribution, emotional manipulation or punishment by her partner. The fear or the anxiety of being alone, or the fear of being mature, independent and self-supportive may mean that a person seeks out a confluent relationship. It may mean to touch the impasse if they were mature and independent and so seeks out another person or group to avoid this, as a means of avoidance.

The opposing side of the confluent relationship is the person has a *need* to be in control then they may meet another to whom this can be fulfilled, this may be met in relationships where one *helps* the other, the person has no intention of helping the person so they can overcome their problems, but to help them into helplessness, and in that way they always have a role to play, always being there to pick the person up if they fail or encounter a problem, and to rescue them.

- **Denial**

In this form of resistance the person may actively deny the thought or feeling, the child who lives with a controlling parent may deny that such dominance takes place, then as a creative adjustment the child may disassociate their self from their feelings, so that they are not aware of this from the parent, the purpose of this denial be to ignore the feelings of anxiety and the reality that they are being controlled. The wife who is in denial that her husband is having an affair and ignore all the signs may be in fear or feel the feelings of anxiety of what would happen if the truth became apparent, that she would have to support her self and to forge a life alone without the comforts that her lifestyle may offer. If she has a traditional marriage in which her partner earns substantially more then it may mean that if she did become aware of his infidelity and they separated then because of her lower income she may have to relocate to a less desirable area and lower living conditions. The same may be for the person who is in denial that his marriage is over but he stays in the relationship just for access to his children, he may make himself believe that he has feelings for his partner, but is it just an excuse to stay in that relationship. The person may creatively adjust to this also by the way they *see* their relationship, and to block the awareness of this. If a person does make the suggestion, then just as with the young child and the controlling parent it will be simply denied. The parent who is dominating and emotionally abusing his wife and children may be in denial at this, choosing to see the world from his own distorted view, that instead of controlling his family he is actually protecting them. If a child who has seen his mother and father argue and fight, then introjects this as the way of being with his own partner when he gets older may encounter parents who are in denial that they have influenced their child in such as way. Denial then may derive from the avoidance of awareness, maturity and responsibility.

- **Suppression**

The person may suppress their thoughts and feelings if it does not fit their self-concept, or they may creatively adjust to this position. The person may repress or suppress their criticism of others, or the person who has a *need* to win the approval of others may suppress any emotions, or the expression of those emotions that are not valued, so if a parent usually shouts and screams (displaying aggression) to his family he may avoid disclosing this to people as it would risk losing their affection or approval. A man who is normally angry or negative in his everyday life may suppress this when he knows his wife is around, as he is aware that being this way would risk his relationship

The person who has a need to be liked by others may suppress their feelings of hostility towards a person or in a situation, this person is

169

manipulating their self to win the approval or the affection of the other, and is that is presenting a false self. These emotions are still there within the person and may be expressed to a person or thing that does not hold the same value, for example the husband who has a need to be liked, or to win the affection of others may put on a smiling face and tell jokes to others (who may believe this and think that he a great guy) however, when he returns home he may release this hostility and anger towards his wife (a real self to his wife and a false self to the people he wants to impress) The person may have creatively adjusted to this position, to hold back parts of their self that are not approved of by others. The person who seeks this approval of others may suppress other aspects of their self, to be accepted. The person who is devoutly religious may not disclose this to his *friends* if he knows that they will may dislike him if he talks about his faith, the child who is highly capable in a certain field such as art or poetry may suppress this to be able to fit in to his family and their values (if his family have the idea that men in that family should work in a manual job) The woman who is highly intelligent and can easily find the solution to problems or issues may restrict this if she is in the company of a person who has the need to be in charge and has some sort of authority over her, such as her employer. She may therefore play stupid so as not to challenge him. In both these examples the person hides parts of their self, and if this becomes an introjection such as *don't be you* the person may creatively adjust to this, and disown feelings or attributes in the search for affection or approval.

- **Reaction Formation**

Reaction Formation is when a person turns the feeling around to be the opposite and the person may rationalise this as a belief. If the person has a need to be liked or to win the approval or the affection of the other, even though the other may be a dominant bully the person may believe that are great and they are great friends, the person may distort, dismiss or discount anything to the contrary. A child who has been involved in an abusive relationship with their parents may be adamant that their parents are the best and that they have never been mistreated, though the evidence would suggest the opposite.

- **Displacement**

Displacement is a process in which the person is aware of the feeling that is present within them but is redirected to someone or something else. For example the employee who feels hostility or anger towards his own manager may realise that if he did express this to him his own career would be in jeopardy, and so this build-up of emotion is displaced to his partner. The term "kicking the cat" originates from this, the person who cannot express his feelings to a person who he views as more important may take it out on people he views as less important. In this example, there is a close link to suppression and feelings or behaviour is being held back or expressed, depending on the value of the person. This is also an example of seeing the other as an object, or being monological, and also an example of aggressiveness. The person is not looking to the other as a unique individual in an assertive or dialogical manner but as an object to express these feelings onto. Displacement may also be a reason for common vandalism or cruelty to animals, as the person *acts out* on unexpressed emotions towards something or someone that is less important. Being less important is not a requisite though for displacement as the person who has an issue or problem with a person who is an authority figure, such as a police officer may displace this onto another subjective authority figure such as a parent or official. The person is aware that hostile action taken against a police officer may result in being arrested, but the same expression towards another who they view as being an authority figure may be less risky, or carry less of a penalty.

- **Rationalisation**

This form of resistance is to arrive at a conclusion that justifies the situation, and to give meaning to their own thoughts, self-concept or beliefs. The child who feels that their parent is at fault and has a desire to be angry at them they may *see* the situation in such a way that gives this a purpose. If the parent gets them a gift they are trying to buy them, if the parent becomes divorced and meets another person then they are abandoning them, if the parent shows concern for the child then they are being intrusive or bossy, if the child is told that they have to eat their dinner then the parent is mean. No matter what the parent says the child distorts the meaning and rationalises to ascribe their own meaning. The person who rationalises may also excuse the behaviour of the other, the abused person may rationalise and say that their partner is just trying to protect or look after them, though this may be from a passive position in which the other superior. The person who is in the other position, the superior position in that relationship may rationalise their own actions, they will not be saying that they are an abuser, a controller or a dominator of their partner but rather with try to *see* it that their behaviour is justified, they may distort information to protect their self-concept and that they are only looking after their family. The person may blame the other to be able to rationalise their own behaviour, and in that is a lack of responsibility for their own actions, such as when a person says "you made me do it." The person may also creatively adjust to be able to see the world in a way that justifies their actions or beliefs, or, just as with the other forms of resistance the person may creatively adjust to block emotions or thoughts.

- **Intellectualisation**

Intellectualisation is similar to another form of resistance called Isolation of Affect (in which the person safely thinks the feeling) and is a form or rationalisation, the person who lives in their head may become analytical and block off their emotions, or just as with the Buddhist lady from a previous chapter who used quotes to communicate with others used this form to create a distance from contact. I have noticed that some professionals seem to talk in a type of official speak when in relation to others that they are working with, and may have developed well used phrases to communicate with others. There is no emotion that drive the words is spoken in a bland emotionless way. The person who distances their self from their emotions may have an array of jokes, quotes or sayings that create a distance from unpleasant emotions, and may be common place in occupations in which a person regularly works in a environment where they are open to seeing people in distress or pain. Intellectualisation may be formed as a creative adjustment to protect the emotional health of such as person, however if we apply field theory onto this then the person who has become emotionally blocked in one area of their life may have repercussions in another, for example the nurse who becomes emotionally hard when working in a hospital and seeing people in distress may become this way with her family if this creative adjustment

172

is outside her awareness.

- **Distortion**

I liken distortion to be a kind of cherry picking of information and may be closely likened or associated with any of the other forms of resistance, for example the person may only *see* some of the available facts to reach a distorted conclusion, the person who wants to see the world a certain way may highlight some areas and disregard others to fulfil a need. The person who is racist and thinks immigrants to leave the country may distort information to justify their beliefs. The father who wants to turn his children against their mother may tell them a distorted story in which the mother left the family home and doesn't care about her children, when in reality the mother fled from an abusive relationship and the father is trying to alienate the mother by telling the children this distorted story. This then becomes an introjection that may be swallowed whole and not questioned by the children, and when the mother calls and tries to see her children, this is also distorted with the message "see kids she is only calling you and can't be bothered to come to the house" when in fact the woman is in fear of seeing her ex-husband again. Distortion can have many faces and purposes, but can be used to fulfil a need, to give a meaning to the self-concept (the person who sees their self to be weak and helpless may distort anything that would challenge their own beliefs) or to manipulate the environment. The person who is angry at his parent may distort the parent's concern and love and accuse them of being bossy and controlling. The child though may be trying to live more independently but, because of the creative adjustments in their life they may be unable to be assertive to their parent, and instead becomes passive aggressive, to try to create a distance from the parent. The person who is a staunch feminist may distort information to give that self meaning, the person who feels that she is hated by other people will distort how she sees and hears to be able to believe that this is real. Distortion can mean seeing a situation from a different perspective, for example the person is not trying to help them, they are trying to coerce them, the person isn't just being friendly, he is trying to get the person to trust them and then he will deceive them, and distortion them serves to give a purpose for isolation or solitude. The person who is passive and have a fear of being aggressive or assertive may distort any situation so they do not have to become assertive or aggressive.

If a man shouts at them they may immediately give an excuse, or take responsibility for the situation, in this it is much like the other form of resistance, rationalisation. A person may distort the meaning of words to reach the desired outcome, the person who is angry at the other will interpret any information presented and twist that to be able to hate the other, the person who wants her sister to end her relationship with her new boyfriend will distort any information she has about this man to try to convince her that she should leave him. The person who distorts the world around them to satisfy a desire or need, may discount, disregard, deny, lie or interpret events to make this possible. It may also be a way from a person to give an excuse or justification for their behaviour. If a person who is depressed and this is part of their self-concept may interpret anything, or distort anything to make this possible, they may walk through their place of work with their head down and say nothing, their contact functions may give the message *stay away from me* and then, when people stop talking to him he will feel justified in thinking that no-one wants to talk to him, and feel down because of this denying that their own actions have caused people to avoid them and distort, or interpret the actions of other people to be able to feel depressed. The same interpretation may be made for the man who distorts anything a woman says to him as being sexually suggestive (this would also be projecting his own sexual desires onto the woman) if she says hello to him with a smile this is distorted into "she wants me" if she laughs when they speak he may think that she is flirting with him. As said before if anything that challenges this happens he will discount it, deny, dismiss or disregard it.

- **Regression**

Regression has be used to explain when a person reverts back to a usually immature behaviour, however from a self-concept perspective I have the idea that it indicates that the self-image or the self-concept is but a thin veneer that person presents to other people, I remember reading once a few years ago the story of some charity workers who after completing a vocational helping course were put in the field to help people in need, they all had the belief that they could overcome any problem and were confident that they had the skills to provide a resolution to any issue they came across. Out in the field though it was different from what they were expecting and they found the experience very demanding. They all complained to the charity manager saying that the tutor of the course had not prepared them for what was to be expected when on placement, but the manager was aware that they did not seem like the confident and self-assured people who believed they could overcome anything, but immature children who were attacking their tutor and suggesting that he was at fault. In actual fact the course tutor has told them of all the dangers and risks of their placement, but as the people on the course thought that they could handle any problem and ignored his advice and guidance, then when they realised that were unable to rise to the challenges of working in that charity, they proceeded to blame the course tutor in a whining and pleading manner to the charity manager, rather than consider that it was their own beliefs and expectations about their self (their self-image and self-concept) that was challenged. I have had a similar experience in have noticed that some people who have the idea of their self as being physically fit may regress back to an immature state if this image cannot be met, previously they may have rationalised or distorted how they saw the world, then when *their truth is not the truth* occurs then the person became immature and started to blame other people, their equipment or that they were feeling under the weather as a viable reason why they could not for example run in a competitive race. I think when a person can be authentic then the need for a self-image is no longer as necessary so regression is less likely due to their own acceptance of who they are and are less reliant on the approval of others, however when a person does have a self-image or self-concept and this is put to the test or confronted then the person may regress. This is different from the person who can own both polarities, to be mature and immature, to be responsible and irresponsible, and to be passive is some situations, assertive in others and aggressive if needed.

Imagine a person who believes himself to be confident, popular and outgoing, and has his props to support this, by having a pretty woman so he looks the part to others. His partner starts to take driving lessons and then he begins to feel the pangs of anxiety, knowing that as she has passed her test she will have more freedom and won't be as reliant on him, of course he has encouraged reliance so he can keep her close. He starts to distort her driving skills as he begins to be more critical and judging, not in a truthful sense, but in a manipulative manner, the purpose being to dissuade her from continuing to take driving lessons. If he is successful and she stops then his anxiety (at the loss of his self-concept) will subside, but the effect of this will be his partner who may have less self-confidence or belief in her self. If she challenges him he may rationalise and say that he is only looking out for her, that there are lots of bad drivers on the road and he feels protective with her. This is just another manipulation though and only serves as an excuse or smokescreen for his ulterior motive.

The self-concept then is a thin veneer, a camouflage or an image presented to other people, and this person regresses to any earlier immature state upon feeling uncomfortably when feeling the feelings of anxiety, in this person it is manipulation, though in another it may be anger.

- **Sublimation**

Sublimation is a form of resistance in which the person redirects the feeling into a productive activity and may be similar to other forms of resistance such as displacement or deflection.

I say this that with regards to the person's own self-image or self-concept it may be more preferable to redirect their energy or feelings towards something else, because of their own thoughts or beliefs about their self in relation to the other. The young person who has feelings of anger directed to his negligent parents may focus this attention onto sports, he may take up boxing to focus this anger there instead. If he were able to be assertive he may voice his concerns to his parents, and engage in dialogue with them and to find hopefully a resolution. His own beliefs about his self and his parents may mean that this is not an option and so he feels he has to accept his lot in life and focus this anger or resentment elsewhere. As the person always has the capacity to creatively adjust he may find that he has a talent or aptitude for the boxing and this may form part of his own self-image, what got him involved in boxing initially though was the his situation and the inability (outside his awareness) to influence his environment, that is to say to feel that he can talk to his parents about his thoughts and feelings. There are many books written by authors who have lived in oppressive regimes and had little opportunity to change this by standing against the regime, and so allow these feelings to be directed towards writing, poetry, art and other forms of expression. The term regime is situational and may also include living in an oppressive family or in one's own situation that is confining. Sublimation, like distortion, displacement or rationalisation is another form of avoidance, in that the person avoids the presenting issues or feelings for a variety of reasons and instead focuses their energy towards someone or something else. Sublimation may also have the purpose maintaining a rigidity in their self-concept, for example the person who is living in an dominant relationship may have (creatively adjusted) feelings of low self-worth, and living in that relationship sustains this belief, if the person became more assertive this would challenge their own idea of who they are, so instead the feelings are deflected somewhere else, but that does not facilitate change of growth, such as, if the person enrolled on an assertiveness course then things in that relationship may change, and this would mean that how they viewed their self would also be brought into focus, but if the person redirected their attention towards writing a journal or painting then their situation can remain the same, and of course this would continue to sustain their own self-concept of being of low self-worth and not capable.

- **Avoidance**

Avoidance has many faces and implications for the self-concept, with the polarities of the person who identifies with one polarity may avoid situations in which the other side will be evoked, the person who sees their self as happy, positive and cheerful may avoid any situation in which the opposite is presented, they may see the world as being safe and secure (through their projection of their own idea that they need to be safe and secure) and distort anything that would impact on this belief. The person who has the need to be positive and happy when encountering a person who has recently gone through a crisis may cherry-pick what they hear to only focus on the positives, or to distort or deflect what the other is saying to be able to avoid talking about the other person and the crisis they are going through, they may bring up topics to further deflect from the person, but remain with the façade, such as "oh, that's too bad you've been through that horrible divorce, but, where are you going on holiday this year?" the person may seem like they are interested and listening, but it only for the purpose of picking any areas to focus on the positive, which is part of how they see their self. The formation of their self-concept though means that the person *has* to be positive, for the fear of what being negative means (which would mean touching the impasse or the implosive layer) Interestingly, the person who has the opposite need, that they are negative and have a need to see the world through those eyes, may only focus on the parts of what a person is saying to be able to be negative and

177

pessimistic. There may also be some rationalisation and denial in the person who has to be positive, as they may justify to their self that they are "just trying to cheer the person up" though this is done because of the avoidance of drawing attention to the negative parts of the person and what they have been going through.

The person who is normally aggressive in relation to other people may avoid any situation in which they would have to be passive, the woman who has a hatred of men may avoid any situation in which this would be questioned, and so they both stay in their own world where their beliefs have a meaning. The person who sits and plays his games console may be avoiding responsibility, the person who looks blankly at his smart phone may be avoiding having meaningful relationships. Just as the person who spends much of the time on social media may be avoiding close relationships with the people around them.

If we look at the symbol again;

The person may avoid anything that is not part of their self-concept. (Section two) If it is part of the person's creative adjustment to talk in a low droning voice (the purpose outside their awareness being to not attract other's attention, or to bore other people) then they may avoid any situation in which they would talk in different manner. The same could be said for any other aspect of the contact functions, areas of assertion or polarities. There may also be the avoidance of responsibility or maturity, that the person does not accept responsibility for their own actions or the repercussions of their behaviour. It is easier then to push this responsibility onto someone or something else, the mother can feel that she can have a large number of children, but it is the government's responsibility to take care of them, or the person who blames their parent for their behaviour. The person who does not wish to accept responsibility for their own actions may distort the stories they tell to attribute the blame onto someone else. I remember once a young man telling his friends a distorted story so that all the blame for his actions were attributed to his parents, the young man then did not have to accept responsibility for his actions, and his friends *bought into* his story (a manipulation of the environment) and also blamed his parents. The same can be said for maturity, the person who resists being mature may become involved in a relationship with a person who will carry this burden, she can continue to be immature and not make decisions, while her partner takes on this responsibility. The person who does not wish to be mature may alter how they see the world, or come to the belief that there is nothing they can do, and through this self-justification the person can reasonably say that since they cannot influence people around them (perhaps rationalised after a bad experience) so then they can give up and only look after themselves. The mature person takes ownership of their life and takes a responsibility for their own actions on other people, as well as to their self, the mature person is aware of the choices they make. The person who avoids responsibility may become detached and not take anything seriously they may say "i don't care about anything" to show what appears to be a sign of defiance, but it that is just a denial and the fear to say "i care about something" because if a person can say this, then so is the responsibility and the choice to do something about it. The person who says that they do not care, as well as not taking anything seriously withdraws from not becoming emotionally attached or responsible and may become detached from others. This may be a creative adjustment, as the purpose of avoidance may be to not be hurt, or to not to be let down, or to be selfish or self-centred and therefore to not have a concern for others.

- **Low Frustration Tolerance**

This final area of resistance is something that I have considered for some time, as I have observed that some people have an aversion to tolerating feelings of anxiety, frustration or pain if their need is not being met. The person with the gambling addiction may feel that they are unable to stop, not because they cannot, but because they will not, and find it difficult to manage the feelings of anxiety when the need is not fulfilled. The person *must* fulfil the need (for example to gamble) for the feelings of anxiety or frustration to subside or dissipate, the feelings and sensations associated when the need is not being met may be emotional or physical. The person is unable or unwilling to endure the anxiety of the short term for the benefits of the long term, and as a rationalisation they may accept that situation, as it is easier to say to one's self "this is just the way I am" and accept that this is just the way it is for them. I remember recently when out walking the person I was with had a low frustration to the feelings of thirst, and went from being relatively relaxed to almost frantic as he asked again and again where the nearest shop was to be able to buy some water. He seemed to have a low frustration to being thirsty and needed immediate relief, instead of being able to tolerate these feelings for a while.

From the view of the self-concept I think that some people can become (for want of a better word) addicted to their self-concept or self-image and fight to maintain it. The abusive husband has his needs met by manipulating his environment so that he is in charge, for example if he and his wife are socialising it may be him that does most of the talking, with his wife nodding in agreement. It would be intolerable or frustrating for him then if the roles were reversed and it was his wife who was the centre of attention and he was on the sidelines nodding in agreement and feeling that he was unable to speak. The husband then, upon touching his impasse or entering the implosive layer would be feeling the feelings of anxiety, as it is *need* (much like the *need* of the gambler) to fulfil his view of himself. The belief of the introjection that this need is derived from may be something like *I am special* or *I have to be noticed*, and the person creatively adjusts to fulfil this. Of course the other side of this coin if I continue with the same example would be the wife, if she has creatively adjusted to live in that abusive relationship then she may have indeed have a poor self-worth, which she has integrated into her view of her self, and as such she may have a low tolerance to becoming the centre of attention. This low frustration tolerance is an indicator when the person journeys from the *me* to the *not me* and may have many implications. Imagine the person who has a need to be independent and in control, the purpose being not to be self-supportive and to be self-sufficient, but from the avoidance of asking people for help as this produces feelings of anxiety. He may have a low frustration to the feelings of anxiety if he encounters a problem that he cannot solve such as a medical problem in which he must visit a doctor. He may ruminate for while or live in denial, he may creatively adjust to desensitise his self from the feelings of pain as the medical issue gets worse until he eventually succumbs and goes to the doctor. As he is very independent he may gain a considerable amount of knowledge so he can maintain he self-concept and talk to the doctor as an equal, and not as an (as he sees it) inferior person asking for help.

The same may be said of a person who wants to be seen as ill, as this means that they are taken care of by other people, if they are convincing they can live this way for many years and convince family members, doctors and other officials so they can remain this way. They may be avoiding responsibility and the feelings of anxiety may occur any time they are asked to take control of their own life, the person may have a low frustration tolerance to taking responsibility for their own life and forging their own path. There may be a manipulation of the environment as they convince others of their own self-image, but also a manipulation of their self as they adapt the way they talk, dress and other ways of interacting with others to fulfil this need. The person may be in the position of *I am sick and want to get help, but I don't want to get better.* Getting better means taking responsibility (which would mean touching the impasse or those feeling of low frustration tolerance) so the person may continually relapse, which would also have the purpose of fulfilling the need to be sick, that they may feel down or withdrawn as they have relapsed again. The opposite of low frustration tolerance is high frustration tolerance, and the person may have creatively adjusted to endure a lot of anxiety or frustration, especially is part of an introjection. As I have said previously, as I lived in a deprived area when growing up desensitised myself to the feelings of cold, so much so that in my later years I was reluctant to installing central heating at my house, as I rarely felt the cold. I had desensitised myself in this way, and when going to work, which had heating I would start to sweat as it seemed so hot in that building, it was not that it was that warm in my work place but that my body had adjusted to the cold.

The person who believes that is it their purpose (from an introjection) to take care of others may come to believe that it is their role to take on the many hardships of caring for someone who is ill. They may start working in helping occupation and work long stressful hours, or find a person who is in need and become their carer. If a person is manipulating their environment they may seek a partner to change, and restrict their growth, doing everything for that person, so they can be put into a position to be able to care for them. They may think nothing of spending most of their time caring for others, but little time on their own self-care (this is an indicator or a person who rationalises taking care of others as a vocation, however has the purpose of fulfilling a value of low self-worth, and placing their importance as being second to others, to become people-pleasers)

This person while having a high frustration tolerance to endure many stresses may have a low frustration tolerance to putting their self first, and may put off anything that would mean pampering their self or engaging in self-care. The person though may justify going on holiday once a year and spoiling their self, but is not in the spirit of prizing and respecting one's self, but in a distorted or rationalised type of way, they may feel that have to work hard to be able to treat their self. If this rationalisation was not in place then they may again feel the feelings of anxiety as they touch the impasse, as the *me* becomes the *not me*.

As the self-concept provides a direction, meaning and purpose (no matter what that meaning or purpose that is) The meaning of resistance serves some important functions, such as if we view that anything outside the self-concept is something that creates anxiety, so it is that many forms of resistance can protect a person from that, and that the person does not have the internal support to be able to overcome or challenge that anxiety. The forms of resistance then become part of the self-concept, but outside the person's awareness, the person just *is* and simply is their way of being in the world, it enables the person to exist, and rather than attack or try to dismantle them, I think it is important to try to understand the resistance and to understand what it is supporting.

Resistance may keep at bay perceive threats to the self-concept, but in doing so may also push away support, as the person touches on the impasse. I do not see that the forms of resistance are on the border of the self-concept, but are rather interwoven into the fabric of how the person exists, to understand the resistance is to understand the person's beliefs, how they structure their thoughts, the way they speak, the words they use and other styles of contact. If a person is to break through their resistances then I feel that it is important to know how they support the self-concept, as it not only protects, but also affirms and gives meaning. For example the woman may creatively adjust and gain weight to protect herself from sexuality and men (making herself unattractive) though this is outside her awareness she may fail at diets, not because she cannot follow a diet plan, but of what it means to be attractive to men. If she has gained weight as a result of a poor self-worth then this may be assimilated into her self-concept, and by losing weight she may gain a higher self-esteem, she may have a low tolerance to the feelings of feeling good about herself and so sabotages her own efforts. If low self-worth is part of how she views her self she may fail at any attempt to lose weight. I write here about a person's weight, but this is what is phenomenological to the person, I could have written college or education in the place of weight, and the person who resists being successful may talk herself out of going to college and stay in a menial job, the person with the low self-esteem may try to enrol at college but something may always seem to happen to mean that she does not complete a course. The resistance that takes place here affirms the person's own belief of their self, and protects them from the impasse, of anything that would cause anxiety. The person who gains weight to make herself unattractive to men, may find it easier to be overweight that to explore her sexuality, the person who stays in menial job may be afraid to explore her academic potential. The resistance then supports the self-concept.

If a person has a resistance to be vulnerable in relationships, then may create a self-concept in which they must be busy, and have the goal of being financially successful. The person is only chasing this goal as it means that they are too busy to form or seek a relationship, and may instead feel justified in saying that they are *too busy* for a relationship. If they do become involved with a person then they may again have a great excuse to only partially enter that relationship, as they can plausibly say they are focused on their career. They may keep the relationship light and emotion free or seek a predominantly sexual relationship. The person's fear of a close relationship is the driver for a busy career and the desire to be financially successful (as opposed to successful in a relationship, or in the own self-awareness)

The person though who desires to be in a relationship because of what it means to be alone may have developed a high tolerance for people with whom she is not compatible, in that she may believe that it is better to be sad than to be alone. This would be different then to the person who resists being involved in a relationship until she meets a person who she feels happy with and she can enjoy life and to share experiences with. The first person enters a relationship because of a the avoidance of being alone (the avoidance of anxiety) the second persons enters a relationship to share her life with a person she chooses to be with. The forms of resistance may guide the self-concept to an outcome that protects it and nurtures it, this is the difference for me between self-concept growth, that is to say the person only grows within the limits of their own self-image or self-concept and organismic growth, in which the person grows in their search to become an authentic person free (mainly) from the influences of creative adjustments and introjections, the person only interested in growth within the self-concept lives within the boundaries of their own beliefs and forms of resistance, the person striving for organismic growth may actively seek out their own existential impasse, to experience the *not me* and feel the feelings of anxiety and being vulnerable as opposed to the comfortable feelings of the *me*. The *me* is after all just a collection of beliefs, about their self and the world around them. An example of growth within the self-concept would be a mother who resists giving up her role of mother, even though her children has grown up and left home, she may begin a course to work in a school, a nursery or some other helping role in which she can be a *mum* there instead. There may be a fear to ask "if I am not a mum, then what am I?" and instead her resistance to this anxiety may guide her towards a job or role where this question is never asked, something that may mean she steps outside her *self* and to try something that doesn't involve being a mum. Interestingly there may be a monological stance, as if she has the desire to continue being a mum, then people that she may interact with in that role only serve to give meaning to this, and she may (outside her awareness) encourage others to treat he like a mum. (Manipulation of the environment) Being a mum is her own familiar territory, and like the person who could not tolerate the feelings of thirst, so it was for the person who could not put down the *mum* role.

As we can see the self-concept is a very complex composite of thoughts, beliefs values, contact functions, levels of assertion, polarities, introjections, creative adjustments, zones of awareness, the areas of resistance and their function and purpose for the person. The person is existing, and from that may grow in the direction of the self-concept, to follow a path within the boundary of the impasse. I would like to explore further the implications of the person who lives their life within the self-concept, before we move onto the final chapter.

I remember once a few years ago encountering a man who was full of self-pity, and this seemed to impact on all areas of his life, he had what seemed by any standard to live a pretty comfortable life, had a career and had little money worries. He would rationalise anything anyone said to him to be in a negative light and seemed to see the world in which he was worse off because of conditions that were outside his control, if anything good did happen to him he would avoid mentioning this, and then when I asked about his new car or motorcycle he would deflect this onto another area. I saw him recently and he was still same way. I had the thought that he was engaging in a form of self-pity, and that he was seeing the world and disregarding anything positive that happened to him. For me, self-pity is a form of self-care and for this person (after I was talking to him for a while) discovered that his father was a very cold and distant man (who rationalised that he had to be this way to build a successful business to look after his family) and considered what would happen for a small boy growing up in that world. The man wouldn't let people feel sorry for him and presented as a tough and hard masculine man, though this may have again be a smokescreen, or a role as he tried to be like his father (the search for affection or approval as he sought recognition from his father by emulating him) but was open to this form of self-pity, for although no-one else could be allowed to take care of him (and he put up a steely defence to any person that tried to show concern or support) he was able to feel sorry for himself. I thought about the role of creative adjustment and how this person had adjusted to life with his father and the implications for his self-concept, and how he related to people. This way of being had many ramifications as he seemed to be unable to accept help from people and resisted any feelings of concern towards him, when I saw him he always seemed to be starting a new relationship, and when I asked him about this he said that "women were needy and were always looking for attention" or which I interpreted as a form of projection, that he in fact was needy and looking for attention, however, when this attention was given he would be reluctant to accept it, if indeed he ever did, I thought about the introjection that lead to a creative adjustment *I want your support and affection, I can never have it, but I can give it to myself* and this was a foundation to his life and how he viewed the world. I noticed that outwardly with women he would appear confident, dressed impeccably well with designer clothes and drove an expensive car, he showed a developed interested in any women that he spoke to, so I was not surprised he would have no trouble in finding a woman to start a relationship with, and I thought about how his new partner adjusted to this, for each relationship was kept light and superficial and that had no depth leading the woman to guess what was going on as this man kept himself emotionally distant and closed off from her. The last I saw him I he was still talking the same way and had a different woman with him.

If he did meet a woman who had a *I need to help other people* creative adjustment or introjection this woman may damage herself trying to *help* a person who is resistant to receiving any type of help, or to engage in a close and personal relationship, in which a person can be vulnerable to another person. For him to be vulnerable to another person this could constitute touching the impasse and the *not me* and so would create anxiety or fear. The woman if she were unable to *help* another person, in this case this man then she may feel guilty if she cannot fulfil this *need*, the need to help another person. A toxic relationship may occur then with a person who needs to help another person and a person who resists any type of help or support, but presents as someone who exhibits a form of self-pity.

The woman's form of helping then is not really helping the person, but to satisfy her own introjected beliefs as to how she should be a person, and this belief becomes a *need* for that person. Helping this man could take the form of assisting him to understand why he is distant in relationships, but yearns for the support of others, to be understanding and to not allow herself to *buy into* or to be manipulated to fulfil the role he is inviting her to take, and lastly to engage in her own self-care, to end the relationship when she realises this man is not ready or unwilling to give himself to another person and to let another person know him (as this would create vulnerability for his self) however if helping is part of her self-concept she may be drawn into this toxic relationship and may then creatively adjust and this may lower her own self-belief or self-esteem as she has a need to help, but the man will not let her help him.

I think a need or desire to help and to be understanding or inclusive to other people is a good thing, but if the person *has* to help another person, then they may be open to being used by another person who like the man has a need to be helped (but in his case he resists this) and this may form in my view a range of issues, for if a person who has a need to help meets a person who needs to be helped how can there be any growth, and instead we have two people who have growth only in their self-concept and not by trying to understand how they exist in the world this way and strive towards an organismic growth. Interestingly in this example this may also may involve a projection of the opposite of the part of the polarity that is untouched, the person wanting to help may project the opposite (to be helped, to be weak, to be vulnerable) onto another person, and the other may project the untouched part of their polarity (to be responsible, to be strong) onto the other, the driver that creates this is creative adjustment and introjection, and the beliefs (outside their awareness) as to how they *should* be a person. The formation of these *shoulds* by their necessity mean that everything outside that should is avoided, and so forms part of their own structure of their resistances.

I have often thought about the role of passivity and the implications for the person, and what the person avoids to give this passivity a meaning. They cannot normally be assertive or aggressive, though they may engage in being passive aggressive, so how can a person who is passive overcome their environment, for example, if I want to know about a person, or to be noticed by another person how can I go about this? If the person is passive to avoid being judged by the other, then they may try and please the other, they may ask questions about the person to elicit a sense of approval or affection, the person who has this need may resist any form of assertion or aggression as in doing so will jeopardise how they receive praise from others. Stepping aside from this I have thought about a ways in which a person can know about a person without asking about them, I have wondered if a person can become a *mind-reader* and to make intuitive guesses about the other person (much like myself making an analytical inference about the person who was invited to the course group) or to gossip about the other person. It may be easier to gossip and to guess about the person than to just ask them, as this would create less anxiety. This thought came from observing a person who wouldn't enquire about a person, or to talk to them to discover who they were, but instead to sit as if in silent judgement of the other, observing the other to form an opinion and make assumptions such as "he is talking about himself so this means that he is arrogant" and is a form of denial (at their own passivity and the implications of this) and distortion, as the person is making hypothetical guesses on their own view of the person, instead of the self-question of "why am I sitting here making guesses about a person instead of talking to him" to form an opinion. I feel that when this passivity (or when it becomes the previous example then it becomes a form or passive aggression, as the person is attempting to form an opinion of the other without making any type of contact) is exaggerated then the person may become kind of spiritual and relies on their *sensing* or *intuition* of a situation, group or person and if is integrated into the self-concept then the person may pride their self on their sensing and intuitive skills as to know a person without even talking to them. I do believe that some people can develop their sensing skills and to become aware of situations or people without dialogue being spoken, but, for some people who are passive this may has been a form of creative adjustment, and the avoidance of being assertive, or even aggressive (aggressive in the sense of having a query and then asking the person) The person who makes intuitive guesses though about a person without speaking to them and who prides themselves on their skills may be in avoidance or denial, saying that they don't need to talk to a person to know them they can sense them, this *me* of being aggressive or passive aggressive is preferable to the *not me* of being assertive. They may also be in denial that they could be wrong, since any guess, supposition or inference always lends themselves to the balance of probability that it is wrong, so the person who stays quiet and silently judges the other who is speaking and projects their own beliefs onto the other (such as "if I was speaking so much I would be arrogant") or resent the person for doing something, or being something that is outside their way of relating to others (this way of being may be in the implosive layer or beyond the impasse and as such create feelings of anxiety in that person, which is then either denied, suppressed, avoided or rationalised and instead the person has the feeling or sense that the person is being arrogant) and the person is being judged from that view, in a passive aggressive way.

The person may be speaking though because they are nervous as their own internal sensing suggests they are being silently judged, or that they have a wish or desire to engage in dialogue with another person. The person may also have a love of the subject that is being talked about, or may be manipulating their environment to discuss this issue. The person who is the silent judge and relies on their sensing or intuitive skills based on passivity and the fear of being assertive may reach a speedy conclusion without considering all factors, or the consequence and sequence of the event or person speaking, and their own silent way of being within that (the person who engages with another who is quiet may talk more to fill the void of silence, little aware that they are being judged for this in a negative or critical manner)

The passive person then having developed these sensing skills may have initially became passive as a means of creative adjustment or introjections, and becoming a person who relies on these sensing skills may be a further example of self-concept growth. It is easier to not question this, as if these belief about their self is challenged then it may mean touching the impasse, and therefore anxiety as the person move from the *me* to the *not me*. The person then who is passive and holding back much about their self, to adjust to the world according to their beliefs may become to resent people who are assertive or aggressive (the opposite of what they are not) or may chase after them or find this person attractive or appealing, not because they actually are, but as they represent an aspect of the person that is avoided, and may create a confluent relationship.

I often wonder about a person who has a need to be surrounded by people that support their self-concept or to live or search for a place where this has meaning, such as the person searching for a spiritual connection travelling to India, the person who has a desire to be admired and works in a self-depreciative role or job involving helping others, the person who views themselves as intellectual seeking comfort in the company of others who share this, the person with strong religious values who looks for others who are the same. Although there are many introjections and creative adjustments that form the self-concept in this way, it is the seeking of others that support this that is of interest to me. The person who feels that they have to go to India to seek spiritually may be doing so because those beliefs and way of being are not challenged in that country, but in this country they may face ridicule or strange looks of they dressed in the attire that feels most comfortable or within their own beliefs, the message then would be *I can only be me with people that accept me* the person may then feel they must adjust their self to the introjected values and beliefs of where they live, and may feel they have to hide who they are, to create a *false self*. By seeking others that substantiate their beliefs they are gaining an acceptance and an approval, so they may feel that they must associate with others who will give them acceptance or approval. I remember reading once about a strongly religious man who instead of going to church to be surrounded by a people who shared and approved of his views he took his beliefs out into the world and engaged with people who challenged and questioned his beliefs, this person did not need the approval of others to follow his way of life, and instead by living his life with authenticity and assertiveness he endeavoured to be genuine and alive, free from the confines of introjected beliefs and values, or the need to be surrounded by people who approved of him, he lived his life by the values that were important to his self. This authenticity may create resentment in others, for if a person has the courage to try and live an authentic life, in a world where others are holding their self back and creating a false self so as to *fit in,* then it may be easier to question, judge or ridicule the person, rather than question their own values and beliefs, and how they themselves have creatively adjusted to live within their own world. It may be easier or less anxiety provoking then to have an idea of who you and to surround yourself by people who share this, the intellectual can be intellectual with anyone, but he may restrict his self and present a false self when engaging with others he may think will view him negatively, the person who has those strong religious values can be that way anywhere, but restricts that part of himself when engaging with people who would

challenge that part, and so he creates a false self to present to others to whom he cannot win approval or affection. The person who has a love of reading, or a hidden sexuality, of painting soldiers, drawing pictures or engaging in pottery and restricts this because of the anxiety of what it means to be judged by another may be living an inauthentic life, particularly if this way of life is not shared or valued by others.

If I adjust myself and create a false self to live in the world, do I view myself as an object to adjust, or a person who is living and existing? I believe when we hold back parts of our being to be able to have the approval of others we turn ourselves into an object in which we mould (creatively adjust) ourselves to whatever container (or world) we are in, and when that involves adjusting our self to the values of others we have the introjected message *don't be you, be the way I want you to be* and this can be a strong introjection as to how to be a person, which may create its own anxiety or depression if we cannot live to those views, we may also have a dull ache inside our self as we have an idea that we are living an unfulfilled life. It is my view that if we live as an image, or a self-concept that are treating ourselves like an object, an object formed of beliefs values, contact functions, levels of assertion, polarities, introjections, creative adjustments, zones of awareness and the areas of resistance, the person is existing with the container of the self-concept, even if that constitutes presenting a false self to others within their world. How can there be authenticity within this container, it is only when we push the impasse, to move from the *me* to the *not me* that we can understand the boundary of what the *me* means (like the fish in water) how it is given purpose, how the person *sees* the world from that position and also how person manipulates their self and the their environment to give their self-concept a meaning. The person who is deeply religious may realise that they are only that way in the company of others with whom their views are approved of, and may feel anxiety if they disclosed their religious views at their place of work. Touching the impasse mean daring to be someone different, to stretch the idea of who they are as a person, to question and acknowledge their old views and beliefs and the purpose of what their resistances meant to them. It may also mean the death of that old person and the search or embarking and the daring to ask that question *if I am not this, then what may I become?* I believe that when a person can ask this question of their self that are taking responsibility for their life, to embrace the impasse and to know that the feelings of anxiety that kept the person in the container of the self-concept is now an avenue to understand one's self, such as why do I feel anxious when I speak in a group, why do I feel anxious is I do not tell jokes to gain affection or approval, why is it easier for me to be a manager and to distance myself from others, to reduce the anxiety of letting another person know me as a person, instead of a manager. Why is it easier for me to be submissive and passive to others instead of taking charge of my own life and voicing my concerns? When we think about Field Theory and how *the field is a unitary whole: everything affects everything else* when the person starts to question their world and existence, instead of looking for miracles in the world they may start to see their own life as miraculous, and to acknowledge, the wonder that is you.

In the next chapter we will look more closely at emerging from the self-concept and what this means to you, as the self-concept can become its own goal, we shall look more closely at the goals of a limited self-concept and the existential path of a person who challenges the idea of who they are as a person, and while this can be enlightening it can also be daunting path as the person leaves the security of the *me*.

*

You are confined only by the walls you build yourself.

Andrew Murphy

191

Chapter 3

Emerging:
From Monologue to Dialogue

to suffer one's death and to be reborn is not easy

Fritz Perls

In this, the final chapter i would like to talk about emerging from the self-concept and what this means, with the above quote from Fritz i do agree that there is a kind of death from certain parts of the self-concept, and in a sense the person is being reborn.

I would like to give an example to highlight this, a while ago I was watching a television programme about a man who had been in a serious accident and had lost the use of his legs, he was paralysed from the waist down and was confined to a wheelchair. He had started to feel depressed knowing that he would be this way for the rest of his life, and anxious at the thought that everyone was looking at him and pitying him. This man though previously had been an long distance runner, cyclist and swimmer and competed in events that incorporated these sports, he was athletically gifted, or rather, that he had spent many hours nurturing and practising, honing his natural talents, and had a determination and motivation to practice, whether that was running, cycling or swimming whatever the weather and time of day, in fact, if he was training for a big event he would get out of bed at 4 am and go on a 20 mile run before work, this man's had a steely unflinching focus, an inner drive to achieve his ambitions and goals.

The television programme never focused on the man's life outside this area so I am unsure what the creative adjustments or introjections were that influenced this man to be so driven, but they were there and integrated into his own self-concept. He was becoming depressed as he could not live up to the idea of the way he should be (an able-bodied and athletic man) and anxious at the thought of people pitying him, but previously he had been ok with people looking at him and clapping as he competed in events, and even offered advice and tips to other athletes, so he was fine at attracting attention in ways he thought were positive (that it was ok for him to attract attention in an admiring, advising or helping way, but not in a pitying way) He later was able to *put down* the valuing of his self in this way, and gained an acceptance of who he was as a person, and though he knew he could not compete in these types of events again, he could focus on what he could do in spite of his injuries, and so he had a specially build 3 wheeled bike made so he could continue cycling, he also learned that he didn't like to be looked at in a pitying manner because of the value or confirmation or his own worth from how other people viewed him.

This man then, was able to gain an awareness of his self and liked that he enjoyed pushing himself physically in different sports. His motivational drive and enthusiasm for doing this meant that he could have done anything, but that in whatever he did he would push himself to the limits of what he could do. This man emerged from his old self-concept, challenged his idea of who he was and grew through it, yes he could have become depressed and anxious because he could not live up to the idea of his self, and isolated himself from others so he would not let himself be valued by others in the way he though they were *seeing* him (perhaps a form of projection) but instead he used some of qualities that were part of his old self-concept and integrated these into his renewed sense of self, his high motivation and determination. In this sense the old self was dead and he was reborn into something new.

I don't see that creative adjustments or introjections are necessarily bad or negative, but when these become part of a self-concept and a *this is who I am* belief that it can lead to rigidity and an inflexibility when faced with (as with this person) a different way of life caused by an injury, and the awareness that he was confirmed by how others viewed him, it was ok for him to be seen as a an athlete but not as a person with an injury and confined to a wheelchair. This man owned the injury, and rather than avoid he embraced it, though he realised that he could no longer cycle 100 miles on a bike, he could use his self-determination to push himself in other areas of his life.

This way of being and the emerging from a self-concept may also be used for a woman whose children have grown up and the role of *mum* is no longer as necessary, she may no longer feel she has to care for another person, or to have a person dependant on her, but can choose to highlight her nurturing and empathetic side of her self to care for others, if she so wishes. She can volunteer in a caring role or develop a career that focuses on this, of if she decides to put down all the role of mum (and is aware of the *guilt* that may ensue if she cannot be *mum,* to fulfil that role or self-concept) she can explore other areas of her self, she may utilise her attributes of patience and tolerance, or her organisational skills that were utilised in the mum role that can now be used in a career or job. What she can do by emerging through her self-concept is to put down what she wishes to put down and to carry or integrate the qualities that she decides to.

The same may be said of a father who has the need to be important and has used his family so he is the patriarch, the person in charge, the dominant person in that household, he may be full of rationalisations as to why he should be in charge, but upon knowing or gaining a knowledge of his self-concept and the manipulation of his environment to fulfil this he may not *need* his family to sustain his idea of his self and so can, instead of controlling his family so it means he is in charge he can encourage his family, instead of taking over and restricting his children's growth, he can be a source of support, and to encourage his children to overcome problems or issues (that previously he would have solved to exemplify his idea of his self)

The self-concept is a monological self, that is to say, I see myself or have the image of myself of being a certain way from many creative adjustments and introjections, which means I *see* others from that point of view or perspective, it also means the manipulation of self to fulfil this image, and the manipulate of the environment to give this a meaning. As we emerge through this, as we challenge and understand the many ways of our being, and as we make a choice with the acceptance that it is our responsibility to make that choice (rather than the manipulation of self and environment that others or the world is in charge of our life) there is a *death* of that life, of that self-concept.

Although we shall explore this later in the chapter, the monological self is a self that is a culmination of introjections and creative adjustments that have formed outside the person's awareness, the person is merely living in their world, this collection of beliefs and values (about the self and the world) is held in a container that incorporates a role, and in that is an object, so when one is an object (self-concept, self-image or self-identity) then others become an objects from this way of being.

To be born again and to suffer one's death then is no easy task as Fritz has said, and I shall look toward myself for this next example about the process of emerging. As I have wrote in the previous chapters about my own introjections and creative adjustments I had the idea of my self as being strong and tough, as well as being analytical. The self-concept had some benefits, but also negatives as I had cut off other parts of me that were not part of this self, it was easier to be more of a *thinker* and deny or suppress my feelings and emotions, with the rationalisation of *this is just the way I am* as well as being strong in the sense of physically strong and fit, but also independent and self-supportive as a distorted indicator of strength which meant that any form of weakness was disowned and projected onto others, other people needed help, not me, and I was strong enough and had enough knowledge to be able to do this (manipulation of self and environment to achieve this – Field Theory) as well as gaining knowledge in many areas so I rarely had to ask for help from anyone. I missed though the strength that comes from being vulnerable, to touch the impasse and to grow as an organismic person, for that is real strength and the courage to discover those disowned parts. It was easy back them to help other people (in a monological sense) as I wasn't really helping people, I was sustaining my idea of who I was, *people* were just objects to give my self meaning, *people* were just reasons for me to justify to myself that I had to be strong, analytical and unemotional, the way I *saw* world gave meaning to this and a rationalisation that I following a path and that I had a purpose. Touching the impasse, entering the implosive layer of the *not me,* the creation of the Safe Emergency, learning from experiences, being open to the experiential, learning from action and in action uncovered some uncomfortable truths. An awareness of an understanding of an understanding opened many doors to how I saw the world and the emergence of my *self.* The self that emerged through the confines of my old self-concept, to suffer the death of my old self and to be reborn was indeed not easy, and in many ways I am not yet reborn, but on a path towards greater self-awareness. It's easy in life to have a purpose isn't it? To have a knowledge that *this is me* and to have an idea of a meaning to one's existence and anything that goes against that is met with a resistance, and, if the means of resistance fails then the person enters a crisis, an existential crisis.

From our first chapter I mentioned the fish in the water analogy, and I would like revisit it here, for just like the fish the person is swimming in the water, it has adjusted to this to survive and needs the water, just as the self-concept need that particular environment to give itself meaning, when the fish comes to the surface this is tantamount to touching the impasse, it is difficult for fish to breath as it has adjusted so well to life in the water, for a person this would be the same as feeling the uneasy feelings of the *not me*, (the impasse) then, if the fish is unlucky enough to leave the water then as the person entering the implosive layer it cannot live in this, it has not adapted to life in the air and so must return or not live. This is why people find it much more preferable to return to an old way of being, and how for a person to encounter the impasse they must first learn to feel the feelings of the impasse, or to gain a better tolerance of the feelings of frustration when the needs that are part of the self-concept are not met, or that we restrict them long enough to know that they exist, just as the person who has an addiction or compulsion doesn't know they are addicted or feel compelled to act in a type of behaviour or with certain beliefs until that with which they are addicted to (the needs arising from the self-concept) are not met. I think this is why it is easier to regress to an immature state or ruminate (which includes procrastination) on the issue or previous issues instead of an understanding of the possibilities or alternatives to a particular issue, as well as a desire to know how it is that they see the world and experience it in this way. It is less anxiety provoking to stay the same or to regress than it is to grow and challenge the self-concept. We are not a fish, the fish took millions of years to adapt to the air and to dwell on the land, fortunately we can do this in a little less time, we can start to stretch the concept, acknowledging and accepting why the self-concept formed, the resistances that sustain it, and then hopefully realise there is no further need to use others to sustain this self-concept. (Manipulation of environment) When we can see other people as people and not objects, we can move from a monological sense of being to a dialogical person who sees others in an inclusive way, we can grow or emerge into an authentic person.

This chapter then, moves from the second to the third section, the second section of the self-concept to the third section of the emerging self.

This self is not rigid and held in place by restrictive, unreceptive or narrow beliefs, but with an openness and a willingness to experience life and to grow as a person, and to be open to as well as seek out new experiences. If you look at the first and third sections you'll notice that they are the same size but I would like to say that the third section has the capacity to become larger and more encompassing than the first section, because in this section we now have a knowledge and the desire to know who we are, as well as choice and a responsibility into the person we would like to become, the third section can continue on and on as it widens until the person decides that they are happy and content. In the first section the person doesn't have or only has a vague awareness of their self from introjections and creatively adjustments to their world, whatever that is. The person begins with the possibility that they can be anything, but this is restricted and retarded by the world in which they live, the creative adjustment or introjection to be strong, to be weak, to be ill, to have power, to have success, to gain possessions, to win the admiration of others, to seek approval, to be a princess, to be a servant, to be a pauper, to be second to others, to be superior, to react angrily to situations, to be passive, to have a low frustration to anxiety, to have a high frustration to the environment, to talk a certain way, to listen, to blame, to praise, to manipulate , to be manipulated, to have their beliefs and values shaped, to distort, to tell lies, to desensitise, to become too sensitive, to feel, to think, to protect, to be helpless, to be the judge, to be the protector. That which a person can creatively adjust too is immeasurable, with the multiple possibilities that encapsulates the contact functions, zones of awareness, polarities and assertion. The person in most cases doesn't rationally decide to be a certain way to survive in their world they, like the fish adapting to their world because they must, to be able to survive. The fish didn't have the conscious choice to grow gills, just as the cactus didn't have the conscious choice to grow spines and develop tough skin, they merely adjusted to their environment and incorporated these adjustments into who they are, outside their awareness.

This for me is the beauty of this last section, the beauty of awareness, responsibility, choice and growth, the opportunity to either accept or refuse introjections, the willingness to creatively adjust to a situation or the existential choice to not adjust, to have the knowledge that you don't have to adjust, or that you are feeling under pressure from your environment to adjust (as with an employer who may try to manipulate you to get you to work harder, to follow the company introjections) and the ability to choose how you interact with people. Do you *have* to wear designer clothes to win the approval of others, do you *have* to talk about your job when talking to a others, do you *have* to tell jokes to win the affection of others, or do you *have* to be silent or agreeable as someone dominates the conversation with their topic of interest. The answer is no, you do not, but if you do then you do so with the choice that you are willingly doing so, if you actively interested in the experiential (which we shall talk about later) you may purposely explore your sense of self, by putting yourself into familiar or new situations to gain more of an awareness of your feelings, sensing, intuition, beliefs and values, and then perhaps to be open to the experiential or experimental, such as "what happens if I say no to this person?" and then finding out that you feel anxious or guilty at saying this, so you recall all the times you said yes just to appease the other person, not because you meant yes, but because of the anxiety of saying no. (for people who have a low self-worth in relation to other people, or seek the approval of the affection of other people saying no can evoke feelings of anxiety as there is a risk that the other person may not like you, or that you risk their disapproval or rejection, then possibly retroflect or displace feelings of resentment as you say yes instead.) or the person may create a safe emergency when they are aware of the *not me,* the impasse and the implosive layer, as well as an exploration or their self-concept and their own role-playing in relation to other people. This last green section is where we can grow and become a person, a person who with choice, autonomy and self-responsibility can enrich their life with authenticity and organismic growth.

I would like to talk about this further, but for now I'll go on to an experiment, and while I am on the subject an experiment in the sense of this book has only the purpose to try out different ways of being for your own awareness, to listen or speak differently and then to experience the result, as well as understanding of what it means to be you that you speak or listen that way, the *me.* When I was planning this book I had the idea whether to include a lot of awareness experiments, but thought to myself that this would constitute a form of introjection, so the experiments that I have included as well as this next experiment has the purpose to raise your awareness of your self.

I am guessing that one of the reasons you have chosen to read this book would be an active interest in yourself, and that you are willing to be open to exploring your self, and to discover who you are as a person, both in how you exist now as well as to be open to the possibility to what you may become. This last experiment is called The Impasse, and in it we shall touch on the *not me*.

Awareness Experiment – Touching the Impasse

As I was developing this experiment I was thinking that it is a relatively simple idea for an experiment, just be *not me* and sense what it feels like, but after considering this further I realised that this is probably the most difficult one of all in this book, as in previous experiments the purpose being to raise your awareness of how you exist in this world, this last experiment is designed for you to touch on the opposite or the *not* me, and this is an area that we have spent a life avoiding or resisting, to stay within the safety or the comfort of the self-concept, so to challenge that would be to question the purpose of our life, and the meaning that we ascribe to our life.

It's a bit like going to the gym and lifting weights I think, if you lift a heavy weight before you are ready then you'll get injured or strain yourself, and the experience may even put you off going to the gym, so for this experiment just like going to the gym for the first time lift some light weights to get used to exerting yourself this way, then when you get the hang of it and better at experimenting with your self then you can progress further (and lift heavier weights) as you grow as a person. The impasse is always present, and I invite you to always be open to experiences and to be in touch with your inner felt sense.

I would like to take us back to the experiment in Chapter 2 the Living in Your Shoes Experiment, I asked you to write down all the qualities and the characteristics about yourself and asked such questions as "do you take on responsibility or do you let other people take the initiative and tell you what to do?" "are you passive in conversation or do you lead?" as well as asking other questions about clothing and beliefs about yourself.

I asked you to keep this list, so I would like you to go back to it and pick one of the qualities, polarities or characteristics that involve listening or speaking. The purpose is for your own awareness and not for the other person, but how you relate to others, so I would like you to consider if you listen to others or prefer to talk more, and whether this is again relational, do you listen more to your parent, manager or friends and listen less to your children or partner, are there some friends you listen more to, as some less. (The reason for this is that you may have a need for affection or approval from some people but not others, or is your sense of worth or acceptance greater with some people and less with others) So pick a person with whom you listen more and talk less, such as your partner, child, friend or work colleague. Now I would like you to simply talk more, I would like you to grade this yourself and be aware of your own feelings of anxiety and how uncomfortable you are, you are moving from the *me* to the *not me* with this person. As you are talking more I would like you to express opinions, direct the conversation, disagree with the person, or agree with them and give them an explanation as to why you agree or disagree.

Just like with the gym analogy I would like you take it light, it may be that a simple "yes" "no" or "I don't agree with you there" that evokes feelings of anxiety in your body. These feelings of when the person touches the impasse invite us to go back to the security of who we normally are, and within the boundaries of our *self*. This is the basis for me for Low Frustration Tolerance as the person regresses or uses a form of resistance to return to the self-concept and the *this is who I am* belief of their self. There can be no growth in this, except growth within the self-concept, this is a safe way of being, and if we want to be authentic it means pushing the boundaries of the impasse of who we think we are, which is that collection of beliefs and values in a container.

This beauty of this experiment is that our resistances become alive here, as we experience talking more to a person that we normally listen to, we may be challenged by rationalised thoughts such as "he is more important than me and I shouldn't be speaking" "i am taking up his time" "i am not saying anything important" he will not like me for speaking too much" "I am not interesting enough to be listened to" and in that we become not only aware of our own self beliefs but also the nature of our own resistances and what they mean personally to us, the person who has any of those internal beliefs is also giving their self a good reason to stay quiet or agreeable and listen to that person. As we become aware of this then I would like you to become aware of your own self-beliefs and why they are relational to the other person, I would like you to consider that how it is you can speak with no problem to a person who you trust, or that offers you acceptance and how it is that you feel you cannot speak, or find it difficult to speak to a person who you view as more superior in some way, or that you feel that you are only conditionally accepted by that person, there may be other reasons for this difficulty or ease in speaking to a person and for that I would like you to consider your own truth. For example the woman in an abusive relationship may have learned to stay quiet or risk her partner criticising her comments or putting her down, if she did speak up more then it would create tension in that relationship, as her partner may view her voice as competition or a threat to his dominance.

We could grade this awareness experiment more as you lift heavier weights, you could actively talk nonsense, start talking and boasting about your achievements, tell jokes that are funny, that aren't funny, take you time speaking (if previously you have rushed out opinions to this person) or add pauses and reflections inviting the other to wait for you to continue. If you grade this up a level and you touched the impasse further or made the choice to say to yourself "right, I know I feel uneasy speaking my thoughts to this person, but what would it mean if I pushed it further" and decided to take over the conversation, to direct or command the conversation, to judge the other or to offer compliments. This *not me* would be like to entering the implosive layer and I would suggest that a safe emergency be created, or to gradually stretch the self-concept where you are comfortable saying no, yes or lightly disagreeing with that person first. Once this becomes integrated into your self-concept and you have stretched the self-concept then the more involving responses may be more accessible. Although this experiment is being used to highlight being in conversation to understand the impasse, to feel the feelings of anxiety, to understand the boundaries of our self-concept and to become more aware of (and desensitised) to the feelings of anxiety and the physiological responses (inner zone of awareness) associated when we touch the impasse, this can also be used if you are in a group, lecture, meeting or other social gathering, to voice your concerns or thoughts for the purpose of actively searching for the experience that it evoke in your self .

As we have conducted the experiment in speaking, the opposing polarity of this would be listening, a lot of people are adept at speaking, giving advice, ordering others, directing conversations and so on, so for these people the need to win is to take over or lead conversations, their tone of voice, articulation, emphasis and other areas of speech have been honed so that they can direct or lead conversations (and would also mean that if you conducted the speaking experiment with a person like this they may view is a competition and quickly overwhelm you as you talk about your own thoughts, all this means though is that you would reach the impasse sooner) they may tell jokes or be negative, positive, indignant or belligerent or talk with praise or compliments, they may speak in such a way as to distance their self from other people, or talk so as to create a confluence or to be unchallenging and agreeable to other people and their opinions.

Listening then may mean touching the impasse (with the exception of people who listen to fulfil a role or need, or to be passive, submissive or people-pleasers, though listening may also mean that a person is being a silent judge and passive aggressive) for people who speak for the purposes of directing attention to their self for whatever reason. I would like you then to conduct the same experiment but for the purposes of listening, it's the same format, to consider your own view of people in that it may be easier to listen to the boss and show an interest in him that it is to listen to your partner or someone else and to take an active interest in that person. I would say that if you do have an idea of someone that has no bearing on your own self-worth or acceptance then this may be a good person to become more aware of your own processes with. (You may listen to others for approval affection or to substantiate your own position in a group or relationship with another person, like the millionaire who sits silently as he listens to his mother talking, but yet commands or expects the attention of others and is a very poor listener to others he views as inferior)

Now, the simple thing is, just listen to the other, this may involve taking an active interest in that person so you have to ask some open-ended questions, if you feel you want to problem solve to give advice or to put yourself into a judging, critical or evaluative role, then you have become aware of your own self-concept and the drive to fulfil this, and this would be your own impasse as you are not doing what you would normally do. If you do normally speak more than you listen then, then you may been feeling the urge to take over and to speak, I urge you to resist this (an indicator of low frustration tolerance) and stay with the anxiety of the impasse.

Having listened for a while and asking questions to the other person that only serve to fulfil the aim of listening I would like you to now speak a little and give opinions and thoughts about what the other is saying, let the person lead the conversation as you respond to the person and their topic of choice, you are talking and conversing on the other person's topic and this may also touch on the impasse as you cannot fulfil your own self-concept to take over and to talk about yourself.

This last part of the experiment I would like you to return to your normal self and to direct the conversation and talk or listen as you would, I would like you to consider what it is like to return to your self is it easier to return to you speaking or listening self, does it feel superficial, what was it like to listen exclusively to the person and to ask questions to enquire more about them, to start to converse while letting them lead the topic, before returning to your normal way of relating. What were you experiencing to touch the impasse and then return? Was it easy to slip into listening to others or was it a challenge?

Touching the impasse means being able to tolerate the feelings of being uncomfortable, and this an added beneficial aspect of this experiment, this is why I have purposely resisted grading the experiment and to invite yourself to moderate yourself in this, the child who begins to walk, the person who learns a new language and the person who is taking driving lessons learn at their own pace and within the boundaries of what they feel comfortable, as so in that I invite you to learn to experiment with your impasse within the tolerance of your own feelings and resistances. I have included here talking to another person, to find out where you are in relation to the other, and this is another important aspect of self-learning and knowledge of your self-concept, with the purpose being an increased self-awareness you can experiment and experience what it means to talk and to listen to different people in your world. You may even begin to experiment with people you don't know, the person at the bus stop, the person in the queue at the shops, the person next to you at a concert or social event, gaining an awareness of what it means to be you in relation to people you encounter as your live your life, and to discover who you are as a person. This also has the benefits of growing and stretching your self-concept as you discover and practice new ways of relating to people and to experience the feelings associated with these new and different encounters. It is also my own belief that when we can see a person as a person and not as a need of the self-concept,
then we can decide make a conscious choice as to how to relate to others.

Although this experiment is over then I invite you to move onto the other qualities and characteristics that you wrote down about yourself, and as we are continually growing to add onto this, then this list can grow as you become more aware of your internal sensing, when you are aware that you are feeling anxious as you touch the impasse to slow it down and to internally enquire "what is happening to me here" and to take an active interest in your own sensing and beliefs in different situations and with different people, as well as the outcome of those beliefs and what happens when we challenge them, or take them away.

For example, a person who *must* wear expensive clothing could visit to a discount clothing retailer and purchase some cheap clothing to wear, and this would be an experiment to experience the *not me* and the impasse in that particular area, they may feel insecure or of little worth or approval if the people they associate with share the same values of this person and their introjected or creatively adjusted self-concept, If they arrange a night out and wear ordinary clothes this may bring about the impasse if they have the self-concept belief that they are special and superior and the clothes they wear give a meaning to this, it may also be an indicator of the thin veneer of the self-concept of their feelings of having to *fit in* mean having to wear expensive clothing, and by wearing ordinary or cheap clothes then it means they do *not fit in* and so touch on the anxiety of the impasse when the demands of this thin self-image or false self is not met. This experiment would be done in the same manner as the previous two, in that this would be graded to the tolerance and growth of the person. So a person who was actively embracing self-growth and a pursuit to discover who they are as a person and their own meaning of clothing may visit a charity shop and choose older clothes to be opposite of what he believes he should wear, to experience the feelings of the impasse in the form of the safe emergency. Of course, as with talking and listening, this may also mean that a person who has creatively adjusted to have a low self-worth or self-esteem may wear older or worn clothing and actively avoid wearing any clothing that directs attention to their self, their impasse would be to wear expensive clothing and to experience the feeling evoked as the touch the impasse of the *not me,* and then it becomes more apparent the meaning they ascribe to their own clothing, all those years of the manipulation of self to reinforce the self-belief that they are of little value, highlighted by wearing expensive clothing and touching the impasse. I think we can find out more about our self, when we become or touch on that which we are not.

This duality, or the experiencing of what it means to inhabit both sides of a belief or value highlight the not only the impasse but also the meaning of the objects that the person puts a belief onto, clothes are no longer just clothes, but an indicator to their self and to others how successful, important or what status a person is. This is the same for speaking and listening, it is not just talking and listening, but highlights areas of meaning and significance for the person's own self-concept. This may also be met by rationalised beliefs as to why the person has to behave this way, or the distortion of event to make this a justifiable reason. (such as "the kids have to wear expensive clothing otherwise they get picked on at school" while this may be a viable reason, the truth may be that they view their self as important or have to live up to the expectations of others and are projecting this onto their children)

Such other areas of touching the impasse may include all the areas of this book, such as experimenting with different polarities, different areas of assertion, use of props, make-up and jewellery. (Experimenting with make-up may be an effective way to touch the impasse as to wear makeup is a strong introjection as to how to be a female, the person may touch the impasse if she attempts to leave her house with no make-up on at all, she may feel the feelings of anxiety at this possibility)

The person may experiment with posture, paralanguage, their use of their body (the person whose self-concept is to be muscular and they wear loose baggy clothing to hide their physique, may touch the impasse if they cannot be viewed by others the way they want to be seen) their voice and other areas of the contact functions. They may also experiment with their beliefs and rigidity of these, that people *must* or *should* be a certain way, the impasse may be touched if the person tries to suspend their beliefs and values and talks to person as a unique person (it may fulfil the need of a person's self-concept to *see* a person as being a certain way, for example "I hate people who are overweight because they are a drain on the NHS" this belief may fuel their need to be angry, as it goes against their own values and beliefs)

The impasse experiment has the benefit of tasting what we are not, but also that which we are, if we are interested in whom we are as a person and our own growth then we can learn new ways of relating to others, and to gain a flexibility in our beliefs and responses. I believe though that just as with the gym analogy and lifting weights that we have to practice and go to the gym regularly otherwise we lose muscle, so it is with the experiential and experimenting with our self, we have to embrace it so any change or growth becomes integrated into your growing self-concept, and as this grows, then it is inevitable that you grow also.

The Creation of the Safe Emergency, Embracing the Experiential

The Safe Emergency is what I would like to think as a safe form of risk taking, the risk being when we become that which we are not, to touch the impasse by using our self as an instrument, to try out new ways of behaviour, new ways thinking and responding, to be focused on how our emotions are evoked in a particular environment or with a certain person. I don't believe there is much of a substitute for experience, as it is a valuable form of learning about who we are, in the safe emergency we can also practice new behaviours or reactions. The person who feels that they must behave a certain way to attract the attention or the approval of others may test this, by behaving differently, by asking questions instead of their usual listening style, or conversely by listening instead asking questions. It may begin with a sensation that something isn't right, a dull feeling of anxiety that grows as they direct the awareness to their self, the person may realise that to keep the feelings of anxiety at bay they react in different ways, such as telling jokes, withdrawing, talking more or taking on a role, and if the person chooses to they can continue this and practice in the safe emergency.

The safe emergency can be used to slow down a situation to find out what is happening such as a person who, having a feeling that he is taking on the *dad* role when in relation to other people, as he becomes aware of how he is doing this, such as he takes responsibility for others, offering guidance and advice, he may become aware of how he talks, his posture, whether he gives advice, criticises or asks questions, then to consider the purpose for doing this, as it may sustain and give meaning to his role of *dad*, he may also consider whether he is authoritative or nurturing in his role. He may then begin to experience what is like to *not be* him, to put down that role and to try other ways of relating.

The Safe Emergency can be a tool in which the person can actively experience who they are, as the person taking control of their life can manage their learning experience. and how their self-concept is active in how they live. A person I knew had difficulty in saying no to people, so she created an experiment within the safe emergency so as to experience what happened to her self when she said yes to people, and then when she practised saying no. She played this experiment out in her place of work and found it very difficult for her to say no to people with whom she wanted to like her, to win their approval or affection, so as she was committed to learning from her experiences she tried out saying no. This wasn't in a direct "no" way of responding, but if a person asked if she could complete a task she would say she was busy on another duty and didn't have the time. Over a number of months she found it easier to say no to these people, and as she did she noticed that her anxiety at saying no diminished. What she was doing I believe was conducting an aspect of the impasse experiment, she was experimenting with the *not me,* the person that couldn't say no to people. As she graded her response as part of the safe emergency she practised or experimented with a safe way of saying no, in the form or "i am a bit busy now, but as soon as I am free I'll let you know" if a colleague asked her to complete a task. She was then able to experience the feelings and beliefs of what it meant to her to respond this way, this highlighted her own self-concept, introjections and creative adjustments, and how it was that it was important for her to be able to fulfil other people's requests at the expense of her own priorities, as every time she said yes, she was putting her own self second, and by saying no to a person and focusing on her self and needs first this created anxiety, as it challenged her self-concept.

The safe emergency then can be any area that we would like to focus on for an increased awareness, or how we exist, for example the person who has a need to win or to be superior to others may try to touch the impasse by creating a safe emergency in which they try to become aware of *how* they become superior to others, and to gain an awareness of what they are doing to accomplish this (such as talking louder, telling jokes, informing others of their success, talking in a sarcastic, advice-giving, critical or judging manner to others, and what they are feeling when this happens as the self-concept is given a meaning, and the need that is being met by this way of relating.

The person may then experiment by being the opposite, such as asking for advice (if this means that by asking for advice they are inferior) staying quiet and listening to others or asking others about their own interests. (Taking the attention away from their self) There are some areas of learning in this, the person may become aware of the drive or need to be superior, to be better than others, to feels the anxiety as the need is not being met. By touching the *not me,* the person can experience what this means, the drive to return to their self-concept, and also the person is learning a new way of relating to others, as well as a knowledge or how they exist and relate to others, that is to say how they have configured their world so they can be superior. The person may realise that he lives in competition with others, so it is that his need to be superior is in relation to others, and more precisely what others. This then becomes monological as he views the other not as a person, but as an object to be better than.

If this person viewed financial success as a means to means to be superior to others he may create another safe emergency by working in a voluntary capacity for no financial reward. In the safe emergency the person may become aware of their self-concept, as well as an awareness of their own sensations and actions, an awareness of their feelings and responses, and an awareness of their wants, needs, values and beliefs (from the perspective of living within the self-concept as well as touching the impasse)

Another aspect of the safe emergency is that other people may respond or react differently to the person as they try out or experiment with new behaviours and ways of being. The person who finds it difficult to say no, may create animosity or resistance from others as she learns to be assertive and to be able to say no. The other though may be used to piling her work onto this woman, or knowing that as she "never says no" she can ask her (or rather tell her) to complete tasks and to take advantage of this person. When the person says "no" the other then, having gotten used to using this person to compete tasks may put more pressure on her to not say no. This is another part of field theory as the person grows and changes there may be resistance from other parts of that person's world, in this case the people in that person's world who may *see* the person a certain way, then if the relationship changes the other may try to get the person to go back to the way they were. This would be true of the person who has been in an emotionally abusive relationship, for if the person has creatively adjusted to become passive or submissive to an aggressive or dominant partner, then any *growth* in that person may be met by resistance or resentment by the dominant other. The person then, when conducting a safe emergency may create the experiment and grade in such a way to gain an awareness of *how* and in what circumstances they are being passive or compliant, the awareness of the feelings of being put into a submissive role and their own beliefs and values. The person may come to the conclusion after conducting the safe emergency (such as being aware of how they are when talking to the dominant other about where to go on holiday, she may become aware that the other is dismissive, discounting and regards her opinion with little value, leaving her with a lower self-esteem and self-value) that she has progressively integrated and creatively adjusted to the introjection from her partner (that she is inferior) in that relationship. The *not me* then would be met by a defence from the other person, so she may be left with the question as to whether to be assertive with the other, to try to assist him to be more aware of his actions and their consequences, or to decide to leave.

The experiment though may bring about the choice that the person doesn't want to face, for if she has creatively adjusted to this life, then she may have little self-support and believe that she is unable to exact change, or that she has the strength to live alone (another tool the dominant man may use to control his partner, by saying that she couldn't live or survive without him, which she may also integrate into her self-concept) and also that she may have adjusted to believe that she cannot think or accept responsibility for herself, if her partner has made all the important decisions. The safe emergency then could be graded to incorporate these areas as the themes emerge as to how she exists, by experimenting with taking responsibility for her self, by thinking for herself is undoing and understanding the previous creative adjustments, and bringing into her awareness the anxiety that will be met by doing this.

The safe emergency can be used on any of the qualities, values of characteristics that you have written down as part of The Shoes experiment, and you can use create a place to focus on your functioning, thoughts, beliefs and processes. There are no hard and fast rules for this, but an exploration of your being and how you relate to others. You may think to yourself " I am nice" and become aware of *how* you are nice to a person, do you put the other first, do you listen as they speak, do you get up and let the other person sit down if you are on the bus, do you hold a door open for the other if they are walking into a store or do you ask someone that is important to you and enquire about their life and interests. All the time while you are doing this becoming aware of your bodily reactions, your tone of voice, how you are hearing, your gestures and body movements. Then as part of the same experiment to reverse this, to incorporate the opposite of nice, by trying to put yourself first, to take over conversation, to walk through a door and make the other person wait, to jump in front of a queue with a rushed excuse, to take an item you have bought back to a shop and speak assertively. Then while you are doing this also become aware of your bodily reactions, (such as speaking faster, feeling your pulse raise and starting to sweat a little, feeling that your values and self-beliefs screaming out silently as you internally say to yourself "this isn't me." Then, when you have experienced both, you can bring to your awareness that you are *nice* because being the opposite means that you are going against your own beliefs (from introjections) which is a creative adjustment. You are being nice, because of the anxiety of what it means to be self-centred, egotistical, nasty or ill-mannered, not that you actually exhibit these qualities, but your own self-talk and rationalisation as you avoid not being nice. As you continue to experiment this way you may come to the realisation that being *nice* has worked its way so much into how you view yourself and integrated itself into your self-concept that there is a resistance to being what you see as the opposite, even if that means your interpretation of what being nice means, has the consequence of you putting yourself second to others, and in some way an excuse to be passive.

If you do continue with this experiment and practice this different way of being the *not me*, then maybe eventually you will start to own this (just as with the analogy with the gym) and you will be able to *choose* which way to react and to interact in any type of situation, yes you prefer to be nice, but there now is less resistance to being the opposite, to be assertive, and you can now become that if the situation is called for. Just a with a person who is normally assertive and takes pleasure with being able to be this way, but can touch on his aggression if the situation calls for this, such as if he is being threatened and he needs to defend his self. When the person can react from both polarities he challenges the old way of being and the contact functions that supported this, and he may be able drop the *I am nice* role, and become a person with whom *being nice* is not something he *has* to be, but chooses to be. He has integrated both polarities, or as much as he is comfortable with, and to live his life with more authenticity.

The impasse is not something that is feared because of the feelings and bodily sensations it evokes, but the doorway to a further enquiry to what that means to the person and how they exist, and the search for awareness and self-knowledge, for if the person becomes aware of how and why they exist then they have a choice in the direction of their life, no longer is it staying within the confines or the container of the self-concept, by an active exploration of the impasse though the use of the safe emergency in the many areas who a person is.

If we look at the symbol again:

We can see that as section one narrows with the effects of creative adjustment and introjection, the person restricts who they are and what they believe they can be or become, this restriction however means that as the person identifies with, or adjusts to certain characteristics then the other parts are for want of a better term *switched off*. When I was younger I used to work in a noisy and dusty factory, and become so accustomed to the banging of the machines it became filtered out, so my hearing has adjusted to working in that environment. For a while I thought I was becoming hard of hearing (which may have been a possibility if I had continued to work there) but after embracing the experiential I realised that part of my hearing had switched off due to creative adjustment. I practised listening when walking, listening to the river, the birds, passing buses, and when listening to music I would discriminate the various parts of the music such as the drums, vocals, lead, bass and rhythm guitar, and when in conversation I would focus on the subtle intonations and inflections of the persons voice, listening to the change in how the person spoke as they moved from topic to topic. I was in effect undoing the creative adjust from working in the noisy factory by sensitising myself to that which I had switched off from. This is not a world away from the purpose of this final chapter, for as I creatively adjusted in a noisy factory and part of my hearing switched off, so I believe it is that a person may switch off parts of their self, the person who has become passive or submissive and switches off the part of their self that is aggressive or assertive, or the person who feels they *must* be responsible may have disowned (or projected) the carefree or irresponsible part of their self. If the responsible aspects of a person become integrated into the self-concept and part of their identity then it may be given a purpose or a need to fulfil (field theory through the manipulation of the self and environment) the person may configure their world so they are responsible, or emit those signals or way of being to other people that may attract a person (such a person who is immature trying to attract a person who is highly responsible, so they can continue to be this way, and so it becomes a mutually dependent relationship in which the needs are fulfilled in each other.)

The purpose of this chapter, to touch the impasse, to gain a sense of the me, the self-concept and the owned creative adjustments and introjections, to create the safe emergency, to experiment with the *not me*, to move from monologue to dialogue, to become aware of the switched of parts of their self, and then if you choose too then to reintegrate those disowned parts and to gain a greater authenticity. As the person has sealed off those disowned parts, with the need of the self-concept surrounded by and interwoven by resistances with the impasse at the self boundary, creating the need for approval, affection, success or avoidance which may mean that the thought of touching on the *not me* may be met by anxiety. The contact functions, zones of awareness, polarities and assertion are also formed by creative adjustments and introjections and are an integral part of the self-concept, so as you test and experiment, as you taste the disowned parts of your self, touching the impasse and feeling the anxiety or what you are not so you may become to question who am I. The person who has become dependent on others, such as parents, the government or their partner when touching the impasse and being self-supportive may touch on the impasse of maturity and responsibility, that they are responsible for their own existence, the easy answer would be to retreat back into the self-concept, but if he touched the disowned parts of his self and tasted what it meant to be self-supportive instead of dependent on others may realise the freedom and choice that accompanies this, and also realise how much of his self has adjusted to being dependent, such as his beliefs of others as well as his self, the way he speaks, his level of assertion, whether he views the other as a object that exists so he can be dependent on, or a person to respect and value. The person then may be able to feel alive, to feel his own inner values, love and potential, he may have a lessened expectation of other people, and greater self-acceptance, instead of sealing off the disowned parts of his self.

If a person can integrate the disowned parts of their self, to accept the realisation that a *self-concept* is a collection of beliefs and values that has become because of the need to survive in the world. They have the choice and freedom though to accept some introjections and creative adjustments, and to literally *spit out* or reject those which the person no longer finds acceptable or necessary (I no longer *have* to be tough and strong, though I enjoy physical training) then the person, by touching the impasse, creating the safe emergency and the experiential with the drive of discovering more about who they are and to stretch their self-concept. The person may be able to express their self honestly in terms of how they are feeling (instead of manipulating others to achieve the need of the self-concept) for as the person stretches the self-concept, to be open to change and growth, to allow their self to fully experience a range of emotions, both the pleasant as well as the unpleasant emotions (whereas before they would avoid unpleasant feelings because of low frustration tolerance) the person may be able to reach out to their world with an authenticity and greater awareness of who they are, as well as a lessened need to win the approval or affection of others (that only satisfied the old self-concept) the person no longer *needs* to play sick, to have to win, to show off with a fast car or other props, the person can just be. I believe that as the person becomes more self-accepting and to not place *shoulds* onto their self, then they will place less expectations or *shoulds* onto other people.

If the person accepts responsibility for their own existence, that it is their life then there is less manipulation of the environment, the person is responsible for their own expectations, desires, feelings, beliefs and actions, the person is responsible for how they react to others, so if previously the person got infuriated by others and reacted angrily or with hostility through the awareness of being responsible for their self they may not let someone else affect them this way, you decide when and if you get angry, not at the invitation (or manipulation) of another person, you decide whether to be caring, because you choose to and not because another person is playing sick or the victim. This does not mean that you are uncaring, but that is not your purpose in life to fulfil the expectations of others.

Responsibility I believe means self-acceptance and the ability to be alive, to choose our responses, beliefs, thoughts, attitudes, values and emotional reactions. (rather than they be part of a self-concept made up of creative adjustments and unrealised introjections) Responsibility means you decide whether to put yourself first, or to put others before yourself. As I have said earlier in the book, if a person feels they *must* help others as it fulfils a self-concept or need, such as *if people see me helping others then I will win their approval or affection* or *if I do not help others or put other people first then I am of less value, I only exist to help others (people-pleasing)* then this is not a responsible choice, as it is a *must*, if the person can identify through The Shoes Experiment that it is an important quality that they have to exhibit, a quality that they *must* have, then this rigidity can be tested with the impasse experiment, for it the person must be caring as it sets alarms bells ringing with anxiety if they are *not caring* then not only can the person examine how they have configured their life to be caring (since it is an integral part of their self-concept) but also challenge this by being *not caring* or *not me.* This may mean a rationalisation that they have to put others first or a deflection in that it is easier to take care of others than to take care of their self (the person with low self-worth may have feelings of anxiety if they engage in self -care, which is distorted into their self judgement that they are selfish or being self-centred and an reason to take care of others) so the person engaged in the experiential may feel anxiety as they put their self first, which may be construed as being not caring, to identify that caring for them means to put other people before their self, because of their own value of who they are in relation to others (from many introjections and creative adjustments) when the person can integrate the not caring disowned part of their self, which can be a journey in itself as the person learns to engage in self-care through experiential pampering days or giving their self treats such as buying their self new clothes every month and going out for a meal then the person may eventually be able to say "i like to help and care for people, not because I have to or I must, but because I choose to" and this all started from writing "caring" as a quality on an experiment in a book. This person has taken responsibility for their life and existence, and by owning disowned or switched off parts they have stretched their self-concept and taken a step towards growth and authenticity, a move from the monological to the dialogical, that is to say, the person who is being helped is just an object or thing to satisfy the person's need, but, as that need is no longer there, I believe that the other can now be seen as a unique person and not an object.

Responsibility also means not blaming others for their own reaction such as "you made me angry" "you are not taking care of me" "the government is at fault" "my husband left me, I hate him"

Recently, I was in a situation in which people were talking about me, trying to manipulate the opinions of others to be against me. I could have gotten angry and bitter, but instead I tried to lean into their argument, to see their point of view (as it may be correct) and to engage in an assertive manner. I later found that the person was against me because my actions meant that she could no longer be in an advice-giving role to a person, and she blamed me because of it. I pointed out that I was listening to her, but it seemed that she was distorting, or cherry-picking information so as to create an argument, and that while I accepted that this was her view, I could not agree that I was responsible or to accept her blame. My actions in assisting a lady to become more confident and need less support had the consequence of this person not being able go into the helping, or advice-giving role. It was easier to blame me, rather than to question her own need to give advice, in that she had monologically *used* this person, to support and to give advice too, the purpose of her giving advice or help was not to be in a position to let the person grow, but to create a dependency, to be needed. My intervention, in assisting the person to be able to support their self, to become more confident and to not feel the need to ask for advice had the repercussion of affecting another person's need arising from their own idea of their self. Part of this person's self-concept may have also be to be able to blame others if they did not adhere to her expectations, and as such a reason to be aggressive or argumentative, then to manipulate others to be also be against them through the use of gossip and giving distorted information.

The person who for example blames the government for the state of the country, but does not do anything about it is creating an environment is which it will always be this way, for if I have a need that involves blaming, but not doing anything about it then this is tantamount I believe to ruminating. The person could start a campaign, to become involved in local government, to let their opinion have a voice to the right ears and to have the conviction to change or challenge that which they find unjust. I sometimes wonder if this person finds security in blaming, as there is no change, a stuckness. I sometimes wonder if blaming means to judge others but do nothing about it, perhaps with the belief that someone else should do something about it. I once heard a man who talking in the street saying to his friend "why won't someone do something about all these homeless people begging on the streets" and proceeded to blame the council, churches and society for why these people were homeless and no-one helped them. This person was blaming others as to why they weren't doing anything about the problem, and I thought to myself that it is us who are society.

I considered if this was a deflection from responsibility, in that it was easier for him to blame others than to do something himself, as he could have volunteered for a charity that helped the homeless or campaigned to increase awareness of people who live on the streets.

The person who says "you made me feel this angry" is allowing the other to affect her. The responsible person does not allow another person to invite them to react in any way. You cannot *make me* feel angry, I allow myself for you to manipulate me, and evoke those feelings. There may also be an expectation of how the other *should* be, and an aggressive reaction if the person does not follow this. Also, the person who has a need to be angry may *see or hear* what is happening, or what has happened to justify their self in becoming angry. This reaction may also be part of the shoes experiment, as the person becomes experientially aware of their reactions and beliefs or expectations when in relation to their self, or others.

The person who blames her husband for leaving her, may also have the expectation that he *should* be a certain way such as "my husband should always love me and support me" though she may be unaware (or in denial, desensitised or distorting) of her own actions when in the relationship, she may be demanding, not supportive and selfish, perhaps from an introjection where she believes her self to be superior to others, or they are inferior to her, and when he eventually becomes worn down and leaves she may be in shock, wondering what has happened. I think blame in these ways is monological as the other is an object that fulfils the need or the expectation of the other.

As the self-concept becomes its own goal for growth (growing in the direction of the values and beliefs of that self-concept) then the *need* that is present may sabotage organismic growth, that is to say, growth of the whole person. For example, the person who wishes to blame others may resist responsibility as it means if she have to realise her own expectations of other people, or her reticence of doing that she wants other people to do or be. The person who believed their self to be superior to others may resist the opportunity to see people as equals, she may say she is striving towards growth, but will associate with people to who she believes she can justifiably say she is better than, such as volunteering in a hostel or addiction centre. The person who blames the government and ruminates on this so they feel depressed, may create excuses or rationalisations that resists any attempt to stop this, as the person is looking for an excuse to feel depressed.

The person with a low self-esteem who attempts to *get better* may enrol on a course at college, start with the intention that everything will change, the low self-esteem part of her is still there wanting to have a purpose, and so she may find that different crisis's happen then means she rarely finishes any course, and this fuels her low self-belief, this person may also enrol on an internet based course and study with conviction and dedication, but upon completing the course *finds out* that the qualification is not accepted or valid. If the person were to finish a course she enrolled on she may become successful, which would challenge her lows self-esteem. This part of her self may sabotage her growth as she attempts to move into the *not me (success may mean an enhanced belief in her self) The* person who wants to *get better at relationships* but his anger or hostility seems to always impact on them, may outside his awareness choose girlfriends he will get angry with, and as such the relationship will fail (again) and he will move on. Behind this anger is the belief that he is not worthy to be in a relationship. If he were to be in a successful and loving relationship this would challenge his own introjected, creatively adjusted belief as to who and how he is, perhaps he feels unworthy of love or affection, and his use of anger means this will be fulfilled, and no relationship last long enough for him to be loved and given affection. I feel that as one is making a commitment towards growth and the stretching of the self-concept, the is also the pull of the beliefs sustained by many years of creative adjustments that affects the contact functions, assertion, zones of awareness and polarities that, striving for meaning and purpose draw the person back, to the safety and security (and less anxiety as the person leaves the impasse) of the self-concept. I feel that taking responsibility means striving to become a person and to reintegrate the disowned parts of your self, but also an awareness of how the self-concept may act as an attractive lure due to the nature of anxiety when you start to touch on the impasse, and may also serve as a point of regression.

I would like to write a little about how a person may dull their self, to engage in activities that only seem to serve the purpose of wasting time, or to provide a focus away from the possibilities of becoming a person, and as the person has the capacity to continuously creatively adjust then those adjustments become part of the self-concept so I believe that it is that a person may spend an inordinate amount of time engaged in activities that seem to have no purpose or meaning. I am not talking about a responsible and genuine interest in something, but for the purpose of the avoidance of living, and the rescission of organismic growth.

I recall a person who spent most of his free time playing on a games console, he would be waiting in line to purchase the latest game release and would spent hours playing games and trying to achieve points and a high level. I thought to myself, that here was a person who is obviously dedicated to an achievement in his world, the completion of a game. There was no substance to this though as once he finished one game he would move onto another, I asked him if he ever considered going to college or to pursue a career in an area he was interested in, but he looked blank and said that playing games was all he wanted to do. He worked in a factory and when he wasn't working he would be playing on his games console. I thought to myself if this person was living his life and exploring his potential, or if he was avoiding life and what had happened to him previously so that his free time was spent in this activity, so I asked what would he be doing if his console broke, he replied saying that he would be bored and not know what to do. I began to wonder if the creative adjustment away from boredom meant to give himself a purpose, this being spending his life trying to aim for an achievement that had no real meaning, and that this compulsion to spend his life on his console had become a type of addiction, as if he did not play on it he would be bored. There is no growth or aliveness here just a stagnation of a life as the person doesn't explore living, but lives to avoid the boredom of the *not me*. Does the boredom create anxiety, and to dispel that (the feelings of an alive person) the plays another game.

I was thinking about other areas, about people who spend hours on social media looking and commenting on transient trivial material, *liking* a photo or comment or *subscribing* to a person, perhaps for a sense of inclusion or a connection. If the person does not go online and comment or look at other people's pages, photos comments, is there boredom, loneliness, or a sense of not being included? I am not referring to a person who would use online media to maintain a connection to people they would not otherwise have a connection with, such as family members or friends in different parts of the world or country, but the person who *has* be on social media, to spend hours going from page to page liking and commenting.

The same could be said of other types of addiction in this way, the need to get drunk or take drugs in a person's free time, to become obsessed with football or another sport, or looking at videos, or going online in their free time, perhaps even the pursuit of transient meaningless sexual relations may be included here, not because the person seeks out a connection with another person, but to keep the feelings of boredom and the anxiety that follows at bay. I am not suggesting that people who go online and use social media, like sports and follow a team, or get drunk in their free time are only doing so because they are bored, as most people have other interests and moderate their use or time on that activity, but rather the person to whom, as with the person with the games console if the activity or interest becomes the only or one of the few focuses in the person's life. The person who devotes their life to work, may feel uneasy at the weekend, the person who engages in promiscuous sexual relations may feel restless if this need is not met, or the person who spends their life on social media may feel irritable and anxious they cannot go online. Interestingly I see this as a an extension of Low Frustration Tolerance, the person cannot endure the feelings of emptiness, anxiety or boredom and so feels he has to return to his pastime.

All of these can become a creative adjustment and integrated into the person's self-concept, and so becomes a *need* to be fulfilled. For all these I would suggest the impasse experiment, and to become aware of the *not me,* this being the experiential of touching the impasse and the boredom, irritability, restlessness or anxiety as the person becomes aware of what it means to be not them. As the person engages in the experiential they may become aware of the drive to go online, to become aware of the feelings that are evoked when they receive a notification on their phone, and the compulsion to quickly find out who it is that has liked their post or comment.

This type of obsession is not limited to the above, as the person can use running, cycling, weight lifting or any other sport, interest or hobby. The person may devote their life to this and build a career around it, to provide a meaning and purpose, with the benefit of secondary gain of being fit and healthy, that gives a rationalised reason to justify their life path. I believe that when the person *must* run, cycle, lift weights or any other interest then it is an indicator that this activity is integrated into their self-concept the *me,* and the impasse experiment may be used to highlight what happen when the person encounters that which they are not.

This then opens the doors to the experiential, to have an open enquiry into who you are, and belief that you can grow and become an authentic and responsible person. This may begin with the attitude to commit to yourself to learn about your self, to have an active interest in who you are, the needs of your self and how the contact functions serve a purpose.

Through the safe emergency the person can learn during the experience or reflect afterwards on what happened, such as a person who feels they would like to become more assertive and so experiments with this, they are aware of the drive to return to their previous passive way of relating and how this may influence their beliefs and emotional responses (as they have previously been passive, they may feel their heart beating faster and exhibit quicker speech rate as they become the *not me,* the person who is assertive) So the person chooses another to become assertive with, such a taking an article of clothing back to a shop for a refund, this may seem a small experiment, however the purpose is for the person to feeling the feelings of the impasse, the feelings of anxiety and to become aware of their physiological responses while in relation to the other who works in the shop and with whom they are engaging with. The person is desensitising their self to the feelings of the impasse through the safe emergency, stretching their self-concept and learning about their self and challenging the beliefs from their self-concept such as "she'll say no you can't have a refund" "She'll think I am cheeky for taking it back" "i"ll talk too fast and she won't understand me, then I'll blush and start sweating" then, as the person reflects on their actions afterwards, then may discover that these negative self-beliefs about the consequences of being assertive have been a rationalised reason why they have remained passive. As the person becomes more self-aware and responsible they may question and challenge those beliefs, then the person may eventually gain a self-acceptance that they can be any way and do not need the approval of another person. As the person gets more adept at learning from and in experiences, and stretch and challenge their self-concept they may grade the experiments further, this is now little fear of the impasse, a lessened fear of vulnerability into the void outside the self-concept (the implosive layer) so the person may voice their concerns at a public meeting, they may speak their mind and be assertive when engaging in dialogue with another person, if the other does try and dominate the conversation the person may raise this assertively. If it does not succeed and the conversation ends, he will not take it personally as he knows that being assertive means that he does not have to win conversations. The person's original self-concept has grown so that now he feels comfortable being assertive and practising growth as a person. There is no longer the fear of making a mistake, or if he makes the wrong decision, he knows he has the right to change his mind and say no, knowing that he is not responsible for how the other person reacts to this. He can be self-accepting knowing that he can make a mistake and doesn't have to get it right every time, he may even be able to laugh to himself if he does make a mistake or do something wrong.

The experiential is to grasp the experience, like a sponge to wring out all the learning that is possible, to become aware of how a person is when touching the impasse, to be aware of the needs of the self-concept, for example how they are aware they fall into the advice-giving role, because of the avoidance to listen, because if they listen the person may become emotional and they wouldn't know what to do. They have an awareness that it is less anxiety producing to give advice rather than the predicted alternative (from the belief they are incapable of being emotional or to help a person in a crisis) The person can then plan a safe emergency to stretch this polarity, to expand the self-concept, and to practise the *not me,* then eventually the *not me* becomes the *me,* and that which was avoided because of the vulnerability or the anxiety of the impasse is now redundant. The resistance that enabled the person to live is no longer needed or necessary, the person is growing and becoming.

If a person is committed to learning about their self, then the experiential is a door to awareness, and like a river flowing the opportunity to embrace the experience is always there, ready to touch. They may plan experiments, such as the passive person returning the clothing to the store, but is also open to the vastness that the experience is always there to tap into at any point, the person's sense and way of being becomes alive as they savour every moment in life. As they grow through the impasse so much more is now available to them in their life, their self has grown and like myself and my hearing after working in a busy factory and undoing the creative adjustment so it is that a person can integrate the disowned parts the self. They may become open to sights, sounds, people, voices, smells, touch and their intuition, their felt sense (since touching the impasse means to become aware of their internal sensing) everything may become sharper and more concentrated, instead of *switching off* parts of their self, the parts that are not part of the self-concept, the person is willing to experience the *switching on* of these disowned parts. I believe that when you can achieve this level of awareness, that everything is sharper and more intense, then with field theory in mind this may affect other areas of the person's life, they may become overwhelmed by the sights and sounds of busy places or a crowded pub or nightclub, and realise they had a desire to travel only for the purpose of achieving an *experience* when now they are aware that the *experience* is always around them, ready to embrace at any point. The person then, having gained this awareness may choose a simpler life, and become more spiritual as they realise that they do not have to *seek* a connection by joining a group, wearing certain clothes, getting tattoos or identifying with a certain religion or belief. The connection to the world is always present, in their own sensing and intuition, the smile of a person walking down the street, the smell of a bakery, hearing a person laugh, the appreciation of being in the natural world, feeling the wind or the sun, feeling love for all those around you, the gift of solitude and what it means to be alone, being in a loved one's arms, talking to another person and trying to know the other person for no other reason other that you feel they are interesting or that you sense their presence and feel comfortable, letting your hand feel the roughness of bark on a tree, sensing the energy that is all around us, a knowledge that you are alive and open to the experience of living, and that you are responsible for your own life and existence. This for me, is the connection to the world, and like the experience of the flowing river, is always there.

For a man who has lived his life cut off his emotions, this may be overwhelming, for example the person who believes that to be a man he has to not be emotional or show feelings, this *switching off* may mean that as he engages in the experiential and touches the *not me* of the impasse he grows and becomes more self-aware, he realises that he has denied his feelings after the death of his mother, he may feel the love for his wife that were always there but were suppressed, he feel the love for his child and how proud he is they are at college. As he becomes more aware he may feel the intensity of these unexplored, unacknowledged and unresolved feelings. Yes, the impasse can create anxiety, but as he grows and becomes a person, reintegrating the disowned parts of himself he is free to become both sides of this polarity, he has the choice to be strong and resilient, or sensing and feeling.

For people who have emotionally abused and controlled others, as they may uncover or become aware of some uncomfortable truths, their monological self manipulated others for their own gain, to be able to in control, to dominate and to restrict the growth and autonomy of another person. The person may feel intense feelings of guilt and shame because of the repercussions and consequences of their actions, such as telling their wife they were stupid and couldn't possibly go to college as people would laugh at them, that they were too dumb to drive a car and that the only thing they were good for was to have children and to cook and clean. The man may realise that he did all this because of his own insecurities and that his wife is now affected by low self-esteem, that it may take many years to recover from the damage he has caused to her. If such a man tries to become more self-aware then these uncomfortable truths may become illuminated, as the resistances of rationalisation and denial are no longer required. The unknown beyond the impasse may provide a knowledge of the implications of their actions that they would rather not know. This may not be such a terrible thing, as when this person has an awareness of their self-concept and the way they manipulated their environment then they can also grow, to own or become responsible for their behaviour and to learn and grow, that previously they were dependent on the control of others so as to manage their own anxiety, but as they grow this manipulation is no longer necessary.

I would like to talk about Monologue and Dialogue; I have included these terms throughout this book and would like to describe them. I first came across these terms a number of years ago in the book The Miracle of Dialogue by the author Reuel Howe. Although I have read this book many times each time I read it I seem to focus on different parts of it, and had an idea that just as with life, the book doesn't change but the person does. As a person grows and becomes an authentic person I feel that they may look at events differently or from a different perspective that previously they may have been aggressive in a situation, but now they can be more accepting and tolerant towards others. Part of that change I believe can be caused by the shift from a monological to a dialogical attitude, belief and values.

Monologue

The person Reuel Howe writes about monologue; *in monologue a person is concerned only for himself and that, in his view others exist only to serve and confirm him* Howe (1963 p36) and from this I considered the application of how the person may seek to manipulate others to give his self-concept meaning, that is to say to *confirm him.* Howe further writes (1963 p36) *that communication of such a person is parasitical, anxious and lacking in creative impulses and possibilities. His communication is parasitical because he is not really interested in others and values them only according to the feelings they produce in him. He Is anxious because he seeks confirmation of himself, is afraid of person encounter, and tolerates only agreement with himself and his ideas.*

I began thinking to myself, if a person seeks confirmation of his self, through the manipulation of others then how would he accomplish this? I realised that the self-concept is given meaning and purpose through field theory, the zones of awareness, the contact functions, polarities, areas of assertion and through the use of resistances. The self-concept has a need to be, and provides a secure *this is who I am* belief of their self, and when others *confirm me* then it also gives the self meaning. The woman who believes her self to be superior to others may act in such a way to invite or manipulate others to respond to her in that manner, she may play sick to direct attention towards herself, she may become a manager or work in an authoritative position, she may decide to have a number of children so in her world she is superior. The need to be superior from a number of introjections may be creatively adjusted to in a number of different ways. If others confirm her in that superior position then this gives that self-concept meaning, or *confirms* her existence. From a monological view the person who she manages, or the people she has authority over are not seen as people, she is not interested in a person encounter with the person, as they are only an object or thing to serve her, to reinforce her role. I was once invited to take part in a meeting with a senior manager who wanted to engage with his staff in the organisation I worked for. I arrived hoping to share and discuss some ideas, but it became quickly apparent that this manager was only interested in employees who shared his own views, and disregarded others. I wondered then if this person had decided to become a manager to be able to force his views onto others, that people were no longer people, but again objects to sustain his self. I noticed afterwards that this manager disclosed that he had learnt a lot from this meeting, and that It had been a pleasure to engage with all the staff there. I thought about this and the block to awareness, the denial or the rationalisation that had taken place for this manager in the meeting, and the manipulation of the environment as he endeavoured to show others that he was a listening and inclusive manager, when in fact he was only interested in speaking to others that shared his views.

This in itself may be an introjection, as in a junior manager seeks to gain promotion in that company then for him to progress with this manager he may have to adapt his beliefs to be confluent with that of the senior manager, his manipulation of his self, his creative adjustment means that he may disown some of his own values and introject the senior manager's viewpoints. If this is viewed from an organisational viewpoint then the person who wants to work there may have to adapt or adjust to the view or the values of that company. This may be the case of a man who has an inclusive and dialogical way of being going to work in a busy call-centre that has targets, or a person working in a sales environment where they again have targets. Working in these places, where the company belief may be to view customers as *units* and they must sell to 10 units a day, or for the person in the call centre that they must answer calls from 25 units and make 10 referrals may adjust to the company beliefs and view people no longer as unique people, but as objects or units that only exist to serve the goals of the company. If he integrates these values then as the need organised the field, and everything affects everything else in the field (field theory) then he may become monological and view people in his personal life also as objects. As previously being inclusive and within the spirit of dialogue he may respect his wife and children, valuing their opinions and right to have their own thoughts, but by becoming monological he may become distant and cold, not regarding their feelings and emotions, as they are now objects as well. In other occupations where there is the possibility that people are also reduced to things, perhaps from exposure to traumatic events (such the creative adjustment of a police officer, doctor, soldier, firefighter or nurse *switching off* their empathetic nature due to repeated experiences of seeing people in pain) then the same outcome may happen, this turning off of their sensing and empathetic side may mean that in their personal life they become numb to the feelings of people they are close too.

The person who has the need for affection may creatively adjust so this is achieved, if it is a woman they may feel miserable and anxious when she has no *man in her life* so she may start temporary affairs with a number of men. As she is only focused on her own needs then this means she is seeing the other in a monological way that the other only serves to satiate her need, to fulfil the desire for affection and to reduce the anxiety that becomes apparent if she is alone. There are a number of other creative adjustments that may give rise to this, the woman may feel that a man can only desire her in a sexual manner and as such she responds to him in this way, this is still monological though as she is not trying to know another person, but has pre-judged him based solely on her idea of what he wants, and is responding to him based on her beliefs, as she craves the affection of a man she gives him what she thinks he wants, as well as the belief of what a *man* means to her, as in someone to take care and protect her. This belief of what a man is may be from many introjections, as well as what it means to be a woman, she may have the belief that she cannot be independent and to lead her own life and to have a career, and so needs a man to make this possible, or so that she can be dependent on him.

This is similar to a person who must be liked at all costs, it doesn't matter about the person they are talking to or interacting with, the desire to be liked (and the avoidance of what it means to not be liked, as this may cause anxiety) may influence how she interacts with others, this is again monological as she isn't trying to know the person, to discuss freely her thoughts and ideas, but she is restricting her self in relation to the other, she walks on eggshells around people and may act passively, to please people or to be nice. She may adjust her views to follow that of other people so as not to cause conflict. She may even be able to express anger, if this is in confluence with the other person and their views. The person having the need to be liked may have different boundaries with different people, with a person she views as being important the need to be liked may be at the forefront of her relations (a manipulation of the environment) with that person, and with a another who she believes isn't important she may engage with them in a aggressive or rude manner. The man who is the abuser in an emotionally abusive relationship may put on his *nice* face towards the people from whom he needs to be liked or seek the approval from, but upon coming home, may *switch off* that part of his self and become emotionally abusive to his partner. These people are being monological as the other only has the purpose of serving their needs, he puts on his false self to win the approval of others, then takes it off when he returns home (a manipulation of the self and the environment) and cannot be considered authentic or dialogical.

Another example of monologue would be a man who views himself as unattractive and uninteresting, based from a number of introjections. If a person whom he considers attractive or beautiful becomes interested in him in a romantic or intimate manner, and begins to make her thoughts, intentions or desires known then this may be dismissed by the man, as her views of him do not align to his own ideas of his self. This is monological as the woman's views are at not considered as they do not confirm the views or the beliefs of the man. The man remains closed off from the possibilities of what may become. I hear this occasionally with some people stating "he wouldn't be interested in me" or "she is too good for me" and i believe that these views or attitudes have a monological way of being, as the other doesn't share their own view of their self, and in that is not seen as a unique person who is entitled to their own views and opinions. This may be the same with a person who has the belief that "no-one could ever love me" and encounter someone who wants to love them, the monological stance may infect the relationship and he may create tests or sabotage the relationship, so that it eventually ends, this may be part of a manipulation of the environment as he may, outside he awareness end the relationship through a variety of damaging way, to give his *no-one can love me* introjection a meaning and purpose.

The person basing their opinion solely on a characteristic of another person, such as if they are attractive, wear expensive clothing, have a successful career, are a single parent, of a different ethnicity, gender or sexual identity and so on are being monological as they are only interested in the part of the person that resonates or has a meaning for their self. The person is not viewed as whole person, but fragmented to suit the needs or desires of the other. I remember a person I met who disclosed that she "hated the police" so I enquired about this, asking if she viewed a person as being a person first, or their role? She replied saying that they were police first and people second, and so I replied if this was similar to her hating all men? She reflected on this and realised that she was being prejudicial, missing the whole person to focus only on the part that had meaning for her.

The person who has a monological stance uses others for his own gain, to satisfy his own needs, and when this happens there can be no real meeting of person, no authenticity or genuineness.

I believe that the self-concept is intrinsically monological as others are seen from the beliefs that have been created or influenced from the many introjections and creative adjustments, and the disowning of the many parts of who we are. The person's need for reassurance, for affection, for power, for appreciation, for love, to hate, for confirmation, for success, to influence or to satisfy one's own beliefs about other people mean that other people are not viewed as individuals and are unique, but as objects to serve only and to satisfy the need that is present.

If the person sees another as an object I believe they themselves are also viewed as an object and have a monological view of their self, and may only see the parts they want to see. The person who views their self as being warm and kind, rationalising that they are a benevolent manager or parent may be in denial of how they may display hostility or use coercion to force others to accept their views or means of control, perhaps under the heading of "it's for their own good" taking the perspective that they can see the situation more clearly and the other should just follow their advice or guidance. The person who thinks of their self as warm and caring may offer *guidance* however this is a mask for advice giving or ordering others. It may also mean that the person feels they can criticise the other and their behaviour. This may also be outside their awareness as they have the belief that they are a good person trying to *help* the other. This is part of the self-concept and a fixed view of how they should be, and in that is monological. When a person who states "this is who I am" (meaning their self-concept) then this necessarily means that other parts of that person that may challenge their view will be denied. This view may mean that as the self-concept has a need, then a person is only of worth if they are a hard-worker, a good mum, attractive, a helper, a good dad or any number of other labels or roles. When a person views their self as only being this way this is also monological. The constraint of the belief *this is who I am* suggests rigid boundaries, the person is no longer a possibility of what they may become, of the potential for growth and to exceed their own self-imposed expectations, but a fixed self. We then have one person who has a fixed way of relating to the world having expectations of their self, of how they should be, placing expectations onto how other people should be. The person is monological as he can only tolerate agreement with his self-concept, image or identity, meaning that he has to live within the *rules* of this collection of beliefs, values and attitudes. If he were to challenge this it would mean encountering the impasse, and the ensuing anxiety of the *not me*.

Dialogue

I shall start this section also with the writing of Reuel Howe *dialogue is that address and response between persons in which there is a flow of meaning between them in spite of all the obstacles that normally would block the relationship* Howe (1963 p37)
I remember an occasion a number of years ago, I was being criticised from a person I had no direct contact with, she was telling a woman that was close to me that she should break off contact with me as I was *controlling* and not good for her. (I write this in in italics due to the subjective nature

of what this term means, as the person *telling* the other may constitute ordering them to do something)

I initially got defensive, and that my actions, to try and be supportive to this person was being distorted to imply that I was ordering, she had cherry-picked two occasions from a year of me knowing this woman, distorted them and interpreted these occasions as a *sign* of me being controlling. This normally would have been a block to a relationship, as normally I would distance myself from a person who would distort words and meanings for an outcome, but on this occasion I tried to open myself up to dialogue and to communicate with this person, I was open to the possibility that she would construe my intention as being an attempt to manipulate her, (from her ability to distort events) however I would at least try. We met and spoke, she informed me of her concerns and by listening to her, I got the sense that she *needed* the woman I was supporting, to be able to help her, and now that the woman was becoming more confident and self-supportive then she relied less and less on this woman for support. Feeling the impasse as she could no longer *help* this person she tried to manipulate or distort events so that I would no longer be around, and that she could continue to *help* this woman. I listened to her and how she saw my actions, to try to see the events as she saw them, and also to state my own views. I asked what it meant to have this woman no longer ask her for help or advice, and she then started to withdraw, and started to talk about her loveless marriage and how she was not happy, that helping this woman took her mind off it. By being willing to talk to this person and to have an open enquiry into how she saw the event it could have been possible that I was controlling, however through open dialogue it become transparent that she *needed* to help this woman, and she was attacking me and to say I was controlling so that I would leave and she could continue to *help.* Her way of helping, a monological way (that only served to alleviate the feelings in her loveless marriage) used the other to satisfy her own needs, was not really helping, as but a kind of parasitical relationship in which the other never gets better, but stays sick. The woman never wanted the other to get better as this would mean that she would have to face her life in that loveless marriage, and my intervention to offer real support in which the woman learned to be independent disrupted this.

It is the interaction between persons in which one of them seeks to give himself as he is to the other, and also seeks to know the other as he is. This means that he will not seek to impose his truth and view on the other.

Howe (p37)

Just imagine that, placing no values, no beliefs, no attitudes or prejudgements onto a person. This means his expectations and how he believes that people should be are diminished or made redundant. As a person becomes what they are not, and pushes or stretches the impasse there is less of a need to place expectations or beliefs onto another person. If a person does not impose his truth onto another person, then I don't believe that there would be a need to manipulate their environment, to attempt to change that person.

There may actually be an enquiry into how that person lives and can appreciate their uniqueness. Sometimes, when I look at a person it's like looking at a flower, a tree or a painting, I don't look at a flower and think to myself "oh I don't like the petal" or looking at a tree and want to change the colour or texture of the bark, I just accept it the way that it is. The painting by the artist as well, created by them and their own vision or interpretation that has depth and meaning. I don't look at the painting and want to change it, I can accept it for what it is. I can accept all these, the tree, the flower and painting and appreciate their uniqueness and individuality without the need to want to change them. For me, dialogue means to know a person, and to acknowledge their individuality and being, their right to exist how they choose to exist, without judgement or an evaluation, but with an acknowledgement that they have to a right to be and to live.

When I am talking to a person and become aware of the purpose of their communication, for example the salesperson who walks towards me as I walk into a shop, they do not walk directly towards me in a manner that would suggest engagement, but in a softer, more leisurely style, I notice the way in which they just spoke to their colleague, and the shift in their inflection, syntax, use of language as well as use of questions, they may have been talking in a harsh and critical manner to their colleague, but to me their voice becomes soft and enquiring. I notice this change and wonder about the shift and what it entails, the person has shifted their style with their colleague to myself, so where is the authenticity, is he being genuine with him or with me? Is his style of contact usually this soft and he puts on the harsh voice as he works in a competitive job and this indicates a defensive position? (perhaps a creative adjustment) or has he put on this soft voice and way of being to me who is the customer, is this a tactic he uses to manipulate others to achieve a sale, to get his bonus or to fulfil his target, are his targets that imposing that he has had to creatively adjust, to create a false self to dupe the customer, to appear polite and courteous when his intention is just to create a sale. I wonder about how this person is and the likelihood that his change of voice and way of being is only for the purpose of making a sale, and in that does he view the person standing in front of him (me) as a unique person in a dialogical sense, or just a person in a monological sense, he wants to use me to achieve an aim, to make a sale. I do not judge him, or evaluate at him, but appreciate that this is the way he lives, the way he exists, I wonder as well about whether this person lives a monological life, where others are just objects or things to satisfy his needs, or did he adjust to this following the pressure of working in a target driven environment (an introjection) As he enquires as to my needs I say I am ok, but thank you for asking, he looks forlorn and says that if I need anything please just to ask. He walks back to his colleague as the way in he spoke before is back, and they speak in the same harsh and critical way. I don't want to change him, I am not placing a value onto the way I think he *should* be, I accept him and the way he lives his life. I attempted to be my self in that short relationship, to be genuine, however I do not believe he did, as I believe he was putting on his "sales face" when talking to me.

This for me was an example of confirmation (Mann. 2010 p183) in that I acknowledge his whole being and accept that this is the way he lives or exists

As Mann states *the need for confirmation in many people is so great that if they fail gain confirmation for who they are, they will seek confirmation for who they imagine the other will want them to be, and adapt accordingly.* The person seeking confirmation may adjust their self to what the other person my want (or expect) them to be, even if this is in the person's imagination. The salesperson adapted his style of relating to what he imagined I expected him to be. Did he create a false self, to achieve his goal? I do not see much different between his shift towards his Salesperson self and the false self created by a person who is trying to live in a world full of values and expectation of others, of people that are significant to them.

Hycner (1993 p47) writes that *we will attempt to get confirmation by appearing the way we think the way someone else wants us to be.* The person then, whether to gain approval, affection, satisfy a need, to be appreciated, or to seek reassurance or love may adjust their self to what they think the other wants them to be, and is an indicator of a creative adjustment. The person, having a need to be confirmed by another adjusts their self to the expectations or another. If this is a small child growing up in a disciplined household he may hold back his tears as *boys don't cry* as this is the rules of how a boy should be in that house, so adjusts his self to fulfil this. If this becomes integrated into his self then he may have difficulty showing emotions as he has *switched off* part of his self. *Confirmation recognises and affirms the person's existence, even while perhaps saying that his current behaviour is unacceptable* (Hycner. 1993 p48)

For as with the salesperson, That as I offered confirmation to him, I certainly did not enjoy being treated as an object, and that he attempted to manipulate me so as to make a sale, putting on a false voice and interest in me. He objective is not to know me, but to use me to achieve a sale. I could have said something back on my observations, though this may have been my own passive aggressiveness to do this, to play Mr Analytical and to deduce his intentions, to put him on the back foot, but my observations were just that, observations as I find people interesting as I am amazed at the wonder of people, to live and to exist, not as a puzzle to be solved but as appreciation of the complexity of what it means to live, and to creatively adjust in many different ways.

Howe (1963 p69) writes; *we turn people into things when we value and deal with them only in terms their function or usefulness to us.* I did like to be a *thing* or an object to this salesperson (monological) but was experiencing the moment in relation to this man, to feel what it was like to be a *thing* to him for my own learning and awareness, while confirming his existence and an acceptance that this was just way he lived. I didn't feel defensive and to offer a retort to him but to accept him.

This to me is what Dialogue means, to try to be a genuine and an authentic person and to respond with my total self, and to learn from experiences, to offer confirmation that other people can exist how they choose to, though I do not necessarily agree with his behaviour. I do not feel the need to be defensive or to protect myself. I can appreciate being in relation with another unique person and do not need them to sustain me or to give me meaning or purpose, if there are no defences or guards raised, then it can become one person trying to know another person. I have the capacity and the desire to know another person, whichever way that person exists, with acceptance and valuing their uniqueness, I can meet that person with openness and inclusion.

I was open to *meeting* the salesperson even though he engaged with me in a monological way, he probably used the same lines like a script to whomever he met, so he wasn't really speaking to *me,* he was speaking words in the presence of me, acting as though he was speaking to me. There was no real interest in who I was, but the conversation only satisfied his own self-concern. Dialogue is the genuine meeting between people, and when a person can put down their roles and can genuinely meet another person with authenticity.

By touching the impasse, to feel the anxiety of the not me the person has the capacity to stretch his self-concept, and enter into more authentic relations with other people, if a person talks about bikes to everyone he meets, then by experiencing the experiential, to have an active enquiry into how he relates to others he may realise that he is seeing others as objects, as things so that he can talk about the sport he has an interest in, if he were to embrace the experiential and to listen instead of speaking, he may realise that he is being monological, and creates a subject to talk about to take the stage, to focus the attention towards his self. As he feels the anxiety of the *not me*, he may experiment with listening, and by *being* something different his is learning not only a different way of relating, but also how he directed attention towards himself. He may realise that he used to tell stories as a child to gain the approval, by seeking confirmation (adapting to what he thought his parents wanted him to be) or affection from others, he may also have been in competition with his siblings, and his way to get attention was to tell stories (creative adjustment) and here he is now 30 years later playing the same role with the same manipulations. By experimenting with his truth, and becoming the opposite it creates an anxiety when he experiments with chooses not to play those games. If this man becomes present in each moment, he becomes aware of how he is speaking, how he commands attention though stories, how and what it means to touch the impasse, to touch his own vulnerability and to own that *switched off* part of his self, to listen to others and to appreciate them, to offer inclusion and to try to engage in a genuine way. As Hycner states (1993 p82) *A dialogical attitude is starting where the person existentially is, which includes both his aliveness and his deadness.* When a person can reach the impasse, to feel that feeling, to strive towards an awareness not only of how they live (the self-concept) and to actively experience being them (such as the man becoming aware that he tells stories to get attention) and then to experientially journey towards the impasse, moving from the *me* to the *not me* the person can begin to taste and then reintegrate the dead or switched off parts of his being, he can become more alive, more aware, and to live his life with a greater authenticity.

I had the thought of this a few years ago when out running, I was looking around and as I was running moderately fast everything close to me was a blur, I imagined that if I were in a car it would look even more obscure as I was travelling faster, if I was in a plane looking down all I would see is green fields, but if I slowed right down, then I would see everything more clearly, I could see each individual leaf, the hairs on the nettles, the imprint of the footprints on the muddy path, the way a stream flows against a large boulder in a river. I took this and placed this belief onto my own awareness of my own way of being, I learned to experience what it was like to be me, to sense my values and beliefs and way of living, living moment by moment (instead of running, driving and flying where everything was a blur) I tried to be fully aware of what was happening, I noticed my speech rate and heart rate increase or decrease when in relation to different people, the choice of which words I used depending on who I am talking to and my way of experiencing the world. Then by touching the impasse, being aware of the feelings of anxiety of the *not me* to claim back the disowned parts of who I am. I was becoming more aware of what is happening at any given moment, to slowly observe all my actions without placing value onto them or being attached to them, then to recognise and accept the role they played and the need being met, as well as acknowledging the purposes of resistance, to keep me away from the vulnerability of the impasse. This is a type of self-dialogue and self-acceptance. As Howe writes again: *It is the interaction between persons in which one of them seeks to give himself as he is to the other, and also seeks to know the other as he is. This means that he will not seek to impose his truth and view on the other.* Howe (1963 p37)

I was not imposing a truth onto myself, but by attempting to discover myself, to know myself as I am and how I exist. As with Field Theory, this focus on the moment, this focus on presence had the impact on other areas of my life, for everything became sharper, the sense of aliveness has reached every part of my being, to a larger sense of self.

It was around this time when I had another idea, the understanding of an experience. As I see it, an experience is an interpretation of an event, that is to say how I *see* the event creates the experience. I remember one person I knew a few years ago who *in her experience* all men let her down, were arrogant and full of hate. Notwithstanding the implications of prejudice and possible projection here I offered confirmation of this in a dialogical way, and asked her what it was that created her experience, and she replied that men always let her down, were arrogant and argumentative. I listened to her and she told me stories of all the times that she had been let down by men, and so I asked that if she had the same expectations of me, as i was also man? Her reply was a predictive one, that she said that I was ok now but in time I would become just the same as all the rest, and so I asked that if this was her expectation of me, then she might be defensive now, knowing that (in her truth) I would eventually let her down, and that she may be distant towards me. I tried to be inclusive and enquire just what it was that men did that was argumentative, and she replied "well, they challenge me and don't do what they are told!" and so I asked about how she interacted with men that may have brought this response in her. She realised that she was often more coarse and defensive with men, and used to tell them what to do, and if a man responded in any way that she did not like then it meant that he was creating an argument. She became aware that she was unaware of her own hostility towards men, and this was filtering through in her interactions, in her way of *seeing, listening* and from her way of *speaking* with men. She realised that she was being argumentative with men, placing her expectations onto them, as to how they should be, and had disowned the hostile and aggressive part of her self and projected this onto men, enticing men to respond to her in that way, which justified her own beliefs, and giving her a valid reason to distance herself from men.

I wondered after that how a person's experience of an event can open a doorway to awareness of how they live their life. Part of this woman's self-concept was to be able to be against all men, and by understanding her experience of an event could she open the door to be able to understand how she existed.

I thought to myself, can a person practice or offer inclusion to a person to whom they look at through prejudiced eyes, can they offer confirmation, to accept that person just the way they are, when their thoughts are coloured by their opinions and beliefs about the other?

Inclusion is where a person attempts in a non-judging way to experience both sides of a dialogue, to experience their own sensing, thoughts, beliefs, emotions and feelings as well as to try to understand the other person their feelings and beliefs. This is not enough I feel, for I believe that inclusion is to be able as much as I can to experience what the client is experiencing, but at the same time to not become lost in the person (subsuming or projective identification) but to be centred in what I am experiencing myself. With the lady above who said that men were argumentative, I tried to offer inclusion in trying to experience what it meant to *be her,* all her history and creative adjustments that formed her beliefs, the anger towards men, as well as the fear and defensiveness also, that her beliefs as they were never brought into an awareness could never be understood, her anger and expectations kept people at bay, as I brought my awareness back to my own experiencing I myself felt challenged, that I had to defend myself against her attacks towards *men,* that I had to say that she was wrong and mistaken. I realised that had I replied in a defensive manner then this would have given her the reason to be become guarded herself, (and a manipulation of the environment as she creates a situation in which she can become guarded) and by being aware of my own processes, then in this case I could experience myself (much like the impasse experiment) becoming defensive at her comments, and wondering to myself where these feelings came from and for what purpose.

While Inclusion (as well as presence and confirmation) is a very involving area that could cover most of this chapter, or even a chapter in itself, to be able to genuinely or with authenticity offer inclusion means to understand the fixed views, beliefs and values of the other. To be able to, or to try to *experience the other person, as well as to experience your self* means to view the person as unique individual. If we take ourselves back to the comment from Howe:

It is the interaction between persons in which one of them seeks to give himself as he is to the other, and also seeks to know the other as he is. This means that he will not seek to impose his truth and view on the other.
Howe (1963 p37)

Then, when we do not impose our truth onto another person, and seeks to know the other as he is we can offer dialogue to that person, if we can know the other as he is, free from our own rigid beliefs and expectations, then we can try to *know him*, to offer inclusion. As the person grows as a person, by pushing the self-concept and integrating the disowned parts of his self, by understanding the impasse and stretching it then the person can be more authentic with their self, as well as with other people.

The lady in the example above who didn't see a man as a unique individual but through eyes coloured from her experiences of men, she couldn't offer inclusion to a man, as she had a prejudiced viewed of what a man was. If she challenged that view, if she understood that view and the creative adjustment and introjection that created these beliefs, as well as to understand how she interacted with men, how she spoke, how she listened, her own beliefs and values then she could shine a light onto how she existed, then, if she was willing, to touch the impasse, to try to be open towards men, to feel the anxiety as her beliefs that have kept her safe are questioned. If she is able to gain an awareness of this, then maybe she can see a man as just a person, as an individual, and that it was her that was using the prefix of gender to judge this person, based on her experiences. Her experiences are valid, she may have been in numerous abusive relationships with some disturbing and harmful men. The creative adjustment that lead to her own safety and means of avoidance with men, also gave meaning to the transference, to the prejudicial views of all men, and in that her previous abusive partners are still affecting her current relationships.

Another area of this that could be used for the impasse experiment, would be for her own self-awareness, that she may become aware that she was able to be compassionate, understanding and caring towards women, but not towards men. If she were to become experiential in this she could experiment and try to become caring and compassionate towards men, using a safe emergency. She may feel anxious at this, as her own beliefs and the implications or the consequences of those beliefs become apparent. Coming toward the final area of the book I would like to talk about assertion, I resisted talking about being assertive in the previous chapters, as I feel that being assertive shares many values with Dialogue, Inclusion, Presence and Confirmation.

Assertion

There are many books on assertion and I as I see it all sharing many of the same qualities as dialogue, for you to respect your self as well as to respect other people, to engage in open and honest communication, maintaining your own dignity, to be able to communicate thoughts, feelings and emotions, and to take responsibility for living your own life, but not at the expense of other people.

The same values you hold for yourself you recognise that other people

have the same rights,
the assertive person does not dominate other people to satisfy their own needs. I think that assertiveness is a way to recognise that you are a person of worth, and by confirming your own worth, you value that other people have the same right, just as you have a right to live and pursue your own path and happiness in life, then so do other people. If a person can hold these values then this would impact on their style of communication, for if the person hold these views, then many of the ways of speaking that are aggressive or passive in their origin and direction, such as ordering, directing, bullying, needing to win, warning or threatening, moralising or delivering righteous beliefs, giving solutions, judging or criticising others are made redundant, they are no longer necessary or appropriate, neither is the need for power or influence over another person.
A person who is assertive can speak up for their self, to express their needs while considering the needs, rights and feeling of others.
I think that when a person adjusts to life with creative adjustments and introjections the self-concept is formed. Then to give this idea of their self meaning the other person is viewed mostly in a monological way, that they are an object or thing to satisfy the needs of that person's self-concept. The teacher may righteously say that he has become a teacher to be able to help people learn and grow, but is missing that part of his self that is hidden from his awareness, the need for approval, the need for success or dominance or to reinforce the image of his self that he is intelligent. His students become objects that only serve to give meaning to this image (manipulation of environment) he may have only become a teacher because of the introjections from his parents or others (having accepted that he needs to be a *professional* and to have a *career* to be a person, he enrols at university and becomes a teacher.
Is this person being passive or aggressive? For each person their motivations that drive this would be different, so the person who listens in a submissive way as people tell them what they should do with their life, the person is taking a passive view of their life and their own responsibility as a person to make their own choices. For the person who has a *need* to be liked, to have a sense of worth, to be a success or to win the approval of others then they may aggressively and aim for that career to fulfil that need (manipulation of self as the person adapts their self to achieve their needs) The as the self-concept becomes its own goal the person may *own* the role of teacher (or mother, father, doctor, nurse, police officer or firefighter)

238

and this provides a meaning and purpose for their own life.

Assertiveness then has many implications, for if the person passively takes on the view of how to be a person (and either passively or aggressively give this meaning) through the many introjections and creative adjustments that form the self-concept, then assertion, to be able to communicate openly and to express your needs while respecting others may be difficult. The teacher may pride himself on being *assertive,* later realising that he wasn't really being assertive and respecting other people, but aggressive and as his need was to be seen as intelligent and as a person of worth, he restricted the growth of his students to discover solutions for their own problems, as he was so apt to tell the other person where they had gone wrong and to offer a solution, he was denying the student the possibility that they could solve their own problem.

I think that is why a move to be assertive is to challenge the self-concept, that other people, if they are treated with respect can no longer be viewed as an object or thing, just as they, if they are viewing their self with respect, can no longer be an object made up of many introjections and creative adjustments.

So, the move towards assertion can be a challenging one (as is the shift from monologue to dialogue) as the person stretches their self-concept, the person in his pursuit for approval or affection may feel the anxiety of saying *no,* the person who has a need to win, to be competitive with others, to have to be better than them (it doesn't matter who the person is, they just have to be better than them, and in that they are turned into an object) may find it difficult to say *yes* and to consider the other person as a unique person.

From this then there are a number of principles or rights of the assertive person, I shall name them below, and the shift that may occur as the person emerges from the confines of their self-concept. All of these can be used in the impasse experiment, moving from the *me* to the *not me.*

I have the right to say no, as well a right of when to say yes.

For a lot of people saying no to a person may an extraordinarily difficult thing to do, particularly when they rely on the approval of others, and saying no may mean a fear of rejection, or that the other person will not like them. If part of your self-concept was to always say yes, either through people-pleasing to gain a sense of worth, or a creative adjustment knowing that if you said no you would be hassled, badgered, bullied and cajoled until you gave in and said yes. You may even be good at saying no, but as you have creatively adjusted into a submissive role the other person may not take you seriously. This is a manipulation from the other person, not respecting you and having the expectation that you will do what they want. Saying no, and respecting yourself to stand by your decision may be a courageous thing to do, for if you say no to a person who you know may reject you, then it may bring to your awareness what the other means to you, and all the times you gave in and said yes, they were not in agreement with the other person, but said under the fear of rejection and to win the approval of the other.

To touch the impasse for some people may mean to say no, though this would have significant consequences for the person, particularly if they have always been known for being agreeable or saying yes. The other, knowing you are agreeable may be surprised if you stand up for yourself, and may criticise you for saying no and dismiss or discount you until you fall more in line to what they want or expect. The person who has creatively adjusted to be a person of low self-worth or esteem, may have created the field in which others view her as being of this low self-worth. The abused wife may be called selfish if she says no to her husband and children, they may have gotten so used to getting their own way and their needs met at the expense of the wife and mother, that when she say no (to cooking, washing, cleaning and other menial forms of housework) or asks for some help she may be accused of being lazy, selfish, not caring or not loving her family. They may even ask for their old *mum* and *wife* back and say that everything was much happier then, which may try to place guilt onto her. This is a monological stance from the husband and children, as not respecting the woman's right to say no, and then then try to influence her, to manipulate her back to her old position and view of her self. The housewife may feel guilty then because she said no, believing her husband and children are right, and she slowly slips back to her old self form the pressure of the others. Saying no then may mean to not only challenge your own view of your self, but also others who have benefited from you always being agreeable and passive, and being aware that they may not like it when you stand up for yourself, and try to force you to become passive again. When the person can say no responsibly, it means that when they do say yes, it will be said with authenticity, not said because of the fear of rejection or criticism. Part of being assertive is to recognise that others also have the right to say no, even if you do not like it.

I have the right to be myself, even if others do not like it
This is a big one for me, because as the person grows from the confines of their self-concept then it may mean that some of the people with whom the other associated with may again challenge that person. The woman who has always felt that she has to dress a certain way and to wear makeup and other props to *fit in* with her friends may come to her awareness that she no longer wishes to be this way, and to stop wearing named fashion clothing to have a sense of worth or to be part of that group. As she becomes more authentic, and touches the impasse by wearing ordinary no-frills clothing, to experience what this meant to her, and knowing that wearing these clothes sustained her self-image experiments with not wearing these. Her friends though may not want her to be this way, as they themselves have also bought into their self-image and need to wear named brand clothing and props to *fit in*. The message *don't be yourself, be the way I want you to be* is alive here, if the others were authentic friends it wouldn't matter what clothes she wore, and as an extension of this what job she had, car she drove or measure of success she has. As the person grows in their authenticity and challenges their old patterns of relating and being then so it is I believe that relationships made from the self-concept may become to appear more superficial.

The right to be yourself, to follow your own path, to question introjections and creative adjustments, to make your own decisions and to strive towards being authentic may mean that previous relationships (in which the other person wanted you just the way you were) may end, or if they respect your right to be any way you wish to be, may become deeper and more meaningful, as the person respects how you wish to be, rather than how they want you to be. Being yourself means also that you do not have to change for another person's benefit, it also means that you have a right to live your own life, to be true to yourself, to not creatively adjust to other people, to be an individual (though other people may resent or criticise you for not going with the norm) To live you own life means to not feel the need to live up to other people's expectations. One of the tragedies of life is to live a life that isn't yours, when you choose to be responsible for your own life, you choose to live a life and to forge a path to be your self. If you do decide to live your own life, to state your own thoughts and feelings, to live your own life means as well that you are not responsible for the reactions, the thoughts, the feelings or the behaviour of the other, just as you have the right to be your self.

This is again reciprocal, in that just as you have the right to be your self, to not change for others and to follow your own path, then others have the same right as well.

I have the right to make mistakes
I have often thought that a mistake isn't a mistake; it's just a way of learning. A child doesn't make a mistake when they draw a crayon on the wall, they are learning the boundaries of what it means to live and to adjust in their parent's world. Some people try to avoid making a mistake, to avoid taking a risk or to avoid being vulnerable. Is this the view that doing something wrong is a mistake? I knew a person who would avoid doing anything new in front of other people, in case she made a mistake, she was a very critical and judging person, and I think this was projected onto others, that she would be criticised if she made a mistake in front of other people. Another person who lives to high personal standards and their own high expectation may view that making a mistake is tantamount to a failure, that they have to be perfect every time. This person then will avoid daring to take any risks, and may practice to hone their skills or knowledge so that the possibility of a failure, or of making a mistake is minimised, because of the introjected view of what a mistake means. Other people may latch onto a mistake a person has made, to be able to criticise them or judge them (some people may hang onto a mistake that a person has made for years, as it serves a purpose, such as to not forgive, to be able to create a distance, or to be angry) and in that may try to manipulate them with how they *should* redeem their self. This is of course manipulation of the environment as the person is acting in a judging and advice-giving role (which may be part of their self-concept) however when you make others your judge, you make them your master. Your behaviour may be affected by the opinions of others following a mistake. Part of the impasse experiment is to try new behaviours, new ways of being, to challenge or understand old way of living, and in that making mistakes is part of learning. The person who lives by their own high expectations as to never make a mistake, can never dare to fail. It is part of living to fail, to make mistakes, and in that is the self-acceptance that you can make mistakes. This also means the acceptance that others can be able to make mistakes as well.

I have the right to state my opinion, feelings and beliefs, even if others disagree with this. I have a right to change my opinions, feelings and beliefs. I have a right to change my mind.

I was part of a group recently and stated an opinion that was viewed in a negative way by some of the members of the group, they tried to tell me that my opinion was wrong and how I could be right if I just listened to them, I tried to be assertive to them, to engage in dialogue and listen to their point of view, and replied that although I respected their opinion, and their right to have an opinion that I disagreed with their opinion. They responded in an angry tone, saying that I was again mistaken and then again more vigorously tried to coerce me to change my opinion. I replied saying that I was accepting of their view, of their opinion, but they were not accepting of my opinion and instead of valuing my right to see the issue from a different perspective then were trying to tell me that I was wrong, and to see it from their point of view. (A manipulation of the environment)

As a person you have a right to your opinion regardless of whether others like it or not, and it is also your right to state your opinions, feelings and beliefs, with the view that being assertive means not to satisfy your own needs at the expense of others, or at the expense of other people. So in that it would be aggressive to state your opinions to others if they didn't want to listen, or you were dominating the conversation.

Part of the self-concept may mean that it is too easy to state your feelings, beliefs or thoughts, but use the other as an audience rather than a participant in dialogue. You may come home from work and *off-load* your opinions and beliefs onto your partner, and fail to ask them if you can do this, or ask with an equal enthusiasm about their own thoughts and beliefs. For another person who is passive, it may be easier to be silent or agreeable, to change their opinion or beliefs to suit the needs of others (which may also be part of their self-concept) and it may also be part of the impasse experiment to practice experientially to state your truthful opinion, to risk the vulnerability of being rejected, to not be liked or to win the approval, affection of the reassurance of others. It is your right to state your opinion, feelings or beliefs (not at the expense of others) and as you are a growing person, who can be flexible, you can also change your opinions, beliefs or feelings, even if others do not like this. As you are a flexible person who has the capacity for growth (you are not a tree stuck in place) you have the right to change your mind, even if this inconveniences others.

This acceptance of your self, to be able to state your opinions, beliefs and feelings, as well as the ability to change these, as well as change your mind mean that to be assertive other people have the same rights as you do.

I have to right to judge my own behaviour, thoughts and emotions and to not give reasons or explanations to others (and to not expect others to approve of my actions)

As I wrote earlier in this section, when you make someone your judge, you make them your master, there is only you who can judge your behaviour. It is your right to judge your own behaviour, even if this is met with disagreement with other people. A few years ago I was asked to enrol on a course that would have been beneficial to my employer, but not me. I considered all the options available and came to the conclusion that enrolling would not be in my best interests, the response from my employer was to challenge my reasoning and decision making. I had the idea that they were not interested in my best interests, but the organisations, and was trying to manipulate me to enrol by criticising my judgement. I respected my manager's right to have that opinion, but it was myself who was my own judge, neither did I have to give an explanation for coming to the conclusion I arrived at. Although I was open to listening to the opinions of others, it was myself who judged whether my decision was correct, or in error. I have noticed that people may do this, to ask why you made that decision, not as an enquiry or as an interest in you as a person in a dialogical sense, but in a controlling sense, they are asking for an explanation to be able to criticise, to pick out the faults of your point of view of behaviour, then offer an warning, to give solutions, to offer an evaluation or to direct you towards an outcome.

It is only you that can judge your behaviour, even if others do not like this, part of the introjection that I have seen is a person may seek the approval or reassurance of another prior to, or after a decision or course of action, in a sense to seek the approval of the other person.

Part of the impasse experiment may be make decisions, to judge your own behaviour and to not feel the need to offer an explanation. A person with low self-esteem may decide to go to college, to grow as a person. Other people may ask her why she has decided to do this, to criticise her ability to study. She doesn't have to justify her behaviour, reasoning or actions, or offer an explanation, though she may feel that she *has* to offer an explanation to other people, or to expect others to approve of her behaviour, thoughts or actions.

Part of this is also that other people have the right to judge their own behaviour, thoughts and emotions and to not give reasons or explanations to others.

I have the right to say I don't care, I am not interested or that I do not understand.

Part of being assertive means to be able to say "i am not interested" or "i don't care" in fact, one of the many introjections that a person may integrate into the self-concept is to not be rude of offensive to others, so if a person talks about a subject you have no interest in, you may, instead of being assertive and saying that you are not interested their subject you may become passive or aggressive instead. You may silently listen and show an fake interest in the other, waiting until you can see an exit, or behave aggressively, directing the conversation to another topic, cutting the person off or exiting the conversation. The other person though may be aware that the person has no interest in what they are saying, and would be communicating in a monological way, to view the other as an object or thing to *talk* to. It doesn't matter who the person is, the person talking covers the same topics in the same manner (as with the term to buttonhole someone) regardless of the person they are talking to. It is your right to say "i am not interested" "i don't care" or that "i don't understand" without feeling guilt or shame. Assertion means to be able to state what you are interested in, and what bores you or are not interested in. This may again be part of the impasse experiment, to challenge those old introjections, and to able to state with an honesty or authenticity an ignorance or a disinterest in the other person and what they are talking about, while still respecting their right to be able to talk about any subject they choose, just not with you.

Part of assertion is that other people have the right to say they are not interested, do not care or they do not understand, and that you do not take this personally, they are unique individuals and have their own interests.

I have the right to judge whether I am responsible to find solutions to other's problems.

When I was younger I used to take it upon myself to fix other people's problems, until I became aware that by fixing other people's problems I was restricting their ability to overcome that problem by their self, to develop their own problem solving abilities. In effect I was helping them into helplessness, as they searched for others to find solutions to their own problems. Although that role has long been relinquished I am aware that some people look for solutions from other sources, such as to search online for how to fix a problem, to ask a person or to seek a professional in a particular field. One of the great joys of living I feel is to be faced with a problem or issue, and then to overcome it with your own abilities, even if that mean developing your own skills.

A few years ago my car broken down on my way home from work, I had a tool kit in the back of the car and discovered that the gear linkage had snapped. I sought to find a solution to fix this and managed to create a temporary fix using a bolt and some wire. The easy option would have been to phone for a mechanic, or a recovery truck home, but I thought I would try to find a solution myself.

I think it has become an introjection nowadays for some to not believe in their abilities and do not have the capacity or the potential to overcome their own problems, and instead to search for others to find the solutions for them.

On a slightly different note a person may use manipulation to get others to look after them, by playing sick or helpless, to entice the other to find a solution or to offer them support. The person who is passive or submissive may manipulate the other so they can rectify problems or issues, and if they cannot achieve this them they may attribute blame or responsibility for their self towards the other. I am not responsible for other people and their lives, as each person is responsible for their own life, I can offer assistance, to stand by their side as they make the transition to find the solutions to their own problems, but I will not take over, because if I take over I take away their own self-responsibility. A person is responsible for their own thoughts and reactions, and their own behaviour, particularly if they get angry, hostile or upset if I resist solving their problems. This also means that I am not responsible for another person's actions.

Part of assertiveness is the respect that the other person has the right to judge whether to find the solutions to other's problems as well.

I have found dialogue and assertion have much in common, but fundamentally it the self-acceptance as well as the acceptance of the other that is important. If I can accept myself as a unique person and can acknowledge the other as the same that I will not judge them, blame them or criticise them. If I can see the other as a distinct person then I will be free from projection, transference or prejudice, as I move from the monological view of the self-concept to the dialogical and assertive view of the emerging person (as a growing person) then all the fixed attitudes and beliefs of myself and that of other person dissipate and no longer have meaning. If I have big expectations of myself and others then this can lead to big disappointments, but, it I can accept myself and others with an accepting and inclusive attitude and no expectations then I will have no disappointments. I think that a person can take responsibility for what happens in their life, to decide how they react to situations, and that they have rights that do not have to be sacrificed, unless they make an authentic choice to do that.

As my self grows and I become a responsible and self-accepting person I will no longer have a need to manipulate my environment or my self to get my needs met, there will no longer be a need to seek the approval or the affection of others, no longer a need to win or a fear of rejection or of upsetting people, to seek power of success (to be better than the other) to seek the adoration of other people, or to have power over people or prestige, or to able to influence others. I may be able to view the other not as an object to be better than or win the approval of, but a person who just is, just the same as your self, they are their own unique person who is on their own journey through life. Maybe you can *meet* this person, a person engaging with another person with wonder and interest. As the goals of the self-concept are challenged and as the *switched off* parts of the self-concept are brought back to life then as with field theory, that a field is a systematic web of relationships, and that the field is a unitary whole, everything affects everything else, then any growth in the person has a profound and real effect on the person as they experience and encounter their world differently, that they can be genuine in their relations with others. The move towards dialogue and assertion leads to greater authenticity, as well as self-acceptance and the acceptance of others.

As the person frees their self from the shackles of the rigid self-image or self-concept, and the touching of the *not me,* there can be an increase in the potency of life, that everyday occurrences that were missed before can be savoured and enjoyed, both in the discovery of a person's own senses as well as a wonder towards other people. The person who embraces dialogue and assertion may make changes within their personal relationships, as each moment is special. One person may realise that he has wasted so much time on transient and superficial relationships, that instead of disappearing off the pub when he finishes work he decides to stay at home in the evening, to enjoy special moments that can never be replaced with his family. Another person, realising that he was working long hours to be a success in financial terms, may become more focused on being a success in his relationships with others, He work schedule of 60 hours a week means that he is missing his time with his wife and children, and so he adjusts he life style to be content with a simpler life that means less financial success, but a greater richness in his relationships. The goals of the self-concept from many introjections are now obsolete, in both this people they can relinquish their old ways of being, ways which were integrated into the very fabric of how they viewed their self, and have the potential and the possibility of moving onto a new way of being.

A person then, by touching the impasse, by experientially understanding what it is like to *be me*, as well as to *not be me,* to feel the pangs of anxiety as the unknown is explored and discovered, to regain the parts that have long since be cut off through creative adjustment and introjection can make a kind of transcendence into someone new, to emerge into a different person, and a person who is of your own making, not passively taking on board introjections indiscriminately and without awareness. This *seeing* with new eyes, can provide new meaning, (and the realisation of the amount of energy and focus that sustained the old self-concept) as well as a discovery of an enlarged sense of possibility for their self.

As the person now has a growing freedom to live their life they can create their own way of being. Sometimes when I am out walking I try to live in the moment, to live in each breath, that each moment is another moment of an awareness of being alive, whereas previously I was stuck in a fixed view of my self I can now experience all aspects of my being, the sensing, the feeling, the physical, my thoughts, actions, behaviour and intuition, each alive and an experience to be tapped into at any time. I am no longer a fixed person, but a growing person who is in the process of becoming an authentic and real person. As I can accept this in myself, I no longer place any values or beliefs onto another person, there is no judging, or analysing, no diagnosing, controlling, manipulating or criticising, but an acceptance that the other person has a right to exist how they please, a person may engage in a behaviour that I do not like, but I can still accept the person, but not like his behaviour.

With a growing self-awareness I can decide whether to accept introjections and creative adjustments, or to discard them. I can also accept that I do not have to put myself in situations that I do not enjoy, for years I did not like crowded places as there were too many voices and too much stimulation but forced myself to endure them as I had the idea that if I did not then it would be a weakness. Now that I am more accepting of myself I no longer have to overload my senses by going to busy places and have made a choice to avoid these were I can. For me, there is a depth and richness of experience when in dialogue with one person, and with too many people I get overwhelmed. I no longer put pressure on myself to overcome this, but to accept that it is part of me. The past no longer is the controller of how I live my life, for living in the moment, and living in the present through the discovery of my being means that those influences are just that. As I embrace each moment I am aware that there is a type of *tugging,* a pull towards an old way of being, often surfacing in a thought, belief or feelings, and so I stop and pause and consider this, envelop myself in that experience, wondering where it leads. Very often it is a pull to the old me, the person that would use strength to overcome problems, and I contemplate wondering if the old self-concept every truly disappears, or if it becomes a point for regression. When I let go of that old way of being, through touching and emerging through the impasse I opened the door to what I might be. Sometimes logic is not enough to understand your self and others, I think it is a combination of thinking, feeling, sensing and intuition, and when I experience that tugging, I apply my whole being to the experience it, to understand it. Each moment is an encounter, and in that can be a valuable place for self-learning and awareness. My old self-concept, the physical and strong Michael created its own goal, to provide a path to give this meaning, by working in tough manual jobs and then the emergency services. Following this path though and the switching off of those other parts means also meant living a life that give a purpose to their avoidance, and I feel that more than what we are searching for, is what we are avoiding. Touching the impasse and growing as a person means recovering and integrating those old parts that we have been avoiding, and in that may create its own anxiety. The person who has been emotionally abused may resist and avoid making decisions, and manipulates others to make decisions for her, and so as she touches the impasse, she becomes experientially aware of how she is living as she makes a decision (or even thinks about it) the processes of resistance as well as her own self-beliefs she can experience what it is like to *be me*, and then to touch the impasse, to grade her way of being to feel that anxiety and why she avoided this for so long. This discovery for her self is real, she is experiencing her life and her existence in the moment. She is her own instrument for discovery, she is able to be fully present, and also to be aware of what is experientially happening at that moment, for as she makes her own choice she may feel anxious, and question her capability to do this, and from this emerges her own lack of self-belief, that it is preferable to ask someone else what to do than decide for herself.

She may learn to be more assertive and to embrace dialogue, to put down the self-blame, her *"i should be stronger" "i am a failure as I should be better"* and perhaps the blame of her condition towards others. People spend their life blaming others and carry grudges. It's a great way to not offer an acceptance towards another person, and the self-acceptance of who they and the responsibility that this is their life.. The unwillingness to let go is a sign of the rigidity of the self-concept, as the person is stuck in their beliefs as to how they or the other *should be,* or *should have been.* This may of course become part of the self-concept as the person views their life with despair, and begins to see the world from those eyes. Is she able to let go of that blame then she can take responsibility for her life. Every action, every thing has the potential to be a gateway to awareness, and the discovery of being, as well as the joy of being. As I said in the last chapter, I don't have to travel to a distant land to experience a pleasant experience, I can look out my window, go for a walk, become aware of my own thoughts and feelings or to engage in dialogue with another person. A connection with the world around us is always present and alive in each moment, an appreciation of the simply things in life, a greater patience, acceptance and a greater sense of a personal perspective and spirituality. Each moment is a connection to the world around us and in that can become cherished and divine, affirming and accepting the aliveness and vibrancy in all things. If I put this belief onto a connection with a person, then, I can be authentic and have a real and genuine meeting, to be fully present with the spirit of dialogue with each person, offering acceptance, confirmation and inclusion. Growth and being alive is now part of my being, with a joy that can be said in the words

"I exist and I choose how I live."

*

it is not death a man should fear, but he should fear never beginning to live.

Marcus Aurelius

References

Chapter 1

Perls, F, 1973. The Gestalt Approach and Eyewitness to Therapy. 1st ed. USA: Science and Behaviour Books.

Polster E. and Polster M. (1973) Gestalt Therapy Integrated: Contours of Theory and Practice. New York. Vintage Books.

M.Korb. J Gorrell. V Van De Riet (2002 - 2nd Edition) Gestalt Therapy Practice and Theory) Gouldsboro ME. Gestalt Journal Press

Mann, D, 2010. Gestalt Therapy, 100 Key Points & Techniques. Hove, East Sussex. Routledge.

W.L Smith 1997. The Growing Edge of Gestalt Therapy. Highland, New York. Gestalt Journal Press

Bolton. R PHD 1979. People Skills, New York, Simon and Schuster, Touchstone Books.

Simkins, J. 1976. Gestalt Therapy Mini Lectures. Mill Brae, California. Celestial Arts.

Howe. R. 1963. The Miracle or Dialogue. Seabury Press. New York

Bugental J. F. T 1978 Psychotherapy and Process, the Fundamentals of an Existential-Humanistic Approach. Random House. New York.

Perls, Hefferline, Goodman 1951. Gestalt Therapy, Excitement and Growth in the Human Personality. Souvenir Press. London

Chapter 1a

Polster E. and Polster M. (1973) Gestalt Therapy Integrated: Contours of Theory and Practice. New York. Vintage Books.

Joyce P. Sills C (2010) Skills in Gestalt, Counselling and Psychotherapy. London. Sage

Simkins J.S. (1976) Gestalt Therapy Mini-Lectures. California. Celestial Arts.

Chapter 1b

Joyce P. Sills C (2010) Skills in Gestalt, Counselling and Psychotherapy. London. Sage

Yontef, G. (1993) Awareness, Dialogue & Process: Essays on Gestalt Therapy. New York. Gestalt Journal Press.

Chapter 2

Perls, F (1992) (originally published 1969) Gestalt Therapy Verbatim. Gouldsboro, Maine. Gestalt Journal Press.

Zinker, J. 1978 Creative Process in Gestalt Therapy. New York. Random House.

Chapter 3

Howe. R. 1963. The Miracle of Dialogue New York. Seabury Press.

Mann, D. 2010. Gestalt Therapy, 100 Key Points & Techniques. Hove, East Sussex. Routledge.

Hycner, R. 1993. Between Person to Person, Towards a Dialogical Approach. Gouldsboro. Gestalt Journal Press.

20324939R00147

Printed in Great Britain
by Amazon